CLINICAL PROBLEM LISTS IN THE ELECTRONIC HEALTH RECORD

CLINICAL PROBLEM LISTS IN THE ELECTRONIC HEALTH RECORD

Edited by
Adam Wright, PhD

Apple Academic Press

TORONTO   NEW JERSEY

Apple Academic Press Inc.
3333 Mistwell Crescent
Oakville, ON L6L 0A2
Canada

Apple Academic Press Inc.
9 Spinnaker Way
Waretown, NJ 08758
USA

©2015 by Apple Academic Press, Inc.
Exclusive worldwide distribution by CRC Press, a member of Taylor & Francis Group

No claim to original U.S. Government works
Printed in the United States of America on acid-free paper

International Standard Book Number-13: 978-1-77188-091-6 (Hardcover)

This book contains information obtained from authentic and highly regarded sources. Reprinted material is quoted with permission and sources are indicated. Copyright for individual articles remains with the authors as indicated. A wide variety of references are listed. Reasonable efforts have been made to publish reliable data and information, but the authors, editors, and the publisher cannot assume responsibility for the validity of all materials or the consequences of their use. The authors, editors, and the publisher have attempted to trace the copyright holders of all material reproduced in this publication and apologize to copyright holders if permission to publish in this form has not been obtained. If any copyright material has not been acknowledged, please write and let us know so we may rectify in any future reprint.

Trademark Notice: Registered trademark of products or corporate names are used only for explanation and identification without intent to infringe.

Library of Congress Control Number: 2014948126

Library and Archives Canada Cataloguing in Publication

Clinical problem lists in the electronic health record/edited by Adam Wright, PhD.

Includes bibliographical references and index.
ISBN 978-1-77188-091-6
1. Medical records--Data processing. 2. Clinical medicine--Decision making--Data processing. I. Wright, Adam (Assistant professor of medicine), author, editor

R864.C55 2014   610.285   C2014-905641-9

Apple Academic Press also publishes its books in a variety of electronic formats. Some content that appears in print may not be available in electronic format. For information about Apple Academic Press products, visit our website at **www.appleacademicpress.com** and the CRC Press website at **www.crcpress.com**

ABOUT THE EDITOR

ADAM WRIGHT, PhD

Adam Wright is an Assistant Professor of Medicine at Harvard Medical School, whose research interests include electronic health records, clinical decision support, and data mining. In addition to research, Dr. Wright teaches introductory medical informatics at Harvard Medical School as well as clinical epidemiology and healthcare policy to medical students. He is also a member of the leadership team for the Agency for Healthcare Research and Quality-Funded Clinical Decision Support Consortium, which is focused on developing methods for sharing clinical decision support content. Adam has a PhD in Medical Informatics from the Oregon Health and Science University, and a BS in Mathematical and Computational Sciences from Stanford University.

CONTENTS

Acknowledgment and How to Cite xi
List of Contributors xiii
Introduction xvii

Part I: History and Importance

1. **Bringing Science to Medicine: An Interview with Larry Weed, Inventor of the Problem-Oriented Medical Record** 3
   Adam Wright, Dean F. Sittig, Julie McGowan, Joan S. Ash, and Lawrence L. Weed

2. **Medical Records That Guide and Teach** 19
   Lawrence L. Weed

3. **Clinical Implications of an Accurate Problem List on Heart Failure Treatment** 45
   Daniel M. Hartung, Jacquelyn Hunt, Joseph Siemienczuk, Heather Miller, and Daniel R. Touchette

Part II: Attitudes and Use

4. **Clinician Attitudes Toward and Use of Electronic Problem Lists: A Thematic Analysis** 59
   Adam Wright, Francine L. Maloney, and Joshua C. Feblowitz

5. **Healthcare Provider Attitudes Towards the Problem List in an Electronic Health Record: A Mixed-Methods Qualitative Study** 83
   Casey Holmes, Michael Brown, Daniel St Hilaire, and Adam Wright

6. **Use of an Electronic Problem List by Primary Care Providers and Specialists** 121
   Adam Wright, Joshua Feblowitz, Francine L. Maloney, Stanislav Henkin, and David W. Bates

7. **Distribution of Problems, Medications and Lab Results in Electronic Health Records: The Pareto Principle at Work** 135
   Adam Wright and David W. Bates

Part III: Improving the Problem List

8. **An Automated Technique for Identifying Associations Between Medications, Laboratory Results and Problems** 147
   Adam Wright, Elizabeth S. Chen, and Francine L. Maloney

9. **A Method and Knowledge Base for Automated Inference of Patient Problems from Structured Data in an Electronic Medical Record** 183
   Adam Wright, Justine Pang, Joshua C. Feblowitz, Francine L. Maloney, Allison R. Wilcox, Harley Z. Ramelson, Louise I. Schneider, and David W. Bates

10. **Improving Completeness of Electronic Problem Lists Through Clinical Decision Support: A Randomized, Controlled Trial** 209
    Adam Wright, Justine Pang, Joshua C. Feblowitz, Francine L. Maloney, Allison R. Wilcox, Karen Sax McLoughlin, Harley Ramelson, Louise Schneider, and David W. Bates

11. **Computerized Physician Order Entry of Medications and Clinical Decision Support Can Improve Problem List Documentation Compliance** 229
    William L. Galanter, Daniel B. Hier, Chiang Jao, and David Sarne

12. **Randomized Controlled Trial of an Automated Problem List With Improved Sensitivity** 245
    Stéphane M. Meystre and Peter J. Haug

Part IV: Applications of the Problem List

13. **Incomplete Care: On the Trail of Flaws in the System** 273
    Tejal K. Gandhi, Gianna Zuccotti, and Thomas H. Lee

14. **Leveraging Electronic Health Records to Support Chronic Disease Management: The Need for Temporal Data Views** 279
    Lipika Samal, Adam Wright, Bang Wong, Jeffrey Linder, and David Bates

15. **Indication-Based Prescribing Prevents Wrong-Patient Medication Errors In Computerized Provider Order Entry (CPOE)** 299
    William Galanter, Suzanne Falck, Matthew Burns, Marci Laragh, and Bruce L. Lambert

Author Notes 313

Index 321

ACKNOWLEDGMENT AND HOW TO CITE

The editor and publisher thank each of the authors who contributed to this book. All chapters were previously published in various places in various formats; to cite the work contained in this book and to view the individual permissions, please refer to the citation at the beginning of each chapter. Each chapter was read individually and carefully selected by the editor; the result is a book that examines the use of clinical problem lists in electronic health records from many different perspectives, including their importance, history, possible improvements, and current applications.

LIST OF CONTRIBUTORS

Joan S. Ash
Department of Medical Informatics and Clinical Epidemiology, Oregon Health & Science University, Portland, Oregon, USA

David W. Bates
Division of General Internal Medicine, Brigham & Women's Hospital, Boston, MA, USA, Partners HealthCare, Boston, MA, USA, Harvard Medical School, Boston, MA, USA, and Department of Health Policy and Management, Harvard School of Public Health, Boston, MA, USA

Michael Brown
Harvard University, Health Services, 75 Mt. Auburn St, Cambridge, MA, 02138, USA

Matthew Burns
Department of Medicine, University of Illinois at Chicago, Chicago, Illinois, USA

Elizabeth S. Chen
Center for Clinical and Translational Science, University of Vermont, Burlington, VT, USA and Division of General Internal Medicine, University of Vermont College of Medicine, Burlington, VT, USA

Suzanne Falck
Department of Medicine, University of Illinois at Chicago, Chicago, Illinois, USA

Joshua Feblowitz
Division of General Internal Medicine, Brigham & Women's Hospital, Boston, MA, USA, Partners HealthCare, Boston, MA, USA, and Harvard Medical School, Boston, MA, USA

William L. Galanter
University of Illinois at Chicago, College of Medicine, Department of Medicine, University of Illinois Medical Center, United States and University of Illinois at Chicago, Information Services, University of Illinois Medical Center, United States

Tejal K. Gandhi
Partners HealthCare System and Harvard Medical School, Boston.

Daniel M. Hartung
Oregon State University College of Pharmacy, Portland, OR, USA

Peter J. Haug
Department of Biomedical Informatics, University of Utah, School of Medicine, Salt Lake City, UT, United States

Stanislav Henkin
Division of General Internal Medicine, Brigham & Women's Hospital, Boston, MA, USA and Partners HealthCare, Boston, MA, USA

Daniel B. Hier
University of Illinois at Chicago, Department of Neurology and Rehabilitation, University of Illinois Medical Center, United States

Casey Holmes
Brigham and Women's Hospital, 1 Brigham Circle, Boston, MA, 02120, USA, Partners Healthcare, Boston, MA, USA, and Division of General Internal Medicine and Primary Care, Brigham and Women's Hospital, Boston, MA, USA

Jacquelyn Hunt
Providence Health System, Portland, OR, USA

Chiang Jao
University of Illinois at Chicago, College of Nursing, University of Illinois Medical Center, United States

Bruce L. Lambert
Department of Pharmacy Administration, University of Illinois at Chicago, Chicago, Illinois, USA

Marci Laragh
Department of Medicine, University of Illinois at Chicago, Chicago, Illinois, USA

Thomas H. Lee
Partners HealthCare System and Harvard Medical School, Boston.

Jeffrey A. Linder
Division of General Medicine and Primary Care, Brigham and Women's Hospital, Boston, MA, USA, and Harvard Medical School, Boston, MA, USA and Harvard School of Public Health, Boston, MA, USA

Francine L. Maloney
Clinical Informatics Research and Development, Partners HealthCare, Boston, MA, USA

Karen Sax McLoughlin
Division of General Internal Medicine, Brigham & Women's Hospital, Boston, Massachusetts, USA

List of Contributors

Julie McGowan
Department of Knowledge Informatics and Translation, Indiana University, Indianapolis, Indiana, USA

Stéphane M. Meystre
Department of Biomedical Informatics, University of Utah, School of Medicine, Salt Lake City, UT, United States

Heather Miller
Providence Health System, Portland, OR, USA

Justine Pang
Department of General Medicine, Brigham and Women's Hospital, Boston, Massachusetts, USA

Harley Z. Ramelson
Department of General Medicine, Brigham and Women's Hospital, Boston, Massachusetts, USA, Information Systems, Partners HealthCare, Boston, Massachusetts, USA, and Harvard Medical School, Boston, Massachusetts, USA

Lipika Samal
Division of General Medicine and Primary Care, Brigham and Women's Hospital, Boston, MA, USA and Harvard Medical School, Boston, MA, USA

David Sarne
University of Illinois at Chicago, College of Medicine, Department of Medicine, University of Illinois Medical Center, United States

Louise I. Schneider
Department of General Medicine, Brigham and Women's Hospital, Boston, Massachusetts, USA and Information Systems, Partners HealthCare, Boston, Massachusetts, USA

Joseph Siemienczuk
Providence Health System, Portland, OR, USA

Dean F. Sittig
University of Texas School of Biomedical Informatics and UT-Memorial Hermann Center for Healthcare Quality and Safety, Houston, Texas, USA

Daniel St Hilaire
Brigham and Women's Hospital, 1 Brigham Circle, Boston, MA, 02120, USA, Partners Healthcare, Boston, MA, USA, and Division of General Internal Medicine and Primary Care, Brigham and Women's Hospital, Boston, MA, USA

Daniel R. Touchette
Oregon State University College of Pharmacy, Portland, OR, USA

Lawrence L. Weed
Department of Medicine, University of Vermont, Burlington, Vermont, USA

Allison R. Wilcox
Information Systems, Partners HealthCare, Boston, Massachusetts, USA

Bang T. Wong
Creative Director, The Broad Institute of MIT and Harvard, Cambridge, MA, USA

Adam Wright
Department of Medicine, Brigham and Women's Hospital, Boston, Massachusetts, USA and Harvard Medical School, Boston, Massachusetts, USA

Gianna Zuccotti
Partners HealthCare System and Harvard Medical School, Boston.

INTRODUCTION

At present the physician has to read the entire record and then sort the data in his mind if he is to know all the patient's difficulties and the extent to which each has been analyzed. There is no evidence that he does this reliably and consistently; he and others using the record lose their way, and problems get neglected, missed entirely, or treated out of context.
– Lawrence Weed, *New England Journal of Medicine*, 1968 (1).

Though it seems obvious today, organizing the medical record around patient problems was a breakthrough when, in 1968, Lawrence Weed presented the problem-oriented medical record in his landmark piece "Medical Records that Guide and Teach." Even in today's era of electronic medical records, the problem of conceptualizing and organizing patient data around problems is still a challenge, and most medical records are organized around data sources, such as laboratory results, medications, narratives, and diagnoses, rather than organized around patient problems.

An accurate and up-to-date patient problem list is the cornerstone of the problem-oriented medical record. It serves as a valuable tool for providers assessing a patient's clinical status and provides a means of succinctly communicating this information between providers. In addition, an accurate problem list has been associated with higher quality care.

However, maintaining accurate problem lists can be challenging. Most medical record systems depend on healthcare providers to manually update the problem list. These providers are often time-pressed, and the lines of responsibility are not always clear. Nor is there a uniform standard for what ought to go on the problem list in the first place. Most would agree that ongoing, active chronic diseases belong on the problem list, but self-limiting conditions, resolved problems, risk factors or symptoms for which a satisfactory diagnosis has not yet been achieved are less clear.

Together, these challenges often result in problem lists which are incomplete, inaccurate or out-of-date. Such inaccuracies impair the use of the problem list in patient care, often leading to a vicious cycle, as healthcare providers who feel that they can't rely on the problem list are then less likely to keep the problem list updated themselves. In addition to the direct effects on patient care, inaccurate or incomplete problem lists have downstream effects on clinical decision support, research, quality measurement, care management and myriad other patient care functions that depend on accurate knowledge of a patient's problems.

In this book, we present a variety of perspectives on the problem list, organized into four sections.

In Section I, we present three chapters on the history and importance of the problem list. The first two cover the origins of the problem list, and the third provides important evidence that an accurate problem list is associated with improved quality.

- Although the problem list is widely used, medical records have not always been organized around problems. The problem-oriented medical record traces its roots to the work of Larry Weed. In Chapter 1, we present an oral history interview with Dr. Weed, who turned 90 in 2014.
- "Medical records that guide and teach" laid the foundation for a new way of organizing and storing medical knowledge and patient information when it was published in the New England Journal of Medicine in 1968. The now-ubiquitous SOAP (Subjective, Objective, Assessment, Plan) is derived from the problem-oriented medical record introduced in Chapter 2, which has been cited nearly a thousand times.
- Much of the appeal of the problem-oriented medical record is intuitive; however, its direct impact on patient care has been less-studied. Chapter 3 presents a cross-sectional study of patients with heart failure, comparing those who had heart failure on their problem list to those who did not. The authors found that patients who had heart failure properly documented on their problem list were more likely to receive appropriate evidence-based therapy.

Although problem lists are important, they are used inconsistently. In Section II, we present four studies that look at healthcare provider attitudes toward the problem list from four different methodological perspectives.

- Chapter 4 presents a detailed qualitative look at problem list use by physicians, nurses and other care providers. The chapter uses a mix of interviews

Introduction xvii

- and observation, and uncovers several recurrent themes that help characterize the range of provider attitudes and approaches to using the problem list.
- In Chapter 5, we present the results of a survey and set of interviews. While the methods in the previous chapter were open-ended, this study used a more fixed vignette-based approach to further assess healthcare provider perspectives on the problem list, with a particular focus on what providers think belongs on the problem list.
- Chapter 6 presents the results of a statistical analysis of problem list usage, finding that problem list use differs significantly by specialty. Primary care providers documented the majority of problems, with medical and surgical subspecialties documenting proportionally fewer problems; however, some specialties stood out as frequent users of the problem list.
- In Chapter 7, we look at the distribution of problems, medications and laboratory results documented at the Brigham and Women's Hospital. We found that all three data elements exhibited a power-law distribution, with a small number of frequent items accounting for the majority of occurrences—an extension of the "80%/20% rule." This same power-law distribution recurs with many other natural and cultural phenomena, including language, wealth, commerce and settlement.

In the prior two sections, we considered the importance of the problem list, and provider attitudes towards it. In Section III, we turn towards strategies for improving the problem list. The first three chapters look at the development and evaluation of a body of work from the Brigham and Women's Hospital in Boston, MA, beginning with the development of a data mining method for identifying problems, and culminating with a randomized trial. The final two chapters of the section look at additional strategies for improving problem list completeness from the University of Utah and the University of Illinois at Chicago.

- Chapter 8 describes the application of association rule mining, a data mining technique, to clinical data. We successfully used the technique to find associations between problems, medications and laboratory results, and developed two extensions which are particularly useful for clinical data. These associations lay the foundation for inference rules, which are described in the next chapter.
- Chapter 9 describes the development of a knowledge base for inferring patient problems from other structured data in the medical record, describing both a method and a resultant knowledge base. The method builds off the association rule mining techniques developed in the prior chapter, applying it to seventeen important clinical problems.
- In Chapter 10, we describe a clinical decision support intervention we developed which takes the knowledge based described in the previous chap-

ter, and alerts clinicians when their patients have a potential gap in their problem list. We evaluated the intervention with a randomized trial, and found a three-fold increase in problem documentation by providers who received the alert.
- Chapter 11 presents work from the University of Illinois at Chicago. The authors developed a decision support alert which fired when new medications were ordered without a corresponding indication appearing on the problem list. The authors found that the alert was useful for improving problem list documentation.
- Chapter 12 presents work from the University of Utah, also focused on problem list accuracy. The authors developed an intervention for improving problem list accuracy, and tested it in an intensive care unit and a cardiovascular surgery unit, finding a significant improvement in problem list accuracy in the first unit but not the second. Although the interventions described in the previous chapters at the Brigham and Women's Hospital and University of Illinois at Chicago used structured data, the intervention described in this chapter used natural language processing on free-text narratives.

In Part IV, we consider uses of an accurate problem list, presenting three cases, each different in application, but each depending on an accurate problem list.

- In Chapter 13, the authors review a medical error—a patient who didn't receive an indicated pneumococcal vaccination, despite a history of splenectomy. Although the case is multifactorial, notably, the patient did not have "splenectomy" on her problem list. The authors consider how appropriate documentation might have prevented the error and resultant harm.
- Far from the vision of the problem-oriented medical record, most electronic health records today present data in a mostly source-oriented view. Accurate and complete problem lists, however, open up a number of possibilities for better presentations. In Chapter 14, we describe the possibility of time-oriented data views to support problem-oriented chronic disease management.
- In Chapter 15, we revisit the problem list intervention developed at the University of Illinois at Chicago. Although the tool was developed to improve problem list completeness, the authors discovered that it had another important application—detection and prevention of wrong-patient errors.

The goal of this book is to inform and inspire researchers, healthcare providers, administrators, software developers and policymakers interested in understanding and improving problem lists, electronic health records and healthcare itself. It is our sincere hope that the experiences we describe here can lead to better documentation, better use of information and, ultimately, safe and high quality healthcare.

REFERENCES

1. Weed LL. Medical Records that Guide and Teach. *The New England Journal of Medicine*. 1968;278(11):593-600.

Adam Wright, PhD

PART I

HISTORY AND IMPORTANCE

CHAPTER 1

BRINGING SCIENCE TO MEDICINE: AN INTERVIEW WITH LARRY WEED, INVENTOR OF THE PROBLEM-ORIENTED MEDICAL RECORD

ADAM WRIGHT, DEAN F. SITTIG, JULIE MCGOWAN, JOAN S. ASH, AND LAWRENCE L. WEED

1.1 INTRODUCTION

Larry Weed, MD is known as the father of the problem-oriented medical record, inventor of the now-ubiquitous SOAP (subjective/objective/assessment/plan) note, and developer of the Problem-Oriented Medical Information System (PROMIS). (1) His paper "Medical Records that Guide and Teach" (2) is one of the most-cited informatics papers of all time, having been referenced nearly a thousand times. Over the course of his career, he has worked as a scientist, physician, entrepreneur, and, most recently, health system visionary, and has always been a fierce and tireless advocate for a safer, better organized, more efficient, and science-driven health system. (3)

Reproduced from Journal of the American Medical Informatics Association, *Wright A, Sittig DF, McGowan J, Ash JS, and Weed LL, Online First: 3 July 2014, copyright 2014. doi:10.1136/amia-jnl-2014-02776. With permission from BMJ Publishing Group Ltd.*

On December 28, 2010, JMcG conducted an oral history interview with Dr Weed at his home in Underhill, Vermont using questions prepared by JSA and DFS. The interview was condensed, rearranged, and edited by AW, and is presented here in Dr Weed's own words, with the exception of (1) minor additions, clarifications, and references, indicated in brackets, (2) this introduction and the conclusion, and (3) an epilogue presenting a biography of Dr Weed.

1.2 EARLY LIFE AND EDUCATION

I was born in Troy, New York and then I was brought up in Middletown, New York, and my interests were those of any teenager. I went on to college and then I went to medical school at Columbia [College of Physicians and Surgeons in New York City]. I did various residencies, did biochemistry at Penn [University of Pennsylvania, Philadelphia], had fellowships, and was in the military.

1.3 THE DIFFERENCE BETWEEN SCIENCE AND MEDICINE

I had done research in biochemistry in nucleic acid chemistry in the late '40s and early '50s, and I accepted a double appointment at Yale in the Departments of Pharmacology and Medicine. A couple months a year they would come for me in Medicine and say, "Would you make rounds on a ward with students and house officers?" I would then return to the basic science department and do research and teach.

It was in that process that I realized that a research scientist has one problem and can make time the variable and achievement the constant in his work, whereas a physician on a busy ward has multiple problems and limited time, making the behavior of a true scientist almost impossible. As a scientist, you have a very specific project. That's your research. You work on it and work on it, and you finally get it written up. You get it published in a journal. The scientist works under a disciplined system of review and publication of his work. A physician works in a chaotic system of keeping and organizing data and has no systematic review and correction of his daily work.

You'd think that after all these years of being at Hopkins [Johns Hopkins University, Baltimore, Maryland] and Columbia and Bellevue [Hospital, New York] and Western Reserve [now Case Western Reserve University, Cleveland, Ohio], I would have sensed that there's something wrong. But when you're in an establishment, do as the Romans do. You just get along and do what you have to do to get on to the next job. What do you do to get a degree? And if they say, "Go kill your grandmother," you say, "Well, where's my grandmother? And do you have a gun?" That's the way the academic business seemed to me.

Finally I asked myself: suppose you treated a medical student or resident like a graduate student working on a problem to get a PhD. You would say to the student, "Well, what's your problem?" "Well, Mrs Jones is one of my patients." "Well, what are her problems? Where's the list of her problems? We have to work up each problem. Well, don't you have a record?" The medical record of Mrs Jones must be a medical student's scientific notebook. With a scientist doing research you can see in his notebooks in the laboratory what he does each day. You can see his data, what came out of the spectrometer and so on, and you can examine it.

1.4 THE BIRTH OF THE PROBLEM-ORIENTED MEDICAL RECORD

So I said to these interns and students, "I need a problem list." And they'd say, "Well, do you mean the doctor's impression after he did the initial workup?"

But I'm not interested in somebody's impression. I want a clear definition of the problem, the data that support that definition and what you are doing to try to solve it. If I went to a graduate student saying "What's your problem," and they said, "Well, I work in pyrimidine chemistry," I would say, "Specifically what pyrimidine? And tell me, what are you trying to do?"

I realized then—and it was very upsettin —that they weren't getting any of the discipline of scientific training on those wards. When I pick up a chart that is a bunch of scribbles, I say, "That's not art. It certainly isn't science. Now, God knows what it is. The physician who is creating it will have to give it a name." So that's what got me into the problem-oriented record... We started to rearrange the medical records. This was not easy. But after four years we got it going.

There are four sections to the problem-oriented medical record: the database, the problem list, titles, and numbered plans for each problem, and titled and numbered progress notes on each problem. (4) So I can pick up any record, and see for example: Problem No. 3: Hypertension. What were the plans? Let me read the progress notes. Now that's a very defined system.

As you go through such a record, there are four behaviors you should be looking for. Are practitioners thorough? Are they reliable? Are they analytically sound? And are they efficient? What I mean by thorough is are all the data in the required database there? If not you get an F in thoroughness. You then do the same things for the other three behaviors. Now, if you get a Pass in three of the behaviors, but it takes you six weeks to work up a single patient, you're not efficient. And you can't function in the real world. You won't make a living. Nobody or no clinic will hire you. An emergency room will be backed up.

1.5 THE MOVE TO MAINE

Right at that time when I was coming to these realizations, I got a call from Bangor, Maine. The head of the board of trustees was on the other end of the line and he said, "We need a Medical Director up here. Would you come up?"

In those days, in the late '40s and early '50s, Bangor, Maine was a 6-hour train ride through a bunch of pine trees from Boston. You didn't jump in a plane and appear there. And I had a wife and children and I said, "Well, sir, I'm pretty much involved here." I didn't say, "I don't want to get off this academic track and go out in the boonies with a bunch of people in Maine that I've never seen before." So we hung up. Two hours later the phone rings again. He said, "My name is Henry Wheelwright. Does that name mean anything?" I said, "The only Wheelwright I knew is

Jeff Wheelwright who was a classmate of mine in medical school, and a good friend—he was just a great guy." "Well, I'm his father." I said, "Oh." He said, "I'm going to treat you like you're my son, like I treat Jeff, and I want to give you some advice right now. Never say 'no' to a job over the telephone. I'm paying your way up here, get your tail up here." So I went home and told my wife about it—we had to get out a map in those days to see where Bangor was, how far from the academic world.

So I went up there and on the way, I made a list of all the requirements I would have for taking the job, knowing they couldn't meet them. To make a long story short, they met all the requirements. I went to Bangor, Maine to become the Medical Director of the hospital. They really called my bluff. They had five incoming interns and asked me if I would take over. That's when I said to the house officers and staff, "This is the way we're going keep records on the patients. The patient's medical record will be the doctor's scientific notebook." And since I had authority, I demanded it, or I wouldn't come.

I stayed in Maine for four years, and I got the record going.

1.6 ONWARD TO OHIO

But I still had an interest in the biochemistry research that I'd been doing, and I continued my research and teaching at the medical school at Western Reserve. Charlie Burger was one of the students in the medical class there. I told him and other students about the problem-oriented record. I'd say to the students at Western Reserve, "Do you have any idea what all this stuff you're learning in basic science has to do with taking care of patients when you get an internship? You are struggling in biochemistry, learning [the] Krebs cycle. Do you know how the details you are learning now would be used in the care of patients and are you sure you will remember them when the time comes to care for patients?" I reminded them of what Tolstoy wrote about "the snare of preparation" ["The first and most common snare into which man falls is the personal snare, that of making preparations to live, instead of living" (5)] and that John Dewey said that learning and education in the real world means making connections. (6)

1.7 COMPUTERIZATION OF THE MEDICAL RECORD AND LANDING IN VERMONT

At Western Reserve we got the problem-oriented record really rolling in the City Hospital [Cleveland Metropolitan General Hospital, Cleveland Ohio]. Cuyahoga County had put computers in the City Hospital and they asked me to come over and teach medicine. That's when I started to say, "Well, we ought to get a computerized problem list." So that's where the computers started.

Once we got the computer rolling, they came from Vermont and wanted me to come here to really get—and that was in '69 and the '70s—the problem-oriented record going and then a computerized ward at the hospital. [We started] the PROMIS lab in Cleveland and then brought the whole thing to Vermont. (1 ,7)

1.8 THE LIMITATIONS OF HUMAN KNOWLEDGE

Real problems always cross specialty boundaries. If a patient has chest pain, it could be a cardiovascular problem. It could be a lung problem. It could be a spine problem. They could have a broken rib. There can be a hundred causes of chest pain. Well, when a patient goes to see a cardiologist, can she be sure that he knows the symptoms and findings of a thoracic disk [herniation], that doesn't have anything to do with her heart?

Speaking to [a group of physicians] I said, "The problem with the field of medicine is you can't do what the patients think you're supposed to be doing. The patients think you know all 60 or 70 causes of an acute abdomen. But there's not a person in this room who could stand up and say, I know them."

There were a bunch of surgeons in the room, and it was really quite a riot, this meeting. One of them said, "Well, Dr Weed, are you trying to tell us—I've been doing surgery for 30 years–and don't you believe in intuition and experience? You know, you know an appendix when it comes in the door." Yeah, but if it's not an appendix, what you think you sense might be wrong. The patient becomes a victim of your experience.

So I said to these physicians, "You've got all this body of knowledge and you're trying to couple it to everyday action by putting it in people's [medical students'] heads. You're going to give them all these courses. And then they're going to learn to take histories and physicals. They're going to learn all of these details about the patients, and then they're supposed to process it in their head and say, 'Therefore, Mrs Jones, you have appendicitis.' But the voltage drop across that transmission line is enormous. God knows what answer some of them end up with." And they knew they were decompensating. Why am I saying they knew? They specialized. You take the surgery, I'll take medicine. Interns, then cardiologists, hematologists, endocrinologists, and red cell men. Then they formed their own journals.

So finally this one surgeon said, "Well, it sort of makes sense but it's very upsetting. Anyway, I don't accept that experience and intuition aren't something." I said, "Well, I'm not saying you don't have intuitive feelings. What I'm suggesting is that they may be worthless."

So they asked if we could go to dinner together. I said, "Look, if you don't catch onto this right away, it won't help to go to dinner." It'd be like having an abortionist and an anti-abortionist have dinner together so they can settle their differences. They could live together for 10 years and they wouldn't settle their differences.

[By the late seventies, I saw that] we were drowning [the physicians with all the data we could compile in the computer. There was so much there that] they couldn't process it. This brought to mind the poem by Edna St. Vincent Millay (8):

Upon this age, that never speaks its mind,
This furtive age, this age endowed with power
To wake the moon with footsteps, fit an oar
Into the rowlocks of the wind, and find
What swims before his prow, what swirls behind –
Upon this gifted age, in its dark hour,]
Falls from the sky a meteoric shower
Of facts [...they lie unquestioned, uncombined.]
Wisdom enough to leech us of our ill
Is daily spun; but there exists no loom
To weave it into fabric

1.9 DEVELOPMENT OF THE PROBLEM-KNOWLEDGE COUPLERS

[I realized then that] we need[ed] a loom. I used the computer to implement combinatorial thinking and thereby create a fabric of care using data from the literature and data from the patient… the first coupler. Just ask yourself and answer all these questions, then hit COUPLE. There may be 300 questions. [We called it the problem-knowledge coupler. (9–12)]

Two years later, one of the guys in that meeting called me from New York and said, "You know, I was one of the guys fighting with you. I run an emergency training program for emergency room residents. We have 28 residents, we have five rooms. It's a big New York City hospital, and we just missed a 10-year-old girl with an acute abdomen. Do you think this tool [the coupler] would have helped?"

I said, "Well, I'll tell you what I'll do. I will send you—I'll print out the pages. And what you do is you go through these questions."

What I did is I put them in. You just go through these questions with a problem, abdominal pain. Well what do you mean by the right lower quadrant? Well, put it at his fingertips. You click on it to show a picture of the abdomen. I said, "That's the way a coupler works. There's just a bunch of questions." You can teach even high school kids how to use these tools. That's what training should be doing… if we're going to clean up the medical center, we should take the kids that have great hands, great interpersonal skills, and say, "Alex, I don't care what else you do in this world, don't tell me you're a great skier, or you play the cello well, I couldn't care less. Can you do this coupler without making a mistake? Can you feel the spleen? We can use you." He has no doubt that he's got a job and he can do something worthwhile.

If he said this is positive, the machine will know what it votes for. We just go through these questions. We're not going to try to put the knowledge in the doctor's mind. You can't do it. It's a whole different way of moving knowledge.

So at any rate, I said to this person in New York, "I'm going to print the questions on sheets of paper so that you'll just get all the questions in the mail. You're going to sit down with the record of the patient whose acute abdomen you missed, and the resident and the intern and the attending, and you're going to mark on those sheets of paper the ones that were positive. Then I'll fly down and we'll put them into the computer. Then we'll hit COUPLE."

So I sent the sheets of paper to him and I said, "You've got to promise me, when you go through those sheets of paper with the residents, students, and the patient record, you have to mark every question you don't know the answer to because you didn't ask it. Or you don't even know what that test is, when you feel the abdomen. They're simple, inexpensive things that you didn't do. Mark those in red. And then we'll talk about it at the conference."

So I get off the plane. We put the responses in the computer. When we were done I said, "Now, you want me to hit COUPLE, all those findings with all those diseases, but I'm not going to do it." [He replied] "Well, you said you were going to show us." I said, "I'm not going to hit COUPLE. On these papers, half of these questions are red. You want me to hit COUPLE. Then we'll get the wrong answer and you'll say, see, the thing doesn't work. I know how you function. You all went to medical school. Your capacity for self-deception is beyond belief."

One of the residents said, "Well, could we see the findings?" I said, "Yes, I'll show you the findings that were positive. Here they are. Well, you can do automatic outcome studies. We don't have to have typists. They're all printed up. You can do population studies. You're all playing with half a deck. And no two of you play with the same part of the deck."

This one resident that missed the case says, "Dr Weed, I won't criticize you. Would you please hit COUPLE just to see what the machine would have found with half a deck. I'm promising not to be critical."

So I hit COUPLE. [Pause for the coupling results] Well, it says there are four things—from a physiological point of view—that tell you a smooth muscle tube, like an intestine or a ureter, is obstructed. This patient has all four of them. When they're writhing and restless and vomiting and so forth, you want to think of that. Now, in more specific terms, there are eight things in the machine for small bowel obstruction. She's got six of them. The resident looked up and he said, "That's what she had and that's what we missed."

So I said, "Even playing with a half a deck, the machine did better than you."

The couplers are very sophisticated now. But in this case, this was the first thing that came up and the resident said, "That's what she had and we missed it." And some of these questions they'd never even asked. So then I said, "You can page down and read—you get comments about the leukocyte count being normal and there are points about the evidence." Well, how do we know we can believe all this? You click on this and it'll give you [the] reference and the page number. See, you're connecting that patient to the library without having that intermediate, limited human mind in the middle of it.

The coupler builder may not be perfect but he has all day to do nothing but build the acute abdomen coupler. He doesn't have any more patients. You don't know how long it took that person to build that beautiful Honda that you drive out there. All you know is you get in and move your foot and you go. That's the way medicine has got to be. A new division of labor.

To get back to this business, you'd think after this—but one of the surgeons kept saying, "Well, this is impressive, Dr Weed, and on half a deck, you're right. You did get it right. But it's not going to work." And I said, "Why not?" [and he replied] "Well, you can't expect people with not a lot of experience to go mindlessly through all the questions. It takes too long."

I said, "Well, first of all, I wouldn't hire somebody who wants to make $200 000 or a million dollars a year." We could train people to use these tools who are much less expensive. A good practitioner who has the right knowledge tools, hands-on skills, and interpersonal skills. You have to get over the idea that if he gets A's in all his courses he has the best hands-on skills. You must have noticed on the campus that all the best football players are not valedictorians. They may not even get out of school. But for that hands-on thing, they got it. And that other kid, the patients all love her. She's got interpersonal skills that you couldn't graft onto some others if you tried. Of those three things, interpersonal skills, knowledge, and hands-on skills, I can move all the knowledge into tools. I'm going to select the kids who really care about people and have best hands-on skills. That's a completely upside down approach compared to how it's currently done. And then everybody's got high morale because they are doing something useful.

Well, why did this take so long to get going? I wrote the first papers in 1982 in medical journals. That's 30 years ago.

[End of interview]

1.10 CONCLUSION: IMPLICATIONS AND THE ROAD AHEAD

It is hard to overstate the impact of Dr Weed's work on medicine and medical informatics. His ideas led to a fundamental reorganization of the medical record and the introduction of the now-ubiquitous problem list and SOAP note, both of which are taught and used throughout the world. His later work focused on problem-knowledge couplers and the development of significant diagnostic and treatment knowledge bases. He founded a company (PKC) focused on couplers in 1982 and left in 2006. The company was, acquired by Sharecare, Inc. (Atlanta, Georgia) in 2012. (13)

Dr Weed's most recent book, *Medicine in Denial,* an in-depth analysis of "a deep disorder [that] pervades medical practice... [and] exists because medical practice lacks a true system of care." (14) *Medicine in Denial* proposes a new organization of care which has, at its core, four elements:

- A new "Center for Knowledge Building Tools" which would develop and maintain problem knowledge couplers and other knowledge resources
- A training center which would "develop skilled personnel to complete those portions of the couplers that the patients cannot do for themselves, for example, listen to their own heart or lungs, etc."
- A fully realized problem-oriented medical record (POMR) which would encompass a database for each patient, a problem list, plans for each problem, and progress notes
- A center for analysis which would review these POMRs and feed the results back to the Center for Knowledge Building Tools.

This bold proposal for care redesign goes much further than current health-policy approaches like accountable care organizations (15) and patient-centered medical homes. (16) As time goes by and the amount of knowledge instantly accessible via the internet continues to grow at an ever increasing rate, (17) such a vision for ubiquitous human interaction with a computerized, clinical knowledge base (18–20) seems less and less like science fiction and more and more like Weed's vision that is already over 50 years old.

1.11 EPILOGUE: A BIOGRAPHY OF DR LAWRENCE WEED

Lawrence "Larry" Weed was born in Troy, New York in December 1923, and earned an MD degree from the Columbia University College of Physicians and Surgeons in 1947.

Dr Weed is best known as the father of the problem-oriented medical record—a construct he first published on in 1964 and brought to prominence in 1968 with his landmark paper "Medical Records that Guide and Teach" (2) in the *New England Journal of Medicine.* The POMR consists of four components (21):

- The database, a collection of all information known about the patient
- A complete problem list
- Initial plans for each problem, written in SOAP format
- Daily progress notes, also organized by problem and written in the SOAP format.

The concepts of the POMR, particularly the problem list and the SOAP format for progress notes, are now ubiquitous. The POMR has been described, studied, or discussed in over 2000 academic articles as well as countless medical textbooks, is a cornerstone of medical and nursing education, and has had its positive effects documented. (22 ,23)

After developing the POMR concept in Bangor, Maine, Dr Weed put it into action at Cleveland Metropolitan General Hospital and then as a faculty member at the University of Vermont (UVM), where he led development of the PROMIS. (1 ,7) PROMIS was the first clinical information system to use a touch screen terminal. PROMIS was driven by a large medical knowledge base that was initially developed by Dr Weed and his wife Laura Weed (1) and later by a team of clinicians, librarians, and systems analysts. PROMIS was organized entirely around the POMR concept, with the nurse beginning to populate the database, followed by the patient, who would complete a 275-question review-of-systems. Medical students and residents then added additional information, and documented a physical exam—all in structured form. Once the database was populated, the problem list was constructed, plans were developed, and progress notes developed. The knowledge base required to support all of these modules was vast, and eventually specialists were brought in to extend it. When UVM sought, in the 1990s, to implement a comprehensive new electronic health record, their biggest challenge was that no system available had the level of functionality and the richness of clinical knowledge contained in the PROMIS system.

Dr Weed left UVM in the 1980s to start PKC. PKC focused on the development of couplers, which link medical knowledge to problems using combinatorial logic. (9–12) In many ways, the couplers were a maturation of the knowledge base development Dr Weed did for the PROMIS system. Several years after Dr Weed left PKC, it was acquired in 2012 by Sharecare, a consumer-focused site founded by Mehmet Oz (of the Dr Oz show) and Jeff Arnold, founder of WebMD.

In addition to his work developing the POMR concept, building PROMIS and leading PKC, Dr Weed has written five books: *Medical Records, Medical Education, and Patient Care: The Problem-Oriented Record as a Basic Tool* in 1970, *Your Health Care and How to Manage it: Your Health, Your Problems, Your Plans, Your Progress* in 1975, *Knowledge Coupling: New Premises and New Tools for Medical Care and Education* in 1991, *Managing Medicine* in 1993 and *Medicine in Denial* in 2011. He has won numerous awards for his work, including the Institute of Medicine's Gustav O. Lienhard award in 1995, and is a founding fellow of the American College of Medical Informatics.

REFERENCES

1. Schultz J, ed. A history of the PROMIS technology: an effective human interface. Proceedings of the ACM Conference on The History of Personal Workstations. 1986, ACM.
2. Weed LL. Medical records that guide and teach. N Engl J Med 1968;278:593–600.

3. Jacobs L. Interview with Lawrence Weed, MD- the father of the problem-oriented medical record looks ahead. Perm J 2009;13:84–9.
4. Weed LL. Medical records, medical education and patient care: the problem oriented record as a basic tool. Cleveland, OH: Press of Case Western Reserve University, 1971.
5. Tolstoy L, Chertkov VG. The Christian teaching. New York: Stokes, 1898. xiv, 210 pp.
6. Dewey J. Democracy and education: an introduction to the philosophy of education. New York: Macmillan, 1922. xii, 434 pp.
7. Schultz JR, Davis L. The technology of PROMIS. Proceedings of the IEEE. 1979;67:1237–44.
8. Millay ESV. Huntsman, what quarry? New York and London: Harper & Brothers; 1939. ix, 94 pp.
9. Weed LL, Hertzberg RY, eds. The use and construction of problem-knowledge couplers, the knowledge coupler editor, knowledge networks, and the problem-oriented medical record for the microcomputer. Proceedings of the Annual Symposium on Computer Application in Medical Care. American Medical Informatics Association, 1983.
10. McGowan JJ, Winstead-Fry P. Problem Knowledge Couplers: reengineering evidence-based medicine through interdisciplinary development, decision support, and research. Bull Med Libr Assoc 1999;87:462–70.
11. Weed LL, Zimny NJ. The problem-oriented system, problem-knowledge coupling, and clinical decision making. Physical Therapy 1989;69:565–8. [Abstract/FREE Full text]
12. Weed LL. Knowledge coupling: new premises and new tools for medical care and education. New York: Springer-Verlag, 1991. xxv, 362 pp.
13. Sharecare Inc. Sharecare Announces the Acquisition of PKC Corporation. 2012 [cited 3 Feb 2014]; http://www.sharecare.com/static/sharecare-announces-the-acquisition-of-pkc-corporation
14. Weed LL, Weed L. Medicine in denial. CreateSpace, 2011.
15. Berwick DM. Launching accountable care organizations–the proposed rule for the Medicare Shared Savings Program. N Engl J Med 2011;364:e32. [CrossRef]
16. Stange KC, Nutting PA, Miller WL, et al. Defining and measuring the patient-centered medical home. J Gen Intern Med 2010;25:601–12.
17. Gillam M, Feied C, Handler J, et al. The healthcare singularity and the age of semantic medicine. In: Hey T, Tansley S, Tolle K, eds. The fourth paradigm: data-intensive scientific discovery. Redmond, WA: Microsoft Research, 2009.
18. Greenwald R. And a diagnostic test was performed. N Engl J Med 2005;353:2089–90.
19. Frankovich J, Longhurst CA, Sutherland SM. Evidence-based medicine in the EMR era. N Engl J Med 2011;365:1758–9.
20. Friedman CP. A "fundamental theorem" of biomedical informatics. J Am Med Inform Assoc 2009;16:169–70. [Abstract/FREE Full text]
21. Williams L. Complete guide to documentation. Lippincott Williams & Wilkins, 2008.

22. Fernow LC, Mackie C, McColl I, et al. The effect of problem-oriented medical records on clinical management controlled for patient risks. Med Care 1978;16:476–87.
23. Margolis CZ, Mendelssohn I, Barak N, et al. Increase in relevant data after introduction of a problem-oriented record system in primary pediatric care. Am J Public Health 1984;74:1410–12.

CHAPTER 2

MEDICAL RECORDS THAT GUIDE AND TEACH

LAWRENCE L. WEED

The beginning clinical clerk, the house officer and the practicing physician are all confronted with conditions that are frustrating in every phase of medical action. The purpose of this article is to identify and discuss these conditions and point out solutions. To deal effectively with these frustrations it will be necessary to develop a more organized approach to the medical record, a more rational acceptance and use of paramedical personnel and a more positive attitude about the computer in medicine. Eventually, for every physician all three areas will be an obligatory part of his professional environment if he is to play a significant part in the total health-care job that will have to be done. The organization of the medical record should be a matter of immediate concern to practicing physicians and students; the degree of involvement of any individual practicioner with paramedical personnel and the computer will vary with the particular environment and facilities. Developments in all these fields are far more advanced and immediately applicable than many realize, and concern with them is neither premature nor impractical.

From Weed LL. Medical Records That Guide and Teach. The New England Journal of Medicine 278 (1968); Copyright © 1967 Massachusetts Medical Society. www.nejm.org/doi/full/10.1056/NEJM196803142781105. Reprinted with permission from the author.

2.1 NEW TECHNIQUES MUST BE ADOPTED

Among physicians there has been uncritical adherence to tradition in the first phase of medical action, which is the collection of data, upon which complete formulation and management of all the patient's problems depends.

Routine completeness is expected of physicians in the history and physical examination regardless of specific indications, whereas initial laboratory determinations are arbitrarily relegated to an "only-when-indicated" category. Subclinical disease may thereby be missed. Extravagance is then paradoxically demonstrated by the ordering of excessive and inappropriately selected follow-up laboratory and x-ray examinations for the problems clinically evident. Thoroughness and order in the whole process decrease drastically and indiscriminately as work pressures build up, so that finally among physicians there is a remarkable spectrum of behavior from the compulsively elaborate to the sketchy and haphazard. In the field of medicine it has never been clearly determined what the minimum, effective initial data base needs to be.

In the face of the confusion concerning the necessary quantity of data, the initial collection of data should be made as significant and complete as possible. The only limitations should be the discomfort, danger and expense to the patient. If useful historical data can be acquired and stored cheaply, completely and accurately by new computer and interviewing technics without the use of expensive physician time, they should be seriously considered. That this is already so is strongly suggested by the work of Slack, [1, 2] and by results of present efforts in our clinic using trained interviewers and computerized approaches to the recording and printing of narrative, historical data. By such measures every patient can be guaranteed a minimal recorded data base of historical information routinely acquired by a trained interviewer or by direct patient interaction with an organized series of branching questions presented on a television screen terminal. The doctor will always be expected to read this information, enlarge upon it where indicated, and integrate it with that which he himself elicited. In this way the recorded historical data will not be based on a single encounter with anyone, and busy physicians, who represent a wide spectrum of abilities, habits of thoroughness, attitudes and levels of efficiency, will not risk important omissions.

Paramedical personnel, armed with questions and interviewing technics, and with multichannel analyzers, pulmonary-function tests, electronic instruments for studying all systems (particularly the cardiovascular system) and simple routines to assess the musculoskeletal system can create a sound data base rapidly and accurately. At this institution (Cleveland Metropolitan General Hospital, Western Reserve School of Medicine, This work has been under the direction of Dr. Charles Burger and Mr. Eugene Lovasy.) there has been developed a computerized physical examination whose performance requires a high level of thoroughness and precision, but a significant part of it can be performed by paramedical personnel. The "print-outs" from the computer of both the interview and the physical examination are in readable narrative form with only the positive findings printed out under the appropriate system heading. Nurses properly trained could guarantee a certain high level of excellence in breast, abdominal and pelvic examinations. They already do Papanicolaou smears and have nonmedical cytologists interpret them. Having established a large data base in the computer for a large number of patients over a long period of time, we should study it, restructure it and eliminate that which is nonproductive.

Properly trained paramedical personnel can both contribute greatly to the data-collection phase and help teach it. The medical faculty must become far more interested and expert in teaching the analysis of medical data, the complete formulation of the problems, and the disciplined following of each. When these things are done in a complete and rigorous fashion, many problems emerge in a single patient.

2.2 ORGANIZATION OF THE PATIENT'S MULTIPLE PROBLEMS

Whereas a good scientist focuses on a single or very limited number of problems, pursuing each until he finds a solution, the physician is asked to accept the obligation of multiple problems in a given clinical situation and yet to give each the single-minded attention that is fundamental to developing and mobilizing his enthusiasm and skill. The university education a physician receives suggests that his attitude should be scientific in focus, but the multiplicity of tasks that confront him during his clinical training often defeats this goal. He can act as a scientist, however, if he is able to organize the problems of each patient in a way that enables him to deal with them systematically.

It is here that an organized approach to the medical record can help. At present the physician has to read the entire record (often illegible and handwritten) and then sort the data in his mind if he is to know all the patient's difficulties and the extent to which each has been analyzed. There is no evidence that he does this reliably and consistently; he and others using the record lose their way, and problems get neglected, missed entirely or treated out of context. One solution is to orient data around each problem. Each medical record should have a complete list of all the patient's problems, including both clearly established diagnoses and all other unexplained findings that are not yet clear manifestations of a specific diagnosis, such as abnormal physical findings or symptoms. [3 4 5] When the data warrant, these findings can be crystallized into a specific diagnosis. The "problems list" then is not static in its composition, but is a dynamic "table of contents" of the patient's chart, which can be updated at any time. Separate problems all found to be part of the same entity or diagnosis may be combined. The list is separated into active and inactive problems, and in this way, those of immediate importance are easily discernible, and a compact history of the patient is embodied in the complete list. Once such a list has been established all subsequent orders, plans, progress notes and numerical data can be recorded under the numbered and titled problem to which they are specifically related   For example, if we know that the patient has a perforated ulcer, it is so stated; if we are not sure, we honestly state the problem as "abdominal pain" and immediately update it on the original list to perforated ulcer only when the evidence allows. Lists of "impressions" and guesses fail to convey the exact level of resolution of a problem and may result in premature interruption of diagnostic action. Students must be taught to acquire a capacity for the "sustained muddleheadedness" and the tolerance for ambiguity that Whitehead considered so essential when difficult unexplained findings are dealt with. A diagnosis is a step forward only when it can be sustained by the evidence at hand.

Inherent in the problem-oriented approach to data organization in the medical record is the necessity for completeness in the formulation of the

Medical Records That Guide and Teach

```
9/10
Pt. received 40 units of regular insulin yest. because of 3 & 4+ urine
sugars. Got 2000 cc Amigen yest. & 500 cc D,W. Was febrile all
night up to 40 at 8 PM this gradually came down to 39. 8 PM yest.
suctioned & coughed up c̄ return of ½ cup of thick white sputum —
cultured also blood cultures. Was in must. tent c̄ mucomist overnight.
At 4 PM yest had B-R base. Sputum smear unremarkable — WBC's
but no bacteria.

9/10-12:30
10 o'clock urine 2-3+/0. Given 10 U. reg. ins. at 12:30 PM. Temp.
down to 38? Suctioned N.T. ō little return. However during suctioning
pt. vomited 100-150 cc green fluid. Proximal jejunostomy tube drain-
ing well now.

9/11-9 AM
Urine 3+ given 10 U reg. insulin. Pt. was hiccuping all night & this AM.
Levine tube passed c̄ 900-1000 cc bileous fluid removed. Jejunos-
tomy tubes have been draining minimally. Will have Levine tube down.

(THREE PAGES OF SIMILAR NOTES FOLLOW UNTIL 9/26/67)

9/26
Last night 10PM had seizure like behavior and acting strange. Ap-
parently hallucinating. Blood sugar didn't register on destrostix. Had
been given 10 units reg. insulin at 8 PM after IV glucose returned to
nl. This AM vomited up brown black fluid 300 cc + for occult blood.
NG tube had been put since 5 PM yest. NG tube replaced & some ma-
terial small amt. withdrawn. Pt. now NPO ō NG. tube to Gomco.

9/27
Still febrile — Ampicillin 1 g qid — continued; Blood cult. drawn to
check if septicemia still present. Chest x-ray today shows infiltrate in
(R) lower lobe. No effusion. Sputum grew out pseudomonas but Dr.
_____ elected not to treat this.
ON SERVICE NOTE (please read revised problem list and please use
#'s shown)

10/2-6 PM
#1 Chronic Relapsing Panc.:
   b. Diabetes: will continue moment-to-moment Rx of spot urines for
      now. Today c̄ only 10 U regular insulin pt. spilling mainly 2-3+.
      Plan: BLD sugar tomorrow
   c. Panc. insuff.: will begin Cotazyn-B
#2 Complications Following Laparotomy:
   c. Post op ileus: KUB tomorrow. Pt. now tolerating ice cream and
      occ. candy. bs. poor; s̄ gross distention; stool passes regularly →
      fistula

Imp: prob. resolving now
Plan: KUB and continue small feedings
   d. Sepsis: afebrile now on Ampicillin. see flow sheet. Reculture
      tomorrow.
   b. RLL Pneumonia: Film of 9/28 shows some ↑ in this process.
      Will repeat P.A. chest tomorrow & cultures.
   e. Colonic-Cutaneous Fistula: Continues to drain semi-formed
      stool several times per day; the problem is that stool drains
      onto granulating abd. wound.
      Plan: culture stool; Remove some non-func stay sutures; Freq
      dressings & consider colostomy bag for fistula

10/3
#1 Chronic Relapsing Panc.:
   c. Panc. insufficiency: Cotazyn-B will be begun (special purchase)
      and will evaluate effect on absorption and/or stool content
      by measuring amt of fat
   f. Pain: pt. still requires freq narcotics. Neurosug will eventually
      perform epidural block and depending upon results will con-
      sider cordotomy
#2 Complications Following Laparotomy:
   b. RLL Pneumonia: Chest x-ray today shows marked resolution of
      previously described infiltrates; pt. has been afebrile —
      sputum recultured (see #2d).
   c. Post op ileus: KUB today shows little improvement from film
      of 9/29. Ba in same position in colon which is distal to
      fistula. Despite this x-ray findings will continue to feed (see
      #2f). Bowel sounds poor and abd. seems slightly more dis-
      tended. Will give oil retention enema to try to clear distal
      colon.
   d. Sepsis: Pt. has been afebrile, cultures repeated today; o (M)
      heard today; has been on Ampicillin x 9 days. Although po-
      tential still present this problem is under relatively good con-
      trol.
   e. Colonic-Cutaneous Fistula: all stay sutures removed today and
      wound is well granulated but constantly bathed c̄ stool.
      Colostomy bag applied to try to control this drainage. Eti-
      ology of fistula? but may be serving decompressive function.
   f. Malnutrition: Total protein = 6.1 c 2.1/4.0 = A/G in 1965. Wt.
      has ↓ from 141# ——→ 113# since adm.
      Imp: little resolution of ileus. in fact, most of food stays in
      stomach probably; this remains the main problem; other
      as above fairly well controlled except malnutrition.
      Plan: as above plus give gastro-graffin per NG tube and watch
      progress; avoid surgery.
```

FIGURE 1: Sequence of Notes Extracted from a Complicated Record. In the first, unstructured portion, facts and phrases are presented that suggest difficulties in many systems, but the confusion in such a tangle of illogically grouped bits of information is such that one can not reliably discern how (or if) the physician defined and logically pursued each problem. On 10/2 a new physician took over, and the improvement is apparent. By reading the titles alone of each of the progress notes one begins immediately to grasp the nature of the case. In this and in all other figures, the record is reproduced as originally phrased, without editing.

```
                Plan was to pass N.G. tube if Dr. _____ (E.N.T.) found no lesion and
                  he did not on exam today — force feed via tube for a few weeks.
             #5 Depression — patient agitated during nite — lost weight — given
                  Thorazine 25 mgm @ midnite (had 75 mgm Elavil yesterday)
                  today semi-responsive unable to take orally and has low grade
                  fever.*
                P.E.:
                  B.P. 140/70  P. 80 & reg.  T. 101*  R. 32/min.
                  Responds to voice occasionally — pain regularly — not
                      intelligible speech.
                  EENT — nl. except dry mucous mem.
                  NECK — supple — carotids nl.
                  LUNGS — clear, acrate well.
                  HEART — NSR — Gr. II sys. Murmur — ô gallop, rub, etc.
                  ABD. — soft, obese — ? RLQ tenderness & ? RLQ mass.
                  P & R — deferred
                  NEURO — responds as noted — DTR's symmetrical, de-
                      pressed ô pathologic reflexes.
                  SKIN — several ecchymotic areas & superficial abrasions
                      marked generalized edema — waxy turgor to skin.
                  CHEST X-RAY — cardiomegaly

               *See footnote for fever of unknown origin.

                  WBC — 10,000+
                  Urine — not obtained
                  Imp. Same Plus — #Fever unk. origin†
                  Plan — Adm. for observation
```
```
5/13
 #2 Anemia — will recheck Hgb. Hct. today — to get IM Fe — 20 cc
                Imferon
 #4 Edema — malnutrition — #16 plastic tube inserted yesterday.
 #5 Depression — perhaps a little more responsive. Wants water P.O. —
                off psychotropic drugs.
 #6 F.U.O. — will insert foley cath. to preserve skin; and evaluate
                U.T.I.;540 cc; Mic — neg

5/15

 #4 Edema — nutrition — tolerating NG feeding
     750 cal. — 250 a q 3 — will increase to 350 a q 3 — 1,000 cal/24°
     (This record continues on for the next six months, with gradual evolution
     of all the problems and remarkable resolution of some, such as the edema,
     the poor nutrition, and the psychiatric difficulties. Problem-oriented
     discharge summaries facilitate rapid assessment of cases such as this.)

†The pattern of the physician's thought is suggested as he discusses the
 semi-responsiveness under the Depression, momentarily couples the
 fever with both and then quickly decides to follow the fever as a separate
 problem under fever of undetermined origin after finding a supple
 neck and no localizing signs. Should he have done a lumbar puncture
 before he decided to leave the semiresponsiveness with the depression
 and drugs, but formulate the fever as a separate problem? A problem list
 and titled progress notes reveal the context in which thoughts occur and
 actions are taken. Knowledge of content without context can be useless
 or even misleading.
```

FIGURE 2: Record, Randomly Taken from the Files of Two Physicians Currently Conducting a Busy General Practice in a Small Town in Maine, Showing the Approaches Advocated. The internship training of these doctors was based upon problem oriented patient records and care. One may not necessarily agree with the medical decisions, but the manner in which each problem is formulated, pursued and related to the other problems makes it possible for one to assess quality rapidly in terms of the physician's thoroughness and analytical capacity. There have been minor, but useful, modifications in form since the time of the rotating internship of these particular practitioners nine years ago. In the initial plan, not only the number but the title of each problem is used, facilitating even more rapid audit of the physician's approach to a particular situation. It will also be noted that problems #8 — Hiatus Hernia — and #9 — Diverticulosis — were not listed at the time of admission even though they were known. All significant problems should be entered as soon as they are known, noting but not omitting those that are inactive or resolved. Also, progress notes should follow a form similar to that seen in Figures 3 and 4, in which the physician first discusses the problem from the patient's point of view (subjectively, Sx), then states all appropriate objective data (Obj.) pertinent to the patient's problem, states current treatment (Rx), gives any new interpretations (Int.) and, finally, discusses the plan for the next interval.

```
              PROBLEM LIST                    Obj – ASO neg. RH factor – not significantly ↑. Repeat sed rate
6/17  #1 Rheumatic Heart Disease                    – films of shoulders, elbows, wrists
        a. Mitral insufficiency               Rx – symptoms exacerbated by ASA – some relief by heat
        b. Atrial fibrillation                Plan – a. uric acid, serum glob, LE prep
        c. Compensated congestive failure TTB        b. observe
        d. Cardiac catheterization          #8 Family Problems:
        e. Successful cardioversion           pt. has been upset lately by husband's constant admonitions not to
      #2 Presumed SBE                         over-do herself and his general over protective attitude. Today was
      #3 Mild Diabetes Mellitus – adult onset very upset, depressed and crying – it is now obvious that more
      #4 Repeated pulmonary embolism          fundamental conflicts exist in this marriage. Husband drinks, is
      #5 Post. Inferior Vena Cava Ligation    jealous of attention she gives the children, etc.
      #6 Allergic dermatitis                  Plan – have asked her to have husband call me and will get a greater
9/3   #7 Arthralgia                                  feel for the situation starting with the part of the conflict
9/8   #8 Family problems                             revolving around her medical condition

8/5 – CARDIOLOGY                          9/23
TEMP – 36.5  WEIGHT 73.6 kg
                                          Was pelvic (& pap) done during adm? if not, suggest having these
#1 RHD:                                   done.
  Sx – excellent exercise tolerance – does housework, taking walks,
      etc. no SOB                         #1 RHD:
  Obj – wt. ↑ again 4 lbs P 100 reg. c̄ rare PVC BP 150/90  Sx – continued excellent exercise tolerance
      chest – few rales @ (L) base that do not clear c̄ cough; cor. – un-  Obj – wt ↑ 2 Kg B 160/70 P 100 reg; chest – clear; cor – as above
      changed                             Rx – Digitalis 0/100 QD, Quinidine 0/200 qid
  Rx – unchanged – see flow sheet
  Plans – in view of excellent clinical response and exercise tolerance  #5 Post IVC Ligation:
      I am not concerned about rales but will continue to watch    (R) leg now back to normal s̄ edema but (L) leg now swells even
      a. Quinidine 0/200 q2h #300          more and often does not go down @ night – becomes heavy and
         continue other meds               cumbersome
                                           Rx – Naqua seems to help but not taking QD
#5 Post IVC Ligation:                      Plan – a. Naqua QD
  Sx – ō                                          b. refer to peripheral vasc. clinic
  Obj – leg swelling continues to be a problem esp. during the hot       c. D/C Coumadin
      weather                             #7 Arthralgia:
  Rx – unchanged                             Sx – comes and goes but essentially about the same overall.
  Plan – 1. ↑ Naqua to 0/002 QD                 A.M. hand stiffness seems to be her biggest complaint.
         2. Coumadin 0/005 QD                Obj – joint films ⟶ osteoarthritis changes in elbows and hands
         3. protime today                    Rx – ō – heat, rest, ASA
         RTC 3 mos.                          Plan – continue above

9/8                                       #8 Family Problem:
#1 Arthralgias – see EW note 9-3-66         marked improvement p̄ she mentioned to husband that I wanted to
  Sx – continues @ about same intensity but more concentrated in  talk c̄ him. He has not called but has been much improved in his
      (R) arm (exth. done in that arm).    attitude toward her and the children.
```

FIGURE 3: List of Problems and Associated Clinic Notes on a Patient Being Seen in a Busy Outpatient Department of a Large Urban Hospital. This list is a permanent part of the record, and new problems are added as they appear such as the arthralgia and family problems in this particular case. The latter is an example of a good physician who did not limit himself to the strictly medical or organic questions. (Note that all problems are not necessarily dealt with on each visit; the extent of the thought and care given to each situation is clearly defined).

```
Intern's Admission Note:                                    EKG – sinus tachycardia early 1966
67 yr. old white male admitted from OPC for elective T.E.A. of (R)    – WNL late 1966
superf. femoral artery                                     BUN = 15 in 1966; Cr = 1.0, 1966
#2 Generalized arteriosclerosis c̄ localized block at superf. femoral on   U/A in 1966 = WNL
    (R):                                                    BP last admission ranged = 190-140/70-110
  Subj – about 5 yrs. ago had episode of gangrene (R) 5th toe and was   Last BP recorded 10/66 = 140/80
    admitted to _____ where p̄ conservative Rx apparently   Rx – none
    failed and Dr. _____ performed (R) lumbar sympa-
    thectomy which also failed to heal toe. Subsequently lost  #4 Benign Prostatic Hypertrophy:
    (R) 5th toe surgically but still didn't heal well and was admit-  Subj – frequency, urgency, and ↓ stream x 1-2 years, nocturia x 3;
    ted to _____ under Dr. _____'s care where ulcer healed         ō dysuria
    c̄ conservative Rx. Since then has noted slow healing on   Obj – residual in 1966 = 120 cc. IVP 1966 = WNL. cystoscopy in
    feet; had (R) common fem. arteriogram 5 yrs. ago under         1966 = median
    Dr. _____'s direction p̄ translumbar arteriogram failed        lobe impingement on urethra.
    (these records of five years ago are lost currently and pt.    S/P open biopsy in 1966 because of nodule (L) felt by
    gives this info.).                                             rectal – benign prost. hypertrophy, acid phosphatase –
    About one year ago noted onset of severe claudication (R)      WNL x 2; bone series – negative
    leg p̄ ½ block and a little later "burning pain" on sole of  Rx – none right now
    foot. To the present this has worsened slightly. Since that   Negs – ō h/o UTI's in recent or remote past
    time followed conservatively in OPC. Smokes 1-2 packs/
    day; denies ETOH'ism.                                  11/12
                                                           9 PM
  Obj – 11/28/66 had (R) common fem. arteriogram showing local
    block between middle and distal 1/3 of superf. femoral #5 (L) inguinal hernia – reducible:
        Pulses in OPC –  F    P    DP   PT                  Subj – ō
        11/8/67         (R) 2+  –    –    –                  Obj – noted on P.E. in 1966
                        (L) 1+  –    –    –                  Rx – none
                                                             Negs – ō vomiting, pain, or trouble c̄ BM's
        10/26/66        (R) 2+  –   ?+   ?+
                        (L) 2+  –   ?+   ?+                #6 H/O peptic ulcer disease:
                                                             Subj – has had pain in past in epigastrium and in p̄ 1 month it
        Never any ulcers noted on feet in last 1 yr. of OPC visits.    has been worse; burning awakens him at night, relieved in
                                                                       AM by food; coffee and cigarettes make ō difference.
  Rx – pain meds, foot hygiene                                         position makes ō difference; says he's had dark black-
  Negs – neg Kline test (1966); ō h/o diabetes                         brown stool x 1 month.
    FBS = 98 in 1966; ō pain c̄ elevation                                Says he had UGI 5 years ago which showed "very small"
    denies trauma                                                      ulcer "which Dr. _____ said not to worry about."
                                                             Obj – Hct 1966 early = 46-36%
#1 S/P CVA 17 yrs ago:                                            Hct 1966 late = 45%
  Residual (L) hemiparesis and tremor (L) leg – takes Dilantin for   ō guaiacs available; LFT's 1966 = WNL
  this. ō double vision, headaches, or dizziness. ō loss of conscious-
  ness.                                                      Rx – Maalox ⟶ relief
                                                             Negs – ō food intolerance, vomiting, diarrhea, jaundice, chills or
#3 Labile hypertension:                                              fever
  Subj – none
  Obj – ō cardiomegaly 1 yr. ago by x-ray                   Patient Profile:
                                                             lives on pension at home c̄ wife and son; the latter works qd;
                                                             he walks in neighborhood but not far
```

FIGURE 4: Statement of the Present Illness of a Patient Being Seen by a Busy Intern on the Surgical Service of a Large Urban Hospital. It can be seen that this intern writes the present illness in terms of specific problems, discussing the major problem for this particular admission first, even though it is the second one on the original problem list. The patient profile is the portion of the record in which we define how the patient spends his average day at home so that long-term management of his problems will be appropriate to his way of life. The profile presented here should be more detailed so that one might have a more complete picture of exactly how he lives. It is usually the first portion of the record after the chief complaint.

problem list and careful analysis and follow-through on each problem as revealed in the titled progress notes, requiring that the proper data be collected and that the conclusions drawn from this data are logical and relevant. The precision of titled, problem-oriented progress notes and conclusions is directly related to the precision and integrity with which the problems are initially defined. The uncertainties inherent in complex biologic systems make titled progress notes the most crucial part of the medical record. There are never right or wrong single decisions in difficult cases, there are only intelligent and logical or unintelligent or illogical series of decisions carefully or carelessly followed. For certain problems a narrative progress note is not adequate for relating multiple variables.

Data involving physical findings, vital signs, laboratory values, medications, intakes and outputs can lead to sound interpretations and decisions only if they are organized (by means of a "flow sheet") to reveal clearly temporal relations. How often do younger physicians see older ones flip through a record, expound on a single laboratory value, call at random for others in a "stream-of-consciousness" way and give an essay beginning with "in my experience"? Time relations are ignored, crucial data are never brought to light, and wrong decisions forever go unrecognized, because no tracks or logic pathways are discernible in the randomly recorded data.

Flow sheets can be used to facilitate the comprehension and interpretation of multiple interrelated and changing variables. On certain fast moving problems the flow sheet may be the only progress note. The time required initially in setting up a proper flow sheet is small compared to that wasted unraveling and reassembling disorganized and misplaced data. One major goal of clinical teaching should be to designate the problems that should have a flow sheet, the variables that should be included and the frequency with which they should be followed.

When the procedure outlined above has been done manually, a basis for computerization will have been provided, and when it is implemented, all data on a given problem will be instantaneously retrievable in sequence and a physician will be able to focus on one problem at a time, seeing the flow of data over extended periods. He will then be prepared to relate that fully digested problem to the other problems by returning to his up-to-date problem list.

Since a complete and accurate list of problems should play a central part in the understanding and management of individual patients and groups of patients, storage of this portion of the medical record in the computer should receive high priority to give immediate access to the list of problems for care of the individual patient and for statistical study on groups of patients.

It would seem most logical to have the physician enter the problem statements directly into the computer. Work at this institution, [6] after analysis of large numbers of manually recorded problems, has demonstrated the feasibility of using logically grouped displays of such problems on a television screen terminal. The physician makes a choice and, in some situations, will be led through further displays requiring more careful delineation of the problem. For example, he will first be required to state whether the problem in a given organ system is an etiologic diagnosis, a physiologic finding (such as heart failure), a symptom or a laboratory finding (such as an abnormal electrocardiogram). If he chooses heart failure he will be required in the next display, which appears automatically, to say whether compensated or decompensated, biventricular, right or left side. These previously prepared displays enable easy coding and yet give freedom of expression to the physician. This method is a tacit teacher because it requires the physician to formulate his problems consistently, completely and accurately. A large number of such precisely defined problems will provide the necessary data base to allow reliable work by statisticians to be undertaken.

It can readily be seen that all narrative data presently in the medical record can be structured, and in the future all narrative data may be entered through series of displays, guaranteeing a thoroughness, retrievability, efficiency and economy important to the scientific analysis of a type of datum that has hitherto been handled in a very unrigorous manner.

2.3 IMPLEMENTATION OF MORE COMPREHENSIVE CARE THROUGH THE MEDICAL RECORD AND THE COMPUTER

The organization of the record described above forms a framework that easily accommodates psychiatric, social and demographic problems. Usually these are not documented and followed in an organized manner.

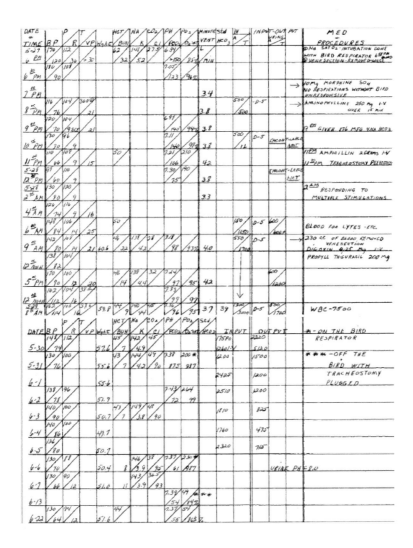

FIGURE 5: "Flow Sheet" Written by a Physician on a General-Medicine Ward at the Time the Data Were Acquired, Not in Retrospect. This represents the course of a patient with a history of tuberculosis and a pneumonectomy who appeared with acute respiratory failure, cardiac failure, trilobar pneumonia and unexplained thyromegaly. One may question some of the data and decisions, but one has no difficulty in rapidly assimilating the course of this complicated cardiorespiratory situation, as seen through the eyes of this physician. Flow sheets should not be limited to patients with acute problems. Many chronic difficulties are best understood and managed by relation of multiple variables over time — daily, weekly or monthly. Patients with hypertension, diabetes and renal and liver disease are among the many who require well structured and up-to-date flow sheets.

2.3.1 PSYCHIATRIC PROBLEMS

In the practice of medicine for many physicians, nonorganic problems have been neither challenging nor interesting. Because of this they have never been listed—even though they easily could have been—with the physician using clear descriptive formulations such as "cries easily" or "family difficulties" if he could not use sophisticated psychiatric jargon. Until all psychiatric problems are consistent objects of the physician's attention and are numbered and titled as such, it will not be possible for him to watch them evolve and thereby learn systematically from his own experience. Furthermore, by ignoring them he has never developed an appreciation for patterns of emotional disturbances, his attitude toward modern technics of analysis becoming at best one of anxiety and perplexity and at worst one of disinterest, ignorance and uninformed rejection.

The computer is making a major contribution in this area. The vast amount of research on the Minnesota Multiphasic Personality Inventory (MMPI) and the computerization of the analyses of the MMPI have made it much more likely, where it is employed, that the patient will gain from his physician an immediate sympathetic understanding of the forces with which he or she is struggling, and much inadvertent neglect and inadequate analyses by the medical profession can be avoided. There are many physicians who reject the help of modern technics on the basis that Osler for three hours followed by Freud for three hours could have done better. Even if this were true, modern technics are not competing in that league, but rather they are competing with hasty "off-the-cuff" five-minute analyses by untrained, impatient physicians who live from case to case and who have no systematic means of learning and improving from a highly organized and recorded data base which is kept up to date.

2.3.2 DEMOGRAPHIC PROBLEMS

Physicians have for years been preoccupied with episodic illness, with problems only when they erupt into symptoms and only with patients who can get themselves to the doctor. At present it is almost impossible to obtain the history of illness from its earliest stages on a sample of the population, or even on an individual. And except for a few pioneers such as Robbins and Hall, [7] most of us do not even think of demographic problems, let alone record, understand and deal with them. As they point out, for a 40-year-old woman whose problem list contains only a fractured arm, we have completely neglected the fact that it may be of major medical significance to her that she is 40 and female and over the next ten years her greatest medical risk is cancer of the breast, and for her a yearly breast examination is the most important part of her care. We are so accustomed to dealing with disease only in the individual and only after it becomes explicit, symptomatic or terminal, that we think people are talking about another field when they discuss health hazards from automobiles, smoking, alcohol, diets, smog, family problems, hereditary factors or mental stress—or just being fat or 40—male or female.

The problem list of the medical record should include demographic problems as well as all others. This will lead to very specific action appropriately timed for preventive procedures and will continually remind us of exactly where in health care our total obligations lie.

Paramedical personnel, such as public-health workers, social workers, psychologists and chemists, are already doing a major portion of the work in this area by collecting data that make it possible to define all sorts of social and demographic problems. Physicians must assume the leadership in providing each patient with a total list of problems, irrespective of who in the medical hierarchy provided the data, and in seeing that therapeutic action reflects some perspective on the total needs of the patient.

When large amounts of demographic data are developed, by means of the computer, a system could be developed whereby input of certain vital statistics on any patient would automatically result in an immediate print-out of his main demographic problems along with the current approaches to their management.

Those who provide total care or who are trying to learn how to provide it, and who naturally integrate findings into well formulated problems should not, and usually do not, feel threatened by a request for a complete list. The specialist who is annoyed or made anxious by health issues in his patient beyond the limited area of his mastery may feel threatened by this strict accounting. Through physicians' inefficiency in getting a broad data base, their past neglect of good record-keeping habits and their neglect of quantity of care as they have pointed with pride to quality, they have almost lost their capacity to handle rationally or even to define large-scale tasks of health care.

2.4 IMPLICATIONS OF THE PROBLEM-ORIENTED RECORD

The structured, problem-oriented medical record provides a focus for constructive action in a variety of "trouble" areas in medicine: medical problems dealt with out of context; inefficiency in medicine; lack of continuity of care; inapplicability of "basic science" facts and principles; "off-the-cuff" and undisciplined rounds and conferences; and, finally, meaningful audits in the practice of medicine.

2.4.1 PROBLEMS OUT OF CONTEXT

Multiple problems may interact, and sophisticated understanding and management of any one of them require a knowledge of at least the presence of all of them. In situations such as the patient with heart failure and azotemia, it is apparent that the right treatment for one may be the wrong treatment for the other, and the need for skillful management is obvious. In other situations the interaction may not be so obvious—as in paroxysmal hypertension, dehydration and hypovolemia [8] and physicians are always risking interpretation and treatment of problems out of context. The medical literature is replete with papers on single entities from series of patients (for example, myocardial infarction, cancer of the colon or pneumonia) in which no complete problem list for each patient was systematically presented. A paper may talk about X per cent mortality for perforated ulcer when, for example, what it should really be saying is Y per cent if heart failure is also on the list or Z per cent if another problem or no others are present. Pneumococcal pneumonia alone may well be a different disease from pneumococcal pneumonia in the presence of azotemia. Potent drugs are administered, and major management decisions made for specific problems taken out of context. It is no wonder that controversies in medicine abound; the present lack of technic for the recording and presentation of data on multiple problems almost guarantees chaos.

PROBLEM LIST

ACTIVE PROBLEMS	RESOLVED PROBLEMS

#1 Accelerated hypertension
  Retinopathy
  Renal Disease	

#2 Hypokalemia — etiology to be determined	
#3 Vomiting — dehydration (CVP — 0, Hct 40)	
#4 Diarrhea — unknown etiology	
#5 Anemia, 2° to renal disease (Problem #1) (Hct normally 30)	
#6	Remote peptic ulcer disease
#7	Cholecystectomy
#8 Exogenous obesity	
#9 (L) Breast mass	
#10	Hx of chronic alcoholism
#11	Hx of GC rxed
#12	Personality disorder
#13 Decreased vision (R) eye possible Central retinal artery occlusion	

#14 Cardiac (M), continuous.
  Never before described ⟶ Chest
  wall flow murmur
  2° to Problem #9 (PN 12/4/67)	

FIGURE 6: List of Problems on a 36-Year-Old Woman. The management of Problem #3, the dehydration, dramatically improved Problem #1, the accelerated hypertension. The volume indicators and other appropriate variables were followed by means of a flow sheet as intravenous volume expanders were given. Aggressive conventional drug therapy of the marked diaslolic hypertension out of context could have had serious consequences.

Until a well conceived problem list is in evidence, so that each is dealt with in context, the fragmentation of care in today's specialty clinics and wards, on rounds and in conferences will never be considered seriously. One must learn how to move easily from a single-minded focus on one problem to attention to the total list and interrelations of multiple problems, much as a biochemist meticulously purifies and studies an enzyme in a scheme of reactions and then returns to consider its relation to the others. He does not, and could not, get basic data on all the enzymes simultaneously in the interest of total biochemistry or the "art of biochemistry," nor does he work on only one and arbitrarily dismiss the others as of little concern. The essential combination of clarifying single problems and integrating multiple problems is greatly facilitated by a medical record that is structured around a total problem list and titled progress notes. Since the body is a complex group of systems, in each of which abnormalities develop that reverberate through the other systems to varying degrees, the specialist, as a responsible scientist, must know the variables in the total system as they affect his specialized judgment and action. A patient's intuitive demand for a "whole doctor" is completely consistent with the demands that good science and knowledge of all relevant factors impose upon the specialist, independently of general discussions of "primary" physicians, total care and humanitarian causes.

Fragmentation of single diagnostic entities resulting from listing separately single related findings is not a legitimate complaint against a complete list of problems. If a complete analysis is done on each finding, integration of related ones is an automatic by-product. Failure to integrate findings into a valid single entity can almost always be traced to incomplete understanding of all the implications of one or all of them. If a beginner puts cardiomegaly, edema, hepatomegaly and shortness of breath as four separate problems, it is his way of clearly admitting that he does not recognize cardiac failure when he sees it. But the important point is that nothing is lost. On the contrary, the interest of more experienced observers is immediately aroused, and some of the patient's problems are combined under a single heading on the original list and are carried one step closer to diagnosis and treatment. The system does not prevent analysis and integration: it merely reveals the extent to which it is performed and it defines the level of sophistication at which the physician functions.

2.4.2 CHOICE OF PROBLEMS AND TIME FOR PROBLEMS

A scientist likes to choose his own problems, determine the time table for action and then spend as much time as necessary. In medicine as now practiced, the patient chooses the problem and initiates the encounter; the physician must react independently of his interests and his moods. Many symptomatic problems demanding immediate care might have had organized care at times specified by a physician in a less acute phase. Since they were never identified in the problem list, they were never followed systematically in numbered, titled progress notes by the too busy doctor, who was dashing off random notes on the acute episode of some other previously neglected situation. A physician should always consciously look at a patient's complete list of problems on the front of the record. If his time is limited he should select priorities, directing attention to those having the greatest potential for moving into the acute phase. The rule should be: when under pressure, do what you do very well; select the problem wisely; and never do all superficially just to get them done. Then the work reflected in each titled progress note can result in a precisely defined building block, and all effort can be cumulative. Lack of time is not a legitimate argument against keeping data in order. Form leads to speed in almost all human endeavors. To the extent that physicians are allowed to study patients and direct therapy in the absence of form (orderly data), they obscure the evidence that reveals whether their actions were or were not complete and justified. We cannot build a sound medical structure on a system that would violate such fundamental rules of scientific behavior on the excuse, "lack of time." Disorganization and inefficiency cost time; the principles of data collection that have been accepted by all other areas in science save time in the long run.

Medical students and physicians can be taught to deal with heavy work loads, set priorities, direct paramedical help wisely and learn efficiency. The medical record is an ideal instrument and focus for achieving these educational goals. We should not assess a physician's effectiveness by how much time he does or does not spend with patients or how sophisticated his specialized technics are. Rather, we should judge him on the completeness and accuracy of the data base he requires at the time he starts his work, the speed and the economy with which he obtains his data for his patients, the adequacy in the formulation of all the problems, the effectiveness of the therapy he prescribes and the total quantity of acceptable care that he is able to deliver.

2.4.3 LACK OF CONTINUITY OF CARE

Lack of continuity of care by the same physician is associated with doctors in training and specialists in medical centers and urban areas to a far greater degree than it is with the community physician with a relatively stable practice. There are many factors that attest to this fact, but the most disturbing is that the chief request of our clinic patients when asked for suggestions about the improvement of their care is in effect, "Could you please fix it so that I won't see a different doctor every time I come? They never really understand, some "pass the buck," and they all tell you different things." The second disturbing factor indicating this lack of continuity is the inefficiency that can be directly traced to multiple physicians. Tests are repeated unnecessarily, results are not followed up, and large amounts of time are wasted by both the physician and the patient even when the records are adequate. A physician familiar with a good record kept by himself can make sound judgments and decisions in one tenth the time that a physician unfamiliar with the record requires.

A complete medical record is essential to reliable continuity of medical care, even with the same physician. A complete highly structured, problem oriented medical record will be invaluable to any physician and is essential to the busy one. A table of contents and a good index facilitate greatly the use of any unfamiliar book.

2.4.4 BASIC-SCIENCE TRAINING, THE PHYSICIAN AND THE MEDICAL RECORD

A great deal that physicians labor over such as the Krebs cycle, phage genetics or membrane theory cannot be applied by them (and often by no one) directly to the complex biologic problems that confront them. The simple quantity of molecular biology and theoretical physiology that is now developing can frustrate and overwhelm anyone if it is not coupled with his research or his continuing development. Since the practice of medicine is a research activity when a clinician deals scientifically with unique combinations of multiple interacting problems, it can be coupled to training in basic science either through the facts themselves or through disciplined approaches to defining problems and handling data.

Collaboration between physicians and basic scientists would occur more frequently if the facts in medical records were structured as they are in scientific documents. It is true, however, that a large body of basic-science facts cannot at present be rigorously correlated with clinical action, and it is also unfortunately true that many basic scientists teaching in medical schools "find it more interesting to explore the fascinating interactions of genetics and chemistry in their uniquely favorable 'non-clinical' material than to bother about 'correlations with' medical and other practical matters." [9] The "infinite elaboration" of details in the laboratory of the basic scientist frequently seems to lead him away from the clinician instead of toward him. Details oriented to specific problems and recorded in an organized manner in clinical charts can do much to make clinical problems attractive to the basic scientist and subject to his advanced technics of investigation and analysis.

Basic-science training could have contributed to clinical performance through the teaching of systematic approaches if the physician had been, as a student, required by the basic scientist to formulate problems and write protocols as well as to perform experiments. It is this capacity to formulate and pursue a problem that distinguishes a good clinician, and a teacher of basic science has failed the physician if he does not teach this discipline but merely dispenses facts through lectures and "cook-book" experiments.

There is one fundamental aspect in the preparation of the physician that the basic scientist is not prepared to teach, Basic scientists are themselves taught to choose and focus on a single or limited number of problems, and they teach neither the philosophy nor the technic for coping with the multiplicity of problems that patients inevitably present. The failure of clinical teachers to develop and articulate an approach to multiple problems has led to a serious discontinuity in the scientific training of the physician. The chaotic medical record is a symptom of this philosophical blind spot. The degree to which we organize the record and elevate it to the level of a scientific document will be a measure of our capacity to develop and teach a workable philosophy of multiple problems.

2.4.5 MEDICAL ROUNDS AND CONFERENCES

In earlier times bedside and autopsy-table teaching predominated, and most of the data used in the discussion were acquired at the bedside. This was a marvelous mechanism to keep physicians and students anchored to the realities of their patients' problems. At present, even though some teaching at the bedside has continued, the collection of data is no longer done exclusively by the physician, and discussion is often a ritual taking place from memory and at random rather than from highly organized problem-oriented manuscripts. This is usually a positive deterrent to rational progress in total patient care. No good scientist would make a judgment or even a recommendation on a single oral presentation of data, nor would he fail to follow up the result. On serious problems scientists usually study their data carefully before meeting with anyone. No scientist would seriously consider medical rounds as frequently conducted as good science, good care or good education. To those involved in care and education, multiple typed copies of well organized problem-oriented records must be at all times available for study and could be the basis for a major change in attending teaching rounds. Such rounds will require that the attending physician study the data beforehand; time that is now spent in presenting cases, determining what went on and giving random displays of erudition will be spent instead in analyzing and criticizing and redirecting the recorded efforts of the physician in solving the patient's problems.

The young physician should be taught to anticipate and indeed enjoy such analyses for the rest of his life.

We should be allowed the luxury of conferences, grand rounds or a clinicopathological conference only when the original data are in good order and completely and carefully presented, but certain educational goals cannot be met by this means. How many teachers of medicine labor under the delusion that they can convey to physicians in one hour or a grand rounds the factual content or the wisdom of their 10, 20 or 30 years of personal experience and evolution in a field? A more realistic goal in teaching is to discipline the physician in the most effective application and growth of his own developing store of factual information through his own disciplined study of actual cases. The computer can make an enormous contribution in this area. (The computer-science aspects of these developments are under the direction of Mr. Jan Schultz.) Problem-oriented medical records can be made easily accessible to authorized individual physicians or participants in a medical conference, who can then be expected to study the patient's data and analyze the list of problems, the plan and the progress notes. Typed summaries of cases containing only selected data are not sufficient for rigorous analysis and medical education.

It is true that this could be and is being done now at this institution on manually constructed problem-oriented records, but the computer will allow immediate retrieval of all the data in sequence on any given problem, graphic representation of data and relations, multiple copies at distant terminals (also used for teaching rounds) and immediate correlation with large amounts of data on similar problems already stored in the computer. Furthermore, when many institutions have similarly developed data banks of patients' records, they can teach and audit one another. Mr. Robert Esterlay is investigating techniques whereby actual rather than contrived problem-oriented medical records can be used as a major source of teaching material for computer-assisted learning of the medical student.

Since the aim is to have the records of current patients readily available, the individual physician or members of a conference can question the doctor in charge of the patient for clarification, pointing out errors or shedding new light on the problems. They may be able to suggest additions to the data base, offering alternatives to the formulation of the problems and the approaches to handling them. By this means a link is forged between education, audit and patient care. Every time someone gets education, a physician will be audited, and at every audit a patient may get better care.

There are those who fear that rigid adherence to the patient's problems will emphasize only the physician's practical knowledge and development and create a tradesman who is dated with the technical expertise of an era, unable to meet new situations in a changing world. The approaches described here will demand of both faculty and student clear thought, a research attitude and a "willingness to apply first principles" to the new situations inherent in the infinite variety of combinations of multiple interacting medical problems. Biologic realities, honestly confronted, facilitate rather than hinder scientific advance. This is the art of medicine.

2.4.6 LACK OF REGULATORY AND FEEDBACK SYSTEM ON THE PHYSICIAN'S OWN WORK

There is no audit by outside authorities on each piece of work as it is completed analagous to what is done in basic science. Basic scientists are monitored by a system that mobilizes the criticism of their peers. Clinical medicine, on the other hand, has tried to substitute qualifying examinations at a single point in a career for a recurring, lifelong audit on each piece of work as it is completed. The strategy and completeness of the physician's own search for data, the depth of analytical capacity in theoretical understanding and therapeutic decisions and the capacity for sustained quality and energy in his daily attack on problems, both esoteric and mundane, are poorly evaluated by any examining procedure that is done at just one point in a physician's career and uses case material besides his own.

Professors of clinical medicine and practicing physicians must be provided with the advantages of an audit whose origin is independent of their own organization.

The medical record can be used in the solution of this audit arid feedback problem if we accept certain basic premises:

1. Premise (1). All the data in the medical record must be identified with a problem to determine whether the data are fundamental to

solving the problem and whether factors such as redundancy, unnecessary delays and unjustified decisions are present.

2. Premise (2). All the data on any given problem must be easily retrieved in sequence and in a completely up-to-date fashion (for example, x-ray and laboratory data must be in the record as soon as they are available). The data are then immediately available to the staff members responsible in a given specialty area for determining whether certain standards for quality are being met. At the outset the staff member will use the same criteria he has always used to assess the quality of management in his area. Eventually, as the data bank grows in both number of patients with a given problem and numbers of variables followed and recorded, new standards for reasonable numbers of tests and good care will emerge.

3. Premise (3). Development of standards for quality of patient care as outlined in premise (2) may evolve easily when a patient has one or several unrelated problems. Conclusions will be more difficult when there are multiple concomitant problems in the same patient (such as cardiac failure, renal failure and malnutrition) the final solution of any one of which is intimately related to the progress on the others. In these particular cases fixed standards of care do not apply, and quality must be determined on an individual basis within a framework of generally accepted principles. The doctor's role in cases of this type may well be likened to that of an analogue computer, which plots specific points on a curve as a function of the time and type of input and the shape of the curve is not known until the input stops.

4. Premise (4). The dimensions of the quality-control problem alluded to in premises (2) and (3) can never be assessed until computerization of the data is accomplished. Manual approaches have not, after all these years, resulted in a widely applicable and practical appraisal. It is through discipline, and rapid effective audits and their demands for explicitness in the definition of problems and the orderly organization of the data that computers could make their main contribution to the performance and development of physicians. Physicians will be able to respond more constructively as

soon as we give them a total picture of what it is that they are doing for specific problems.

The justification for a reorganization of the medical record by identifying all data with a problem is not and cannot be based on any proof that it will in itself guarantee improved quality of care and education. Titles, chapters and indexes in books, well thought out classification systems in organic chemistry and well established rules for presenting data in scientific manuscripts do not guarantee high quality of the material, and no one expects them to in and of themselves. But neither does anyone expect to use the book, work in the chemical field or referee manuscripts if it is up to him to take a mass of incomplete and randomly presented data and organize it before he can even start to deal with the matter of quality. It is hard for nonmedical scientists to believe that we have allowed for this long the chaos in everyday medical data because scientists do not usually write papers on several problems simultaneously as doctors do; they have assumed that physicians have a system and immediately go to the second order of business, which is questions about quality of care. But we have not had a system for progress notes on multiple problems, and we therefore should first find it necessary to organize the record as a basis for beginning the development of a program of quality control. The basic premises stated above have grown from my convictions that it is already accepted in the field of science that all data should be recorded at the time it is acquired and that before it is submitted for analysis and inclusion in the literature of the field, it should be organized and presented in relation to the problem the data are purported to solve.

There may be considerable urgency in these matters, because large amounts of money have already been spent and allocated to the computerization of single components in the hospital complex such as laboratories and pharmacies, with little regard for problem orienting of data and decisions. This proliferation of automated systems within parts of a hospital complex without provisions for a central role for patients' problems make future evaluation of all these expensive efforts difficult. Such automation may be making highly efficient and accurate specific tests and maneuvers, but often it could merely be facilitating rapid action that is not necessarily solving the patient's problems. Daily reporting of an accurate chemical value, for example, has no particular virtue if the problem at hand requires only a weekly determination or no such determination at all. Some of the most advanced and most expensive automation of laboratories today is not coupled with an equally sophisticated problem-oriented clinical situation, and the value of these sophisticated efforts in terms of patients' problems can never be assessed. Laboratories have relied on the assumption that all determinations that are ordered are indicated, and the frequency of given determinations is never overdone, and what is worse, much money has been spent on systems that were never designed to test this crucial assumption.

At present no system is available whereby a medical teacher or member of an accrediting agency can take a patient's record at random, select one of the patient's problems, see all the data pertinent to that problem in sequence and immediately ascertain whether current medical standards are being applied. Such an inordinate amount of time is now being spent determining what was or was not done, and for what purpose, that on a time basis alone a teacher or auditor is rendered ineffective, and abuses may go uncorrected.

Also at present the details of the relation between patients' problems and hospital resources and costs are very obscure. A medical record maintained by the technic described will make possible a fiscal management audit in which utilization of hospital resources and services involved in the care of the patient are a matter of the medical record and can be identified with each specific problem presented by the patient. This combination of facts (clinical problems, hospital resources and costs) will enable the hospital to establish a dynamic unit cost-accounting system similar to that employed by more sophisticated industries. The advantages of such a system have broad and favorable implications for the general management of a hospital in the areas of fiscal planning, organization of resources, measurement of efficiency and daily management of the institution.

2.4.7 ART IN PRACTICE OF MEDICINE

It has been said that preoccupation with the medical record and the computer leads to neglect of the "humanitarian" side and the "art" of medical practice. The most humanitarian thing a physician can do is to precisely know what he is doing, and make the patient as comfortable as he can in the face of problems that he cannot yet solve. There have been major humanitarian and sociologic failings in medicine, but almost all of them can be attributed to our poor behavior as scientists as we have dealt with problems out of context and ignored data relevant to good medical care. It is true that no system will make one kind, thoughtful or sympathetic, but to say that the art of medicine is not dependent on a great deal of discipline and order is to miss perhaps the true understanding of what underlines art in any form. Words of Stravinsky might be applied to our situation: "Human activity must impose limits upon itself. The more art is controlled, limited, worked over, the more it is free." If we accept the limits of discipline and form as we keep data in the medical records the physician's task will be better defined, the role of paramedical personnel and the computer will be clarified, and the art of medicine will gain freedom at the level of interpretation and be released from the constraints that disorder and confusion always impose.

REFERENCES

1. Slack. W.V., Hicks, G.P., Reed, C.E., and Van Cura, L.J. Computer-based medical history system. New Eng. J. Med. 274: 194–198, 166.
2. Slack, W.V., Peckham, B.M., Van Cura, L.J., and Carr, W.F. Computer-based physical examination system. J.A.M.A. 200: 224–228, 1967.
3. Weed, L.L. Medical records, patient care, and medical education. Irish J. M. Sc. 6: 271–282, 1964.
4. Idem. New approach to medical teaching. Resident Physician 13: 77–93, July 1967.
5. Idem. Patient's record as extension of basic science training of physician. Syllabus, case presented at Western Reserve University School of Medicine, Cleveland, OH, 1967.
6. Weed, L.L. and Cantrill, S. Unpublished data.
7. Robins, L.C. and Hall, J. Personal communication.
8. Cohn, J.N. Paroxysmal hypertension and hypovolemia. New Eng. J. Med. 275: 643–646, 1966.
9. Burnet, F.M. Genetics of micro-organisms: Introduction. Brit. M. Bull. 18:1, 1962.

CHAPTER 3

CLINICAL IMPLICATIONS OF AN ACCURATE PROBLEM LIST ON HEART FAILURE TREATMENT

DANIEL M. HARTUNG, JACQUELYN HUNT,
JOSEPH SIEMIENCZUK, HEATHER MILLER,
AND DANIEL R. TOUCHETTE

In the late 1960s, Lawrence Weed successfully advocated for fundamental change in the approach to medical record organization and documentation. [1] In his landmark publication, Dr. Weed identified the challenge physicians face in providing single-minded attention to complex patients with multiple existing and developing problems. His proposed solution would orient data around each patient problem, creating a complete "problem list" displayed prominently in each chart. This Problem-oriented Medical Record (POMR) would be updated at each subsequent care episode. While problem lists have become commonplace in ambulatory practice, there is substantial variation in physician adherence to the use and completeness of information entry. As stated in Dr. Weed's original publication, "Among physicians there is a remarkable spectrum of behavior from the compul-

---

With kind permission from Springer Science+Business Media: Journal of General Internal Medicine, *Clinical Implications of an Accurate Problem List on Heart Failure Treatment, 20(2), 2005, 143–147, Hartung DM, Hunt J, Siemienczuk J, Miller H, and Touchette DR, Copyright 2005 by the Society of General Internal Medicine.*

sively elaborate to the sketchy and haphazard." [1] Today, practice variation is still considered a significant contributor to inadequacies in health care quality. [2–5]

The premise of the POMR is that an accurately defined problem list will directly result in more thorough and efficient patient care. Despite this assertion, there has been little validation that this approach translates into improved patient outcomes. Simborg et al. evaluated [2] consecutive visits in 6 ambulatory clinics to determine the problems identified in the first visit and the follow-up care for these problems provided in the second visit. [6] It was found that problems listed in the front of the chart were more likely to be addressed at the subsequent visit, particularly if there was a longer interval between visits. Recognizing that practice variation continues to exist decades after Dr. Weed's original publication and that expensive physician resources are required to maintain an accurate problem list, we sought to further quantify the impact of this process on patient outcomes.

Heart failure (HF) is a prevalent condition that requires intensive medical management, and it is conceivable that construction and maintenance of an accurate POMR would likely contribute toward enhanced patient outcomes. Several medication classes are known to prolong survival and improve health status in patients with HF and, as such, represent valid process-related quality indicators that are strongly associated with favorable outcomes. [7] Accordingly, the aim of this study was to evaluate the impact of accurate problem list entry for HF on the likelihood that evidenced-based pharmacotherapy has been prescribed.

3.1 METHODS

3.1.1 SETTING AND PARTICIPANTS

This was a retrospective, cross-sectional study involving participating practices from the Providence Primary Care Practice-based Research Network. Participating network practices included 80 practitioners providing care to approximately 200,000 patients in 9 clinic locations in Oregon. All network practices share a common electronic medical record (EMR),

Logician. Problem lists were generated and maintained through physician entry of patient diagnosis. Problem list entries were stored in a dedicated searchable data field, based on the International Classification of Disease, ninth revision, system. There were no limits on number of problems that could be entered per patient. Notes from all patient visits were documented completely in the EMR. Issuing a prescription to a patient simultaneously records that prescription in the patient's active medication list. Paper prescription pads were not used within the network. Patient data including demographics, insurance status, medications, and laboratory values were also available through this clinical database. During the study period, the use of complimentary paper charts was limited to external documents such as specialty consult letters and test results.

The study population consisted of 180 patients within the network who had a confirmed diagnosis of HF due to systolic dysfunction. Patients with HF were identified by query of left ventricular ejection fraction (LVEF) results stored in local echocardiography laboratory databases. Patient charts with any reference to low ejection fraction, congestive heart failure, HF, or systolic dysfunction in the patient chart were included in the analysis. Systolic dysfunction was defined by an LVEF of 40% or less. Patients were excluded if chart evidence of physician awareness of HF diagnosis was not present or if they were deceased, had transferred care outside the network, or their active status could not be confirmed. The definition of active status included documentation of patient encounters (i.e., telephone contact, office visit, or medication refill) before and after the cross-section date of June 11, 2001. Patients identified with systolic dysfunction with or without a problem list entry of HF were selected for analysis.

3.1.2 OUTCOMES AND DATA COLLECTION

The primary objective of this study was to determine the association between the presence of HF on the problem list and treatment with medications demonstrated to benefit patients with systolic dysfunction. Angiotensin-converting enzyme (ACE) inhibitors and beta-blockers have been well documented to improve survival in patients with HF. [7,8] According to guidelines, angiotensin II receptor blockers (ARB) or the combination of hydralazine and a long-acting nitrate are acceptable substitutes for patients intolerant of ACE inhibitors. [7,8] The primary outcomes were defined as the proportion of HF patients with an active prescription for a 1) ACE inhibitor, ARB, or hydralazine/long-acting nitrate combination (vasodilator), 2) beta-blocker, and 3) a combination of a vasodilator and a beta-blocker.

Secondary objectives evaluated the association between HF problem list entry and other recommended therapies (spironolactone, diuretics, and digoxin) and those that are relatively contraindicated in patients with heart failure (nonsteroidal anti-inflammatory drugs [NSAID] and nondihydropyridine calcium channel blockers [CCB]). [7,8]

The daily dose of ACE inhibitor was converted to an equivalent captopril dose based on target doses studied in large, prospective, randomized clinical trials. [9,10] If a particular ACE inhibitor had never been studied in a heart failure trial, then the maximum dose stated in the package insert was considered the target dose. [11,12] The mean captopril equivalent dose and the proportion of patients who achieved the target captopril equivalent dose ($\geq$150 mg daily) were compared between groups of patients receiving ACE inhibitors. [13]

Age, gender, LVEF, serum creatinine, serum potassium, problem list entries, medications, and physician years in practice were collected for all sampled patients. Chart review established the presence or absence of several comorbid conditions with the potential to influence medication selection including diabetes mellitus, hypertension, and atrial fibrillation. The diagnosis of diabetes was defined as the presence of diabetes on the problem list, reference to diabetes in any progress note, hemoglobin A1C$\geq$6%, or a random plasma blood glucose $\geq$200 mg/dl. Hypertension and atrial fibrillation were identified by the presence of a problem list entry or other reference in the medical record for either of these conditions.

3.1.3 STATISTICAL ANALYSIS

Sample size estimates were based on reported prevalence of ACE inhibitor (80%) and beta-blocker (26%) use in patients with systolic dysfunction. [14] Assuming a two-sided test with an α of 0.05 and β of 0.2 (80% power), a sample size of 90 in each group was required to detect an absolute difference of 16% in the proportion of patients receiving beta-blockers. This sample was determined to be of sufficient size to also detect a meaningful difference (20%) in the proportion of patients prescribed ACE inhibitors (84% power). A simple random sample of 90 subjects from each group was selected for chart review and analysis.

All analyses were two-sided and P values≤.05 were considered statistically significant. Continuous variables were described by means and standard deviations and compared using parametric (Student's t test) and nonparametric tests (Mann-Whitney-Wilcoxon test) as appropriate. The statistical significance of categorical variables was assessed using the χ^2 test. Odds ratios (OR) with 95% confidence intervals (95% CI) were used to convey the strength of association for primary and secondary objectives. A multivariate unconditional logistic regression model was used to control the primary analysis for potentially confounding variables according to the methods outlined by Hosmer and Lemeshow. [15] Potential covariates considered were age, gender, LVEF, serum creatinine, serum potassium, presence of diabetes, hypertension, or atrial fibrillation, and physician years of practice. Age and gender were retained in the multivariate model regardless of their statistical significance because of their clinical relevance. Data were analyzed with SAS (version 8.1; SAS Institute, Carey, NC) and SPSS (version 11.0.1; SPSS Inc., Chicago, IL) statistical software. There were no conflicts of interest for any of the contributing authors and the study was approved by the Oregon State University and Providence Health System Institutional Review Boards.

3.2 RESULTS

A total of 793 patients within the network were identified as having an LVEF ≤40%. Of these, 431 (54.4%) patient records accurately included a diagnosis of HF in the problem list. The remaining 362 (45.6%) patient records did not contain HF in the problem list. Twenty-nine patients were excluded for not having a chart note indicating the provider's knowledge of HF. Patient characteristics of the selected samples for both groups are shown in Table 1. Age, gender, serum potassium, serum creatinine, and physician years of practice were not significantly different between groups. Patients with HF listed in their problem list had a statistically significantly lower LVEF compared to those patients in the group in which HF was omitted from their problem list (29.5% vs 31.9%; P =.025). The prevalence of hypertension was 56.7% among those patients with HF present in their problem list compared to 74.4% in those patients whose HF diagnosis was omitted (P =.012).

TABLE 1: Demographics

	Problem List Present (N =90)	Problem List Absent (N =90)	P Value
Age, y (SD)	73.8 (11.8)	74.6 (11.2)	.646
Ejection fraction (SD)	29.5 (7.77)	31.9 (6.91)	.025
Serum creatinine (SD)	1.3 (0.55)	1.4 (0.82)	.737
Serum potassium (SD)	4.6 (0.46)	4.7 (0.71)	.615
PCP years in practice (SD)	18.2 (8.15)	19.49 (7.7)	.279
Female gender, n (%)	35 (38.9)	39 (43.3)	.545
Diabetes mellitus, n (%)	24 (26.7)	29 (32.2)	.414
Hypertension, n (%)	51 (56.7)	67 (74.4)	.012
Atrial fibrillation, n (%)	31 (34.4)	21 (23.3)	.10

SD, standard deviation; PCP, primary care physician.

As shown in Table 2, the use of vasodilators was statistically significantly higher (OR, 3.61; 95% CI, 1.45 to 8.99) among patients with HF present on their problem list (92.2%) compared to patients for whom the problem list entry was absent (76.7%). The use of beta-blockers was higher in the group of patients for whom HF was omitted from the problem list (51.1%) compared to the group in which HF was present in the problem list (42.2%), although this difference was not statistically significant (OR, 0.70; 95% CI, 0.39 to 1.26). These findings remained consistent when the analysis was confined to those beta-blockers with a Food and Drug Administration indication for the treatment of heart failure (i.e., metoprolol or carvedilol). The proportion of patients receiving the combined vasodilator and beta-blocker therapy was also similar between groups (OR, 1.10; 95% CI, 0.60 to 2.01).

TABLE 2: Primary Outcome

	Problem List Present (N =90)	Problem List Absent (N =90)	Unadjusted OR*(95% CI)	Adjusted OR* (95% CI)
Vasodilator therapy†	83 (92.2)	69 (76.7)	3.61* (1.45 to 8.99)	3.23* (1.28 to 8.16)
Beta-blocker‡	38 (42.2)	46 (51.1)	0.70 (0.39 to 1.26)	0.79 (0.43 to 1.45)
Vasodilator and beta-blocker§	35 (38.9)	33 (36.7)	1.10 (0.60 to 2.01)	1.10 (0.60 to 2.02)

*$P < .05$.
†Adjusted for age, gender, and ejection fraction.
‡Adjusted for age, gender, and hypertension.
§Adjusted for age and gender.
OR, odds ratio; CI, confidence interval.

Three distinct multivariate logistic regression models, and adjusted OR, were constructed for the 3 outcome variables and are presented in Table 2. After adjusting for the covariates age, gender, and LVEF in the multivariate model, the odds of being prescribed vasodilator therapy were still significantly higher among patients with HF accurately entered on their problem list compared to those with HF omitted (adjusted OR, 3.23; 95% CI, 1.28 to 8.16). In the multivariate model predicting beta-blocker use, the presence of hypertension was the only statistically significant covariate observed. The inclusion of age, gender, and hypertension in the model did not change the underlying nonsignificant finding in which patients who had accurate problem list entries were less likely to receive beta-blocker therapy (adjusted OR, 0.79; 95% CI, 0.43 to 1.45). None of the covariates were statistically significant in the multivariate model assessing combination vasodilator/beta-blocker therapy. The OR after adjusting for age and gender was identical to the unadjusted OR (adjusted OR, 1.10; 95% CI, 0.60 to 2.02). The Hosmer and Lemeshow tests for all 3 models were not statistically significant, indicating good overall fit. No significant covariate interactions were observed.

The association between individual medications and entry of HF on the problem list were also evaluated (see Table 3). The odds of being prescribed an ACE inhibitor (2.67; 95% CI, 1.37 to 5.20), diuretic (2.5; 95% CI, 1.23 to 5.07), digoxin (2.71; 95% CI, 1.49 to 4.96), and spironolactone (2.36; 95% CI, 1.10 to 5.09) were all significantly higher among patients who had HF on their problem list compared to patients who did not. The proportion of patients who were prescribed medications that are known to exacerbate HF symptoms was also compared between the groups. Analysis found no significant difference in the prescribing of CCB or NSAID in the group of patients with an HF diagnosis present in the problem list compared to those with an omitted diagnosis.

TABLE 3: Association Between Problem Listing and Individual Medications

	Problem List Present (N =90)	Problem List Absent (N =90)	Odds Ratio (95% CI)	P Value
ACE inhibitor, n (%)	72 (80.0)	54 (60.0)	2.67 (1.37 to 5.20)	.003
ARB, n (%)	11 (12.2)	15 (16.7)	0.70 (0.30 to 1.61)	.396
BB, n (%)	38 (42.2)	46 (51.1)	0.70 (0.39 to 1.26)	.232
Metoprolol or carvedilolol, n (%)	23 (25.6)	31 (34.4)	0.65 (0.34 to 1.24)	.193
Diuretic, n (%)	75 (83.3)	60 (66.7)	2.5 (1.23 to 5.07)	.01
Digoxin, n (%)	55 (61.1)	33 (36.7)	2.71 (1.49 to 4.96)	.001
Spironolactone, n (%)	24 (26.7)	12 (13.3)	2.36 (1.10 to 5.09)	.025
CCB, n (%)	6 (6.7)	5 (5.6)	1.21 (0.36 to 4.13)	.756
NSAID, n (%)	11 (12.2)	11 (12.2)	1.00 (0.41 to 2.44)	1.000

CI, confidence interval; ACE, angiotensin-converting enzyme; ARB, angiotensin II receptor blockers; BB, beta-blocker; CCB, nondihydropyridine calcium channel blockers; NSAID, nonsteroidal anti-inflammatory drugs.

After converting individual ACE inhibitor doses to their respective captopril equivalent, the average daily dose for patients with HF present in the problem list was 106 mg compared to 95 mg for those patients who had HF omitted from the problem list (P =.416). The proportion of patients reaching a target dose of greater than or equal to 150 mg daily was not significantly different between groups. Of the 72 patients on an ACE inhibitor in the group with HF on the problem list, 26 were at a target dose (36.1%) compared to 15 of the 54 (27.8%) patients on an ACE inhibitor in the problem list–absent group (P =.323).

3.3 DISCUSSION

The results of this study demonstrate that patients with systolic dysfunction whose medical record problem list accurately contains the diagnosis of HF are more likely to be prescribed recommended medications as compared with patients whose problem list omits the diagnosis. It is also likely that patients with accurate problem lists received more thorough follow-up as evidenced by the trend toward higher ACE inhibitor doses, a finding supported by Simborg et al.6 Although we cannot definitely attribute the benefits seen in this study to accurate problem list entry, patients in this arm of the study would be expected to have survival and hospitalization benefits as a result of higher rates of recommended medication use. [7,9,16] Meta-analysis of large, long-term randomized controlled trials of patients with systolic dysfunction indicates that ACE inhibitor therapy confers a 1.7% annual absolute risk reduction of death over placebo equaling a number-needed-to-treat value of 59 patients per death avoided over one year. [16] If the 20% risk difference in ACE inhibitor prescribing seen in this analysis is truly due to maintaining accurate problem lists, we estimate that for every 295 patients with accurate inclusion of HF, one death due to lack of ACE inhibitor therapy would be avoided over one year. Additional morbidity and mortality benefits might be seen with improved spironolactone, diuretic, and digoxin therapy.

Our results do not support an advantage for beta-blocker prescribing in the group with accurate problem list entries. Additionally, the study does not provide an explanation for the discordant results between beta-blockers and other recommended therapies for HF. There are several potential reasons for this unexpected finding. Cardiologists may more commonly initiate beta-blocker therapy in systolic dysfunction, as compared to primary care physicians. In our study population, cardiologists did not have access to the problem lists maintained by primary care physicians. A second alternative explanation is that beta-blocker use was confounded by the higher prevalence of hypertension found in the group of patients with HF missing from their problem list. Beta-blockers have long been recommended as initial therapy for patients with uncomplicated hypertension. [17] While the inclusion of hypertension in the multivariate model reduces the association by 13% (unadjusted OR, 0.70; adjusted OR, 0.79), it did not completely explain the trend. Beta-blockers were relatively new therapeutic options for HF at the cross-section date, although evidence supporting their use has been available as early as 1996. [18] Their uptake by primary care physicians was still relatively low (roughly 47% overall) and their use may have still been avoided in HF by some physicians. Finally, neither the adjusted nor unadjusted ORs were statistically significant, indicating that chance could have played a role in producing this unexpected finding.

This study was conducted in a practice-based research network in which all clinics utilize a common EMR. The question arises whether the results are generalizable to ambulatory care settings still using paper charts. The EMR used by these clinics, Logician, is constructed to emulate the appearance and function of a traditional paper record. The problem list is displayed on a "summary page" along with lists of the patient's medications, allergies, and advance directives. Problem lists are constructed and maintained manually by physicians. Although the EMR can be used to facilitate disease management activities through electronic searches of the problem list database for patient candidates, no such use of this EMR occurred in the study population to affect the prescribing outcomes for HF during or prior to the time period of this study. Based on the similarities in appearance and maintenance of problem lists, we submit that the clinical benefit of accurate problem list entry is also applicable to patients whose ambulatory record is paper based.

This study has several limitations. The cross-sectional design of this study has many well-recognized limitations. [19] Because exposure (HF problem list entry) and outcome (target HF medication) were measured simultaneously, causality is difficult to establish. Through the use of multivariate regression analyses we were able to control for identified confounders. Unfortunately, other unidentifiable confounders may exist. For example, patients with more symptomatic disease could prompt providers to maintain more accurate problem and medication lists. New York Heart Association functional class, which is not always correlated to LVEF, could not be obtained from patient records and therefore was not evaluated in this study. [7] The severity of systolic dysfunction, as assessed by LVEF, was statistically significantly different between groups. It is conceivable that the two groups were also not similar in functional class. There was also a concern that the difference in the two groups resulted from some unmeasured physician practice characteristic. Thus, a physician practice characteristic (e.g., compulsiveness) might be the true causal factor contributing to both variation in HF therapy prescribing and completeness of the patient problem list.

Finally, this study did not attempt to assess clinical outcomes associated with problem list omissions, but instead examines prescribing rates as surrogate markers for clinical outcomes. Process-related measures known to impact clinical outcomes are also demonstrated valid indicators of health care quality. [20]

3.4 CONCLUSION

Patients with physician-acknowledged systolic dysfunction whose ambulatory medical record problem list accurately contains an entry for HF have a higher utilization of vasodilators, digoxin, and spironolactone compared with similar patients whose problem lists omit such an entry. Additional research is needed to evaluate and quantify the true benefits of an accurate problem list on the care of patients.

REFERENCES

1. Weed LL. Medical records that guide and teach. N Engl J Med. 1968;278:593–600.
2. Wennberg JE, Gittelsohn AM. Small area variations in health care delivery. Science. 1973;183:1102–8.
3. Chassin MR. Is health care ready for Six Sigma quality? Milbank Q. 1998;76(510):565–91.

4. Eddy DM. The challenge. JAMA. 1990;263:287–90.
5. Institute of Medicine. Crossing the Quality Chasm: A New Health System for the 21st Century. Washington, DC: National Academy Press; 2001.
6. Simborg DW, Starfield BH, Horn SD, Yourtee SA. Information factors affecting problem follow-up in ambulatory care. Med Care. 1976;14:848–56.
7. Hunt SA, Baker DW, Chin MH, et al. ACC/AHA guidelines for the evaluation and management of chronic heart failure in the adult: executive summary. A report of the American College of Cardiology/American Heart Association Task Force on Practice Guidelines (Committee to Revise the 1995 Guidelines for the Evaluation and Management of Heart Failure) J Am Coll Cardiol. 2001;38:2101–13.
8. Consensus recommendations for the management of chronic heart failure. On behalf of the membership of the advisory council to improve outcomes nationwide in heart failure. Am J Cardiol. 1999;83:1A–38A.
9. Khalil ME, Basher AW, Brown J, Edward J, Alhaddad IA. A remarkable medical story: benefits of angiotensin-converting enzyme inhibitors in cardiac patients. J Am Coll Cardiol. 2001;37:1757–64.
10. Packer M, Poole-Wilson PA, Armstrong PW, et al. Comparative effects of low and high doses of the angiotensin-converting enzyme inhibitor, lisinopril, on morbidity and mortality in chronic heart failure. Circulation. 1999;100:2312–8.
11. Univasc [package insert] Milwaukee, WI: Schwarz Pharma; 2001.
12. Lotensin [package insert] East Hanover, NJ: Novartis; 2002.
13. Pfeffer MA, Braunwald E, Moye LA, et al. Effect of captopril on mortality and morbidity in patients with left ventricular dysfunction after myocardial infarction. Results of the survival and ventricular enlargement trial. The SAVE Investigators. N Engl J Med. 1992;327:669–77.
14. McAlister FA, Teo KK, Taher M, et al. Insights into the contemporary epidemiology and outpatient management of congestive heart failure. Am Heart J. 1999;138:87–94.
15. Hosmer DW, Lemeshow S. Applied Logistic Regression. New York, NY: Wiley-Interscience; 2000.
16. Flather MD, Yusuf S, Kober L, et al. Long-term ACE-inhibitor therapy in patients with heart failure or left-ventricular dysfunction: a systematic overview of data from individual patients. Lancet. 2000;355:1575–81.
17. The sixth report of the Joint National Committee on prevention, detection, evaluation, and treatment of high blood pressure. Arch Intern Med. 1997;157:2413–46.
18. Packer M, Bristow MR, Cohn JN, et al. The effect of carvedilol on morbidity and mortality in patients with chronic heart failure. U.S. Carvedilol Heart Failure Study Group. N Engl J Med. 1996;334:1349–55.
19. Hennekens CH, Buring JE. Epidemiology in Medicine. Boston, MA: Little, Brown and Company; 1987.
20. Donabedian A. Evaluating the quality of medical care. Milbank Mem Fund Q. 1966;44(suppl):166–206.

PART II

ATTITUDES AND USE

CHAPTER 4

CLINICIAN ATTITUDES TOWARD AND USE OF ELECTRONIC PROBLEM LISTS: A THEMATIC ANALYSIS

ADAM WRIGHT, FRANCINE L. MALONEY, AND JOSHUA C. FEBLOWITZ

4.1 BACKGROUND

Complete and accurate clinical documentation is a critical component of the care process. Medical records serve as an organizing structure for clinical decision making, a tool for communication to other providers, substantiation for billing, data for research and quality measurement and protection in the event of legal process. In 1968, Lawrence Weed, MD, published "Medical Records that Guide and Teach" which introduced the concept of the problem-oriented medical record (POMR) [1] and the ability to create and maintain a structured, coded problem list in a computer system. This advance radically altered medical record keeping, and also had important implications for how clinicians organized patient care and decision making processes.

Clinician Attitudes Toward and Use of Electronic Problem Lists: A Thematic Analysis. © Wright A, Maloney FL, and Feblowitz JC. BMC Medical Informatics and Decision Making *11:36 (2011);* doi:10.1186/1472-6947-11-36. Licensed under Creative Commons Attribution 2.0 Generic License, *http://creativecommons.org/licenses/by/2.0/.*

Today, problem lists are widely used in both paper and electronic medical record systems. The ability to create a coded problem list is a requirement of the Certification Commission for Health Information Technology (CCHIT) for all certified electronic health record (EHR) systems [2] and problem documentation is an element of Joint Commission requirements [3]. Recently promulgated federal regulations for "meaningful use" of electronic health records mandate that physicians must document a coded problem (or a structured entry indicating that the patient has no problems) for at least 80% of their patients in order to qualify for substantial incentive payments.

Meaningful use is, of course, not the only or even primary reason why physicians would choose to use the problem list. First and foremost, problem lists are inherently useful clinically. An accurate problem list helps a physician to track a patient's status and progress, to avoid omissions in care and to organize clinical reasoning and documentation. The problem list is also critically useful when a clinician sees a new patient, giving him or her a "jumping off" point for the visit.

There is some evidence that patients who have accurate and complete problem lists receive better care than patients who do not. Hartung et al. conducted a study of patients whose left ventricular ejection fraction was below 40% (diagnostic of systolic heart failure). In this study, patients with heart failure on their problem lists were more likely to receive evidence-based care for their heart failure than patients who did not: 92.2% received an ACE inhibitor or ARB compared to 76.6% who did not have heart failure on their problem list, and similar patterns held for digoxin (61.1% vs. 36.7%) and spironolactone (26.7% vs. 13.3%) [4].

The problem list is also used for a variety of ancillary functions. For example, electronic problem lists can be valuable for generating diagnosis-specific registries [5]. Quality measurement programs (including "meaningful use" guidelines [6]) may use the problem list to define the denominator for measures, and researchers often identify study cohorts based on their documented problems. In addition, electronic clinical decision support systems [7-10] often depend on accurate clinical problem lists [11].

Despite its importance, the problem list is often incomplete. At our institution, we found that only 59% of patients with CAD have it documented on their problem list, with 62% documented for diabetes and 51%

for hypertension. Similar results were reported by Szeto et al., who found 49% documentation for CAD, 42% for benign prostate hypertrophy and 81% for diabetes at a Veterans Affairs health center [12].

The purpose of this study was to learn why problem lists are so problematic. We chose qualitative techniques because they excel at answering "why" questions, can help us understand problem list utilization from the user's perspective, and can identify contextual and cultural factors that might affect attitudes and utilization [13-16]. In order to better understand clinician attitudes toward, and use of, electronic problem lists, we observed and interviewed a variety of clinicians. To assure the trustworthiness of our results, we triangulated using different methods, multiple researchers and sites, and types of subjects.

4.2 METHODS

4.2.1 SETTING

The study was conducted across the Partners HealthCare system, which includes the Brigham and Women's Hospital (Boston, MA), Massachusetts General Hospital (Boston, MA), Faulkner Hospital (Boston, MA), Newton-Wellesley Hospital (Newton, MA), North Shore Medical Center (Salem, MA) and several other smaller community and specialty hospitals. Partners also has a large community practice network called Partners Community HealthCare Incorporated (PCHI). PCHI practices are independently operated and generally small, with a mix of primary care, specialty and multi-specialty practices.

All Partners clinicians are required to use an electronic health record (EHR)—most use the Longitudinal Medical Record system (LMR), a self-developed, CCHIT-certified EHR, but a variety of other systems are also in use (particularly the GE Centricity Physician Office EMR). The LMR contains an electronic patient problem list tool that allows providers to document coded and uncoded problem entries along with supporting detail. The problem list appears on the summary screen of the LMR (Figure 1). Problem list use is not required and providers receive no specific guidance on use other than basic technical training.

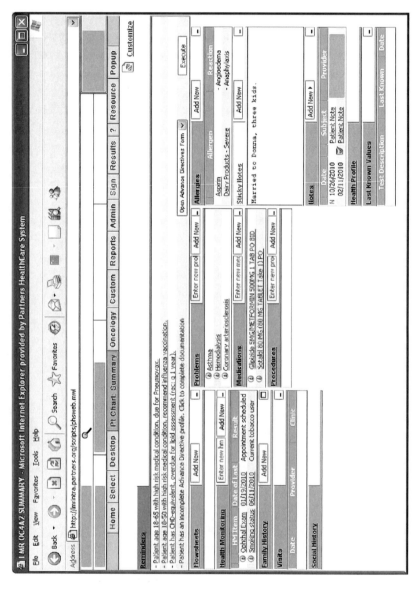

FIGURE 1: The problem list as displayed in the LMR (top center).

4.2.2 SAMPLE

We received IRB approval from the Partners HealthCare Human Subjects Committee. We used a purposive sampling methodology for our study. We began with a list of all medical specialties represented across the Partners network, and selected a representative set of potential practices providing a broad spectrum of medical and surgical specialties, practice settings (hospital and community based, large and small, high and low socioeconomic patient status mix, rural and urban, etc.) and healthcare provider types (physicians, nurses, NPs, PAs, other allied health professionals and complementary and alternative healthcare providers).

We contacted clinicians and practice managers by phone and email, providing each with an information sheet describing our project. When clinicians agreed to participate, we scheduled in-person observations with them. We also purposively sought out particular types of clinicians, asking our subjects whether they could suggest others in their practice to observe. For example, we asked clinicians to suggest potential subjects who were high, typical and low users of the problem list. Occasionally, we would also add additional subjects in real-time if we saw a clinician during our observation who was willing to let us observe him or her on the spot. Data collection continued until a diverse sample of clinicians had been observed and saturation achieved.

4.2.3 FIELD WORK

Once clinicians agreed to participate, we scheduled observations at their site. Where possible we observed them for an entire session or shift (most typically a four-hour session, but sometimes an eight-hour shift or longer). Before the session, each clinician was provided with an IRB-approved information sheet and briefed on the study process by the investigators. We obtained verbal consent from our subjects. Where possible, we observed the clinician's entire use of the EHR and problem list, from pre-visit preparation to the actual clinical encounter (when the patient verbally agreed) to documentation. A two-person team (AW and FM) conducted each observation.

In addition to observations, we also interviewed the subjects during down times in the clinic day, as well as at the end of our observations. These were short semi-structured interviews to explore problem list issues and also gave an opportunity for questions about our observations of the clinicians' behaviors.

We took extensive field notes throughout the observations and interviews, and occasionally recorded parts of interviews. These notes formed the basis for our analysis. Our field methods were based on the participant observation [17] and ethnographic interview [18] methods of Spradley, and were also influenced by the Rapid Assessment Process methods of Beebe [19], as adapted for assessment of clinical information systems by McMullen [20]. We chose these methods because they allow outsiders to relatively rapidly assess culture surrounding a focused area (in our case, the problem list) and to determine common and recurring themes.

4.2.4 DEBRIEFING

After we completed each observation, we met to debrief and review our notes. During each debriefing, we discussed what we had observed, and elicited a set of observations or quotations from each subject, such as "our leadership encourages us to maintain good problem lists" or "the problem list is not complete, therefore I don't rely on it."

4.2.5 ANALYSIS

We conducted a complete analysis of our field notes observations using a grounded theory approach [21]. We used an iterative card sort method to classify our observations into themes. Each of the two observation team members (AW and FM) initially sorted a representative sample of cards into sets, and then met to drive towards consensus to develop a coding scheme. We then did an independent card sort activity categorizing the remaining cards. After four rounds of iterative sorting, the classifications and themes converged, and we re-reviewed our field notes and observation catalog to identify patterns within the themes, and to review classes of providers exhibiting various aspects of those themes. We also did member checking, reviewing our themes with a subset of our subjects to ensure we had accurately captured meaning.

4.3 RESULTS

4.3.1 STUDY PARTICIPANTS

We observed a total of 63 clinicians. Of these, there were 35 attending physicians, 2 fellows, 5 residents, 2 interns, 3 physician assistants, 4 nurse practitioners, 1 nurse anesthetist, 2 nurse midwives, 4 nurses, 2 social workers, 1 pharmacist, 1 massage therapist and 1 acupuncturist. Our sample included a wide variety of primary care clinicians (primary care, family medicine, pediatrics, geriatrics), surgical specialists (general surgery, otolaryngology, obstetrics and gynecology, anesthesiology) and non-surgical specialists (cardiology, medical oncology, endocrinology, infectious disease, emergency medicine, psychiatry).

4.3.2 OBSERVATIONS

The observations were carried out over a nine month period from April 2009 to January 2010. We spent 264 hours observing and interviewing clinicians. Our observations ranged in length from 15 minutes to 8.5 hours. Most observations were initially scheduled for 4 or 8 hours but actual length of each session varied based on provider schedules. In addition, some shorter sessions were conducted spontaneously in the field as described in the Methods section. In one case, observation was stopped at a subject's request because the subject found it distracting. The mean observation time across all providers was 153 minutes.

TABLE 1: Summary of themes

Theme	Aspects and Interconnections
Workflow	• Aspects
	○ Points in the clinical encounter where providers use the problem list
	○ Usability issues
	○ Delegation of problem list use
	• Interconnections
	○ Delegation often depended on attitudes towards ownership and responsibility
	○ Different workflows appeared depending on uses
Ownership and Responsibility	• Aspects
	○ Issues regarding what providers are responsible for maintaining the problem list, and which problems each provider is responsible for
	• Interconnections
	○ Providers felt more ownership when they saw relevance to their practice
Relevance	• Aspects
	○ The extent to which providers viewed the problem list as relevant to their practice
	○ Includes both intrinsic and extrinsic relevance (including authority)
	• Interconnections
	○ Relevance drives use and sense of ownership/responsibility
Uses	• Aspects
	○ All reported uses of the problem list by providers
	○ Included both adding problems and referring to problems, as well as non-clinical uses (billing, etc.)
	• Interconnections
	○ Perceived uses drive relevance
	○ Different uses often require different workflow
Content	• Aspects
	○ Concepts relating to provider opinions on appropriate (and inappropriate) types of problem list content
	• Interconnections
	○ Content relates to relevance, as providers are most interested in adding content they perceive to be relevant
	○ Provider attitudes towards ownership and responsibility affect their willingness to modify problem list content (e.g. to discontinue a problem added by another provider that they consider irrelevant or incorrect)

TABLE 1: *Cont.*

Theme	Aspects and Interconnections
Presentation	• Aspects
	○ Observations related to actual and ideal representation of information in the problem list tool
	• Interconnections
	○ Different workflows and uses may have different optimal presentations
Accuracy	• Aspects
	○ Observations and opinions relating to the general accuracy, completeness and currency of patient problem lists
	• Interconnections
	○ Perceptions of accuracy affect uses and intention to use
Alternatives	• Aspects
	○ Any other mechanism of documenting problem list content other than the formal structured problem list
	• Interconnections
	○ Perception that alternatives are superior affects use and relevance attitudes
Support/Education	• Aspects
	○ Observations related to education and technical training on problem list use and ongoing support
	• Interconnections
	○ Support/education affect perception of uses and relevance
	○ Issues with workflow relate to sub-optimal support/education
Culture	• Aspects
	○ Local, institutional and professional culture around problem list use
	• Interconnections
	○ Cross-cutting theme influencing all other themes

4.3.3 FINDINGS

Across the 63 clinicians we observed, usage of and attitudes toward the problem list varied greatly. Some physicians were punctilious in their use of the list, constantly updating and refining entries in a manner consistent with Dr. Weed's model of the "problem-oriented medical record." Other physicians viewed themselves only as consumers of the problem list—reviewing it from time to time but never modifying or adding. Still others disregarded it entirely—neither viewing nor modifying the list (and in some cases saying they had never even heard of it).

4.3.4 THEMES

We identified a total of nine core themes and one cross-cutting theme to help categorize and explain our findings. These themes describe the full spectrum of problem list utilization behaviors observed (or elicited through interviews) in our sample. Attitudes were variable, and dimensions of variations fit into nine themes: workflow, ownership and responsibility, relevance, uses, content, presentation, accuracy, alternatives, support/education and one cross-cutting theme of culture (Table 1). The results of our analysis are described in full below and include findings derived from both direct observation and clinician interviews. With each quote from an interview or observation session, the specialty of the associated clinician is provided; this is meant only to provide information on the source of the quote and does not to imply that a certain opinion was associated with a given specialty.

4.3.5 WORKFLOW

Clinicians integrated the problem list into their workflow in a variety of ways. Many users would review the list at the beginning of the encounter—in some cases before going in to see the patient, but in other cases in the exam room with the patient present. Some of the frequent users of the problem list used it to guide the entire encounter. During their interview with the patient, they would work through the problem list, asking questions and updating the record problem by problem, and adding problems in real time as new concerns were identified. Other providers held their problem list edits to the end of the encounter (or even to the end of the day or, less commonly, the end of the week when they finished the note for that visit).

In some cases, especially among surgeons, providers would delegate the documentation of problems to other providers, such as medical assistants or physician assistants. In other cases, providers simply did not use the problem list at all, preferring instead to document concerns in dictated notes (see the Alternatives theme) or felt that problem lists were not relevant to their type of care at all (see the Relevance theme).

Within the workflow theme, a series of usability issues also arose. Partners HealthCare uses a coded problem list with a dictionary lookup (and the option to use free-text entries). Providers were often disappointed that the problem list feature could not identify synonyms they might use or misspelled problem concepts. Some providers also felt that adding problems was too time consuming, saying "the summation of clicks is the real problem" (family practice), "it would add 3 hours to my day, which I'm really not interested in" (otolaryngology) or "I would do it if I had the time" (infectious disease).

Some clinicians proposed alternative methods, such as kiosk-based entry of problems by patients, or automated inference of problems. One endocrinologist commented that "to have the doctor entering that stuff seems so retro."

4.3.6 OWNERSHIP AND RESPONSIBILITY

One important related theme is the idea of ownership of or responsibility for the problem list. Many primary care providers felt responsibility for maintaining the problem list, though they also thought that specialists shared responsibility for maintaining the list. There was some disagreement among PCPs about whether specialists should limit their use of the problem list to their own specialty, or whether they should document comprehensively: "it's patient based, not me based" (primary care), "it [having specialists add problems related to their specialty] would make things more accurate, more timely" (primary care), "it's not realistic to have one person in charge" (infectious disease). However, many specialists felt that the problem list was the responsibility of the PCP, and that specialists had little (or no) responsibility for recording problems outside or even inside their specialty: "it's the PCP domain" (psychiatry).

The ownership theme also extended to modification of the problem list. Many providers said that they would be uncomfortable modifying or discontinuing problems added by another provider: "I would never mess with the problem list or medication list" (primary care). Receptiveness towards being on the receiving end of such modifications varied—many providers said they would be fine with changes; however, other providers were more reluctant: "I feel like it's my baby I created for my patients" and "I would be so pissed if they [specialists] deleted" (primary care).

4.3.7 RELEVANCE

Related to the theme of ownership and responsibility was relevance. Many clinicians (especially primary care providers) felt that the problem list was relevant to the care they provided, but specialist opinions were mixed. The more enthusiastic providers said that "the problem list is the bedrock of medicine" (primary care) or that "we live by the problem list" (obstetrics). Many specialists also felt that the problem list was relevant, but some disagreed: "[I'm] just thinking bones" (orthopedic surgery) or "I think problem lists are updated every 6 months by anal residents in [the internal medicine clinic]" (general surgery).

In addition, some clinicians responsible for issues outside of direct medical care did not see the problem list as relevant to their roles. Some social workers reported that they do not diagnose problems, but instead identify concerns that wouldn't generally belong on the problem list. Complementary and alternative providers reported making some use of the problem list "to get a picture of what's going on with the patient, what they've been through and what I can do to help them." (massage therapy) but reported very rarely making modifications to the problem list (though they do write notes).

In addition to direct care, some clinicians were motivated to add problems because they are used in quality measurement and research: "someone's using this data for research, you don't want to use uncoded problems" (geriatrics). Others reported that, even if they didn't find the problem list personally relevant, they were motivated by a pay-for-performance target applicable in certain Partners clinics, by enhanced billing, by peer pressure or by their leadership.

4.3.8 USES

A large number of observed and interviewed providers reported that they thought the problem list was useful. Even some non-users of the problem list agreed that, in the ideal scenario, the problem list could benefit patient care. Many providers reported that the problem list was especially valuable when caring for patients not previously known to the provider (either new patients transferring in, or in coverage scenarios), and direct clinical use was the most commonly reported use for the problem list.

Some providers also pointed out that the length of the problem list (apart from its content) was also an important indicator of a patient's overall health and disease burden. One provider also indicated that a very long problem list in conjunction with a very short medication list is a "red flag" for somatization.

Clinical decision support was also reported as an important driver for problem list utilization. Several providers indicated that they would add problems where they knew they would receive useful reminders (e.g. for diabetes). The LMR also has a "KnowledgeLink" function, allowing users to find reference information for problems, and some users reported this as an additional incentive to add problems. Some users also reported, anecdotally, that they had observed others who occasionally intentionally created uncoded, misspelled problem list entries (e.g. "diabetees") to suppress unwanted reminders.

Certain non-clinical uses of the problem list were also identified. Pharmacists and nurses reported using the problem list to find indications for prior authorization requirements of drugs. Many providers also use the problem list in billing, though some providers felt that this use did not always lead to clinically optimal problem lists, "I think others are padding the problem list for billing purposes" (infectious disease). Finally, several providers indicated that they thought the problem list was important in quality measurement and research, and so they added problems to support these functions.

4.3.9 CONTENT

One significant area of disagreement about the problem list related to its content. There was widespread agreement that active, ongoing, chronic problems belong on the problem list. However, there was considerable disagreement about other types of data. Some providers included resolved problems, acute but likely self-limiting problems, family history, surgical history, symptoms without definite diagnosis (such as chest pain), medical devices, social issues, demographics.

In many cases, providers reported significant nuances in their attitudes towards these data types. For example, many providers thought that "status post myocardial infarction" belonged on the problem list, despite its latent or historical nature, but opinions on entries like "history of urinary tract infections" were much more mixed. The documentation of acute processes, like otitis media and cough, was also controversial—many providers favored documenting them and then inactivating them once resolved, others felt that such problems should only be elevated to problem list entries if recurrent. Some providers also added additional entries like "narcotics contract," and "Jehovah's Witness" to the problem list, though others emphatically believed these to not be problems. This behavior seems to represent a workaround due to a lack of other prominent places to track this information in the information system.

The actions users took in response to subjectively inappropriate existing content varied—many providers complained that they found problem lists to be filled with "junk" but wouldn't want to offend another provider by removing it (see also the Ownership and Responsibility theme), while others aggressively pared details they found irrelevant.

One significant facet of the content theme revolved around coded and uncoded problem list entries. The LMR provides a large dictionary of problem terms mapped to SNOMED, but users have the option to add uncoded terms (which cannot drive decision support) as needed. Many users reported that they did not know the difference between these two problem types (or even that there were different types available) despite an alert shown each time an uncoded entry is added. Some users who were aware of the difference reported a great desire to use coded terms "I bend over backwards to find a coded problem" (primary care), though this desire was often counterbalanced by some concern about the granularity of the problem terminology. For example, the LMR problem list dictionary contains "thyroid cancer," but does not allow for further specification of the type (papillary, follicular, medullary, etc.). Some users expressed uncertainty as to whether it was better to put a coded but more general term on the list, or an uncoded but more specific term. Some users reported that they had requested the addition of terms to the dictionary, but many of these users felt that their requests were ignored and quit making further requests.

4.3.10 PRESENTATION

The LMR provides little support for organizing the problem list—users can reorder the list and mark problems as inactive, but there is no ability to automatically sort or group problems. Many users commented that they would like to be able to group the problem list by a variety of criteria, including chronology, status (active or resolved), disease course (acute or chronic), certainty (established or provisional), organ system or importance. Other users wanted the ability to create a problem hierarchy or otherwise represent relationships between problems (e.g. to show that a patient's diabetic retinopathy is part of their diabetes, and that their diabetes is, in turn, linked to obesity).

Some providers also wanted specialty specific views, or the ability to only show problems that they had entered. Others disagreed with this (sometimes quite emphatically) declaring that it's "bad medicine" (oncology) to only see problems in your specialty, and that "people should not live in a silo of I'm only treating xyz" (anesthesiology).

4.3.11 ACCURACY

Many subjects commented on the accuracy and reliability of the problem list. Some thought the problem list was generally complete: "I usually take it at face value" (primary care), a number of subjects repeatedly stated they could not rely entirely on the problem list because it is not complete or accurate: "If I could trust it, I would look at it," "I don't use the problem list anymore because no one updates it." Providers reported that false negatives (missing problems) were much more common than false positives (incorrect problems). Some providers reported that they had confidence in the problem lists for their own patients, and sometimes for patients cared for by other physicians in their practice, but had less confidence in problem lists maintained by others.

For many providers, the lack of reliability meant that they would still review (and possibly update) the problem list, but that they will augment the problem list with other sources of information such as medications, notes, recent hospital discharge summaries or interviewing the patient (see the Alternatives theme). However, others reported completely discontinuing their use of the problem list, relying entirely on alternatives. We noted a "tragedy of the commons" occurring in many practice settings—providers reported that, frustrated with their incompleteness, they had stopped updating patient problem lists—this disuse then contributed to the further decay of the problem list, causing other providers to also discontinue use.

In contrast to this cycle of disuse, we also found some settings of mutually reinforcing use. A particular midwifery practice made consistent use of the problem list. When asked if the problem list was reliable, one midwife indicated that she could rely on the problem list "because it's always accurate." Asked if she were certain that the problem list was always accurate, she replied "it has to be accurate—we rely on it."

4.3.12 ALTERNATIVES

Many clinicians reported using a variety of alternative approaches to determining a patient's problems in addition to (or instead of) the structured problem list. The most common was keeping a problem list in the past medical history section of their outpatient progress notes. Clinicians also reported reviewing the most recent discharge summary (often cited as a very reliable snapshot of a patient's medical issues at the time of discharge), using the medication list to infer problems (particularly for medicines with a single or narrow set of indications), reviewing billing diagnoses (when available), relying on their own memory of the patient, discussing the patient with other providers or querying the patient directly.

Clinicians gave a variety of rationales for the use of these alternatives. One common explanation was their lack of confidence in the accuracy of the problem list (see Accuracy theme). However, clinicians also reported some specific adaptations to their style of care or personal preferences. For example, some specialists preferred to keep a personal specialty-specific problem list in their note to avoid the "clutter" of the complete problem list. Others said that they preferred to hear the patient describe their medical history in their own words. Finally, some providers kept shadow paper problem lists, reporting that they felt they could better organize their thoughts on paper than in a computer system. These problem lists are maintained outside the patient's standard medical record and cannot be readily accessed by other providers, which may ultimately result in fragmentation of clinical information due to unavailability or unawareness of these additional records.

4.3.13 SUPPORT/EDUCATION

Many users reported that they had received little or no formal education or training on the use of the problem list. Some indicated that they had been informally trained on the problem list during medical education, but this was variable. Within obstetrics, for example, one fellow reported being taught during medical education and residency to thoroughly document problems—another, who studied elsewhere, reported, "I wasn't taught that way," and didn't begin using the problem list until she joined Partners.

Several subjects had received training on the LMR which included a short section on adding and modifying the problem list, but reported that this training was purely technical in nature, teaching them the mechanics of the problem list function in the LMR, but not providing any information on content, responsibility or effective use.

Most clinicians reported that requests for additions to the problem list dictionary were generally ignored, "When there's a problem or bug they work really fast and are really effective. When there's a new feature request it never gets done." (oncology), "I quit making suggestions because they never do them" (obstetrics), though some clinicians did report receiving occasional responses. We queried the Partners Knowledge Management group, which reported that there is a general hold on adding new problems that might impact decision support until after the Partners problem dictionary is fully migrated to SNOMED.

4.3.14 CULTURE

The final theme we identified was a cross-cutting theme of problem list culture. Much of the variation in attitudes towards problem list usage was attributable to various prior themes we reported; however, we noted that there appeared to be a slightly more amorphous notion of culture within practices—some practices and clinicians, otherwise similar, used the problem list more or less than others. This culture seems to be derived from a variety of sources—we observed cultures tied to medical specialties, particular institutions, particular clinics within institutions and particular types of healthcare providers within clinics.

Problem list culture appears to be a complex and multifactorial phenomenon. In many cases, it is driven by formal leadership—some physicians reported that they used the problem list principally because the clinical leadership of their clinic set an expectation that everyone would use the problem list, and followed this with periodic chart audits and feedback to clinicians. This leadership did not always require formal authority—in some clinics, there was a single "champion" without formal authority who encouraged his or her fellow clinicians to maintain accurate problem lists. A culture of problem list utilization can also be driven by a sort of clinical "citizenship." In many settings, providers reported that they often took care of each others' patients, and that they depended on an accurate problem list when providing coverage, so they prioritized keeping their own problem lists updated for the benefit of their fellow providers.

Qualities inherent to a specialty or practice setting, as well as a specialty's larger culture may also drive the formation of a problem list culture. Specialties providing longitudinal care to patients, such as primary care and oncology, had strong cultures of problem list utilization, while episodic care settings, such as surgery, did not have a strong culture around problem list use. However, the obstetrics practices we observed were consistent users of the problem list—though they do provide episodic care (frequently of a surgical nature) their episodes are longer than many other surgeons', they provide frequent, ongoing and sometimes high-intensity care to their patients, and they have a strong cultural tradition of cross-coverage and mutual dependence (when an obstetrician encounters a patient in labor he or she expects to find accurate and complete documentation of the patient's prenatal course written by the extended obstetrical care team).

4.4. DISCUSSION

4.4.1 RECOMMENDATIONS

From our study, it became clear that there was tremendous variation in provider attitudes towards electronic problem list use and, in many cases, considerable frustration. Almost all clinicians (even non-users) agreed that the problem list was important and potentially useful, but many also felt that its full potential was not being realized.

One especially important phenomenon that we detected was a wide range of opinions on how the problem list should be used. This manifested itself particularly in the Ownership and Responsibility, Accuracy and Content themes. Providers expressed widely divergent views on who should be responsible for the problem list, the degree to which problem lists were reliable and up-to-date and the appropriate kinds of information to document in the problem list.

This variability suggests that more research, and perhaps policy setting, is needed to ascertain best practices for problem list usage and ultimately, perhaps, to establish guidelines or policies. None of the hospitals or clinics we studied had a formal policy on who is responsible for maintaining the problem list or what clinical conditions should belong on the problem list. Some clinicians reported an implicit or explicit expectation that they updated the problem list, but none had received specific guidance or training on effective problem list utilization, and several reported uncertainty about ownership of and responsibility for the problem list. The lack of a formal policy may have contributed to the wide variety of problem list use behaviors that were observed in this study.

A consistent policy on problem list use within and across institutions would likely be beneficial for increasing the value of this shared resource for all providers. We believe that clinicians and clinical professional organizations are optimally positioned to devise best practices (and perhaps model policies) and encourage them to do so. These findings also have implications for EHR developers who should collaborate with guideline developers to augment electronic problem list tools.

Developing consensus on optimal use of the problem list would have considerable benefits. Establishing wider agreement could make documentation more consistent, thus reducing inaccuracies and making patient problem information more readily accessible. This, in turn, could further increase use of this shared resource if providers find problem list content to be more consistently reliable and have a clearer understanding of expectations for its management.

Additionally, the federal meaningful use regulation (Stage 1) explicitly mentions the problem list, requiring that "more than 80 percent of all unique patients seen by the [eligible provider] have at least one entry or an indication that no problems are known for the patient recorded as structured data" [6]. This will likely result in an increase in use of electronic problem lists but does little to ensure their accuracy and consistent maintenance. The regulations (perhaps appropriately) do not specify what is or is not a problem, nor, in the setting of a shared record between specialists and primary care providers, who is responsible for maintaining the problem list. To meet this goal, as well as future Stage 2 and 3 benchmarks, more consistent problem list use will be needed.

Here we have identified major themes in provider attitudes and use of the problem list using qualitative methods. Future research should expand this analysis to other sites to test the generalizability of these findings and should incorporate quantitative analysis of provider problem list use. Formal guidelines should then be developed on the basis of these findings.

4.4.2 LIMITATIONS

Our study has some important limitations. First, as is the case with any ethnographic study, our results are inherently influenced by the ethnographers themselves. We adhered to standard ethnographic methods to manage potential bias and to ensure that our data collection frame was open and wide, but it is possible that other observers might develop different conclusions.

Second, though our sample was large and diverse, it was limited to a single health system, and focused specifically on providers using an EHR, which limits the generalizability of our results. Given all providers used the same problem list tool, some of the issues reported, especially those around workflow, may be tied to the advantages and deficiencies of this particular system. It is likely that providers outside of our system, or non-users of an EHR might be systematically different. To guard against the first issue, we explicitly asked our subjects about their experiences before joining Partners (subjects came from a variety of community, academic, military and institutional practice settings) and integrated this information into our analysis. The second issue (focus on EHR users) was inherent to our study design. We would encourage other researchers to explore problem list utilization using similar techniques in other settings and among non-EHR users—such study would almost certainly add additional richness to our findings.

Third, and finally, our study may be subject to the Hawthorne effect (subject reactivity to observation). We did our best to guard against this by encouraging subjects to speak honestly and probing them about whether behaviors they exhibited were typical. We also used the ethnographic technique of triangulation: in addition to observations, we also used interviews, observed multiple subjects in most settings, and occasionally reviewed past records and problem list entries in real time with our subjects to ensure a complete and unbiased understanding of their problem list attitudes and behaviors.

4.5 CONCLUSION

Clinicians do see the intrinsic value in accurate, up-to-date problem lists; however, real-world usage of problem lists is highly variable and often falls short of ideal. We identified important issues regarding reliability of the problem list, as well as lack of consensus (and even confusion) about ownership and responsibility, content and perceived relevance of the problem list. Resolution of these issues may enable more effective and efficient use of the problem list, potentially resulting in improved quality of care.

REFERENCES

1. Weed LL: Medical records that guide and teach. The New England journal of medicine 1968, 278(12):652-657. concl
2. Best Practices for Problem Lists in an EHR [http:/ / library.ahima.org/ xpedio/ groups/ public/ documents/ ahima/ bok1_036244.hcsp?dDocName=bok1_0362 44]
3. Information Management Processes (Standard IM 6.40): 2008 Comprehensive Accreditation Manual for Hospitals: The Official Handbook. Oakbrook Terrace, Illinois: Joint Commission Resources; 2008.
4. Hartung DM, Hunt J, Siemienczuk J, Miller H, Touchette DR: Clinical implications of an accurate problem list on heart failure treatment. Journal of general internal medicine 2005, 20(2):143-147.
5. Wright A, McGlinchey EA, Poon EG, Jenter CA, Bates DW, Simon SR: Ability to generate patient registries among practices with and without electronic health records. J Med Internet Res 2009, 11(3):e31.
6. Comparison of Meaningful Use Objectives Between the Proposed Rule to the Final Rule [https:/ / www.cms.gov/ EHRIncentivePrograms/ Downloads/ NPRM_vs_FR_Table_Comparison_Final.p df]
7. Chaudhry B, Wang J, Wu S, Maglione M, Mojica W, Roth E, Morton SC, Shekelle PG: Systematic review: impact of health information technology on quality, efficiency, and costs of medical care. Annals of internal medicine 2006, 144(10):742-752.
8. Garg AX, Adhikari NK, McDonald H, Rosas-Arellano MP, Devereaux PJ, Beyene J, Sam J, Haynes RB: Effects of computerized clinical decision support systems on practitioner performance and patient outcomes: a systematic review. Jama 2005, 293(10):1223-1238.
9. Kawamoto K, Houlihan CA, Balas EA, Lobach DF: Improving clinical practice using clinical decision support systems: a systematic review of trials to identify features critical to success. BMJ (Clinical research ed 2005, 330(7494):765.

10. Osheroff JA, Teich JM, Middleton B, Steen EB, Wright A, Detmer DE: A roadmap for national action on clinical decision support. J Am Med Inform Assoc 2007, 14(2):141-145.
11. Wright A, Goldberg H, Hongsermeier T, Middleton B: A description and functional taxonomy of rule-based decision support content at a large integrated delivery network. J Am Med Inform Assoc 2007, 14(4):489-496.
12. Szeto HC, Coleman RK, Gholami P, Hoffman BB, Goldstein MK: Accuracy of computerized outpatient diagnoses in a Veterans Affairs general medicine clinic. The American journal of managed care 2002, 8(1):37-43.
13. Kaplan B, Shaw NT: Future directions in evaluation research: people, organizational, and social issues. Methods of information in medicine 2004, 43(3):215-231.
14. Pope C, Mays N: Reaching the parts other methods cannot reach: an introduction to qualitative methods in health and health services research. BMJ (Clinical research ed 1995, 311(6996):42-45.
15. Pope C, van Royen P, Baker R: Qualitative methods in research on healthcare quality. Quality & safety in health care 2002, 11(2):148-152.
16. Sofaer S: Qualitative methods: what are they and why use them? Health services research 1999, 34(5 Pt 2):1101-1118.
17. Spradley JP: Participant observation. New York: Holt, Rinehart and Winston; 1980.
18. Spradley JP: The ethnographic interview. New York: Holt, Rinehart and Winston; 1979.
19. Beebe J: Rapid assessment process: an introduction. Walnut Creek, CA: AltaMira Press; 2001.
20. McMullen CK, Ash JS, Sittig DF, Bunce A, Guappone K, Dykstra R, Carpenter J, Richardson J, Wright A: Rapid Assessment of Clinical Information Systems in the Healthcare Setting. An Efficient Method for Time-pressed Evaluation. Methods of information in medicine 50(2)
21. Glaser BG, Strauss AL: The discovery of grounded theory; strategies for qualitative research. Chicago, Aldine Pub. Co; 1967.

CHAPTER 5

HEALTHCARE PROVIDER ATTITUDES TOWARDS THE PROBLEM LIST IN AN ELECTRONIC HEALTH RECORD: A MIXED-METHODS QUALITATIVE STUDY

CASEY HOLMES, MICHAEL BROWN, DANIEL ST HILAIRE, AND ADAM WRIGHT

5.1 INTRODUCTION

The problem list is a key part of the medical record. At a high level, it lists the patient's most important health problems and gives the practitioner key information to determine the best treatment plan. Good problem lists are known to improve patient care [1,2] and are used as a resource for clinical decision support tools to prevent medical error [3,4]. Yet, there are issues with problem lists that limit their effectiveness. The three greatest are thought to be:

Healthcare Provider Attitudes Towards the Problem List in an Electronic Health Record: A Mixed-Methods Qualitative Study. © Holmes C, Brown M, St Hilaire D, and Wright A. BMC Medical Informatics and Decision Making **12,**127 (2012); doi:10.1186/1472-6947-12-127. Licensed under Creative Commons Attribution 2.0 Generic License, http://creativecommons.org/licenses/by/2.0/.

- No common approach: Practitioners differ in opinion on what should and should not go on the problem list [5,6].
- Completeness (false negatives): major problems are never listed on the patient's problem list [7].
- Clutter (false positives): Minor or inactive problems accumulate on a problem list making the document unfocused and incomprehensible [8].

With the passage of the HITECH act, most of the medical community is now focused on adopting electronic health records that can improve patient care. As problem lists are more readily shared across providers, the above deficits have become more prominent. Yet, to solve these issues the medical community needs to know more about how practitioners are currently approaching the problem list and the logic behind those decisions. This research is meant to provide such guidance and through this knowledge, encourage the development of a common approach.

5.2 BACKGROUND

Lawrence Weed created the problem list in the 1960s as part of his recommendations for a problem-oriented medical record [9]. A simple idea, the problem list soon became a commonly accepted part of the paper medical record and is now used in EHRs as well. The American Health Information Management Association (AHIMA) defines the problem list as "a compilation of clinically relevant physical and diagnostic concerns, procedures, and psychosocial and cultural issues that may affect the health status and care of patients" [8]. At its core the problem list is meant to include the most important factors about a patient (largely chronic diseases such as diabetes and chronic heart disease) to allow practitioners to gain a quick sense of the patient and ensure that significant issues that affect treatment decisions are not hidden within the medical note.

Studies show that high quality problem lists directly link to better compliance with best practices in medicine. Hartung et al. found that patients with known systolic dysfunction who had heart failure listed in their problem list were more likely to be prescribed the appropriate drug therapy than those without [1]. In a study looking at encounter notes across consecutive medical visits at six medical clinics, Simborg et al. found that those practitioners who listed the diagnosed problem on the problem list were more likely to follow-up on the issue than those who did not list the diagnosed problem [2].

Practitioner's ability to quickly appreciate the most important facts about their patients' impacts their ability to provide high quality healthcare. Therefore, when problems are left out or hidden within a long and cluttered list, the problem lists' effectiveness is compromised. In order to improve patient care and reap further benefit from the problem list as a data resource, the medical community needs to create clear, consistent, complete, and accurate problem lists. Unfortunately, the medical community's current approach to the problem list makes inconsistency and error the standard.

5.2.1 THE INCONSISTENCIES

In ethnographic and qualitative studies of healthcare providers, Wright et al. found that healthcare providers' use of the problem list is incomplete, and that attitudes vary across care providers [6,10,11]. Practitioners have developed their own style on how to manage and organize the problem list [5,6]. For example, practitioners may argue that listing a family history of breast cancer directly on the problem list is important for prompting more frequent testing, another practitioner can debate that its inclusion duplicates the family history section and clutters the list. Zhou et al. published similar findings identifying the ambiguity surrounding the definition, use, and benefits of the problem list among different clinician groups, and highlighting the challenges of improving documentation in complex, longitudinal cooperative clinical practices [12].

While these differences are likely frequent, they are problematic for a healthcare system where multiple practitioners are building a patient's medical record together through the EHR. With no common guidelines for how to approach the problem list, issues such as missing problems [1,2] and lengthiness [8] decrease the potential benefits problem lists could bring to patient care.

5.2.2 WHY ADDRESS THE ISSUE NOW?

The nationwide transition to the EHR in the United States [13] brings the possibility to standardize parts of the medical record in order to improve patient care. To comply with meaningful use, practitioners must maintain an up-to-date problem list of current and active diagnoses based on ICD-9-CM or SNOMED CT, clinical coding standards designed to classify diseases, symptoms, and other relevant factors about a patient. In addition, at least 80 percent of all unique patients must have at least one entry or an indication of none recorded as structured data in the problem list [14].

Meaningful use standards are preparing the EHR to enable clinical decision support and population management tools [13,14]. These tools depend on reliable platforms of aggregated data such as the medication list [4]. Yet, the problem list is not currently supportive enough for these tools due to its inconsistencies, specifically missing problems [7] and clutter [8]. The problem list will need more than a common language platform to support these tools [10]. If the problem list were standardized—(i.e. policies and tools were designed to ensure that a patient's problem list was the same regardless of the practitioner(s) who created it)—it could mean improvements to patient care, such as:

- Make it more likely that practitioners identify all the important factors about a patient to determine their best treatment plan [1,2].
- Help to prevent medical errors through clinical decision support tools [3,4].
- Allow for the accurate identification of disease specific populations for quality improvement programs, practitioner report cards, and potential research study participants [10,11].

Further, the problem list is becoming part of the shared medical record across providers and organizations. Specifically, as part of the menu set of meaningful use measures, providers must provide a summary of care record for transitions of care and referrals which must include the problem list [14]. As a likely seed for common shared medical record, creating a common approach to the problem list will be important to reaping the most value from health information exchanges.

5.2.3 CURRENT POLICIES LACK DIRECT GUIDANCE FOR PRACTITIONERS

Policies on the problem lists can be found through a range of organizations such as AHIMA which released best practices for problem lists in 2008 [8]. Other organizations with policies related to the problem list include Health Level 7 [15] and The Joint Commission [16]. Of course, the federal government also included new requirements for the problem list within the meaningful use standards. The impact of these policies has not yet been measured and, with the exception of meaningful use, it is not clear that any of the policies have been adopted widely.

Based on a review of these current policies, most address what administrators should provide for the problem list with the strongest focus on coding. Guidance for how practitioners should approach, manage, and organize the problem list is largely limited to high level definitions about the problem list. From the policy perspective, practitioners are left to their own personal judgment for what to include and not include in the problem list.

Education and training within healthcare organizations does not appear to provide any further guidance for most practitioners. According to Wright et al. education and training towards the problem list among practitioners interviewed was insubstantial, typically informal, and highly variable [6]. Some healthcare organizations in the United States created their own policies towards the problem list, but it is unclear how effective they are at producing valuable problem lists nor are they in widespread adoption across the United States. Therefore, while policies offer high-level rules, specific guidance to the practitioner on how to construct and maintain an accurate problem list is noticeably absent, leaving room for errors and variation in practice.

Policies and EHR tools are likely the best approach to solving the issues with current electronic problem list [6]. Yet, very little research exists on how practitioners make decisions regarding what to include in the problem list and therefore the best common approach to the problem list is unknown. This knowledge would help the medical community move forward in developing such mechanisms.

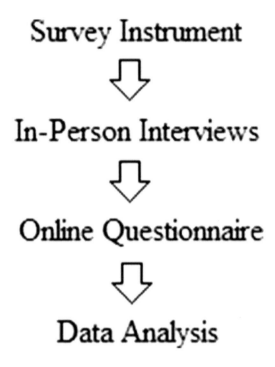

FIGURE 1: Mixed-methods study design order.

The purpose of this study is to develop a better understanding of how practitioners think about and use the problem list. A secondary purpose is to study the extent to which practitioners differ in their decision making and if these decisions vary based on practitioner characteristics such as clinical work experience, specialty, and age. Such research will assist in the pursuit of developing policies and tools that can create a common approach to the problem list.

5.3 METHODS

To identify practitioner opinions towards the problem list and the logic behind their decisions an observational cross sectional study was conducted at Brigham and Women's Hospital (BWH) and Massachusetts General Hospital (MGH). Of note, the EHRs at these facilities allow both coded and free text diagnosis to be entered into the problem list, providing the practitioners with great freedom in how they approach the problem list. This study was granted IRB exemption from the Partners HealthCare Human Subjects Committee.

5.3.1 STUDY DESIGN

A survey instrument was created to identify practitioner attitudes towards the problem lists in areas that were predicted to be variable. Then the survey instrument was administered through a two-pronged approach. First, in person interviews were conducted with practitioners to understand the logic behind their hypothesized actions towards the problem list. Second, an online questionnaire was sent to practitioners to gain numerous viewpoints. For the data analysis stage, both data sets were used in conjunction to create a summarized analysis of practitioner opinions towards the problem list. These steps are outlined in Figure 1 below.

5.3.2 SURVEY INSTRUMENT

Based on the premise that well-meaning practitioners will differ in their views about actions towards the problem list, the survey instrument focused on areas of action towards the problem list that were thought to be highly variable across practitioners. These non-standardized areas were defined and categorized based on the prior research experiences of the study team. These experiences included a project to improve coded problems at a health services organization from a major research university [10,11], an ethnographic study of healthcare providers' use of the problem list [6], and experience with developing an EHR tool which alerts practitioners to potential problem list gaps [17]. Based on the knowledge learned from these undertakings, the areas of focus for the survey instrument are defined and explained in Table 1.

TABLE 1: Details on problem list vignette questions

Question	Category	Potential Controversy	Example
What problems should be included (Broad)?			
1	Family History	Should family history only be listed in the family history section of the EHR or if important enough be included in the problem list.	Family history of breast cancer; Family history of diabetes
2	Social History	Should social history only be listed in the social history section of the EHR or if important enough be included in the problem list.	Construction worker; Non-smoker; Suspected alcohol abuse
3	Surgeries	Should surgeries only be listed in the past surgical history section of the EHR or if important enough be included in the problem list.	Appendectomy; Knee replacement surgery
4	Hospitalizations	Should hospitalizations only be listed in the prior hospitalization section of the EHR or if important enough be included in the problem list.	Hospitalized - May 2006 - MI
What problems should be included (Detailed)?			
5	Latent chronic diseases	Should chronic diseases which are currently not receiving medical treatment be included in the problem list?	Asthma, no symptoms, no medications
6	Non-medical conditions	Should problems that are not a disease, family history, social history, surgery, or hospitalization be included in the problem list?	Medical anxiety; Medication non-compliance
7	Undiagnosed long term symptoms	Should symptoms that cannot be linked to a specific diagnosis of a disease be listed in the problem list?	Chest pain - work up completed, no diagnosable cause
8	Multiple occurrences of transitive illness	Should transitive illnesses that occur multiple times be listed in the problem list?	Multiple urinary tract infections
9	Sequelae problems	Should a disease caused by an original disease be listed in the problem list?	Coronary heart disease caused by diabetes

TABLE 1: *Cont.*

Question	Category	Potential Controversy	Example
Terminology			
10	Use of acronyms	Should practitioners use acronyms in the problem list or write out the full title of the disease?	DM or Diabetes Mellitus; CHD or Coronary Heart Disease
10	Level of detail of problems	What level of specificity should be used to describe a problem?	Diabetes; Diabetes Mellitus; Diabetes Mellitus Type II
11	Listing a sequelae	Should a problem caused by an original disease be listed with the original problem on the problem list?	Diabetes Mellitus Type II with renal manifestations
When to add or delete problems?			
12	Timing (add)	On a problem where it is unclear if it is transitive or chronic, how much time or number of appointments should the practitioner wait until listing it on the problem list?	Back pain
13	Timing (delete)	When a chronic disease is cured or no longer receives medical treatment, should it be deleted from the active status problem list and if so, when?	Diabetes Mellitus Type II; Breast Cancer; Migraines
Sensitive Problems			
14	Whether to include sensitive problems?	Should sensitive problems be included in the problem list?	Depression, HIV/AIDS
15	To include sensitive problems when other practitioners have access to the same record	Should all the patient's practitioners know of all their diagnoses through the problem list in the EHR?	Anorexia Nervosa; HIV positive
16	To include sensitive problems when a patient disagrees with a diagnosis	Should a diagnosis that a patient does not believe they have be listed in the problem list?	Depression; Anxiety Disorder
17	To include sensitive problems when a patient has access to the problem list through an online patient portal	If a patient has access to their problem list through an online patient portal, should a diagnosis that could potentially hurt the patient's feelings be listed on the problem list?	Obesity; Depression

TABLE 1: *Cont.*

Question		Category	Potential Controversy	Example
Who can change the problem list across the following roles:				
	18	Specialist	Should specialists be responsible for adding or deleting problems that they diagnose or treat?	Asthma; Breast Cancer
	18	PCP	Should the PCP be solely responsible for adding and deleting all problems, regardless of who originally diagnosed the problem?	All potential problems
	19	Nurse Practitioner	Should a nurse practitioner be allowed to add and/or delete problems when they care for a patient?	All potential problems
	20	Other RN	Should an RN other than a nurse practitioner be allowed to add and/or delete problems when they care for a patient?	All potential problems

After determining the specific areas to study, the survey instrument was constructed to gather practitioner opinions. This survey instrument has two sections: the first part asked background questions such as clinical discipline, age, medical experience, and importance of the problem list to the respondent measured via a Likert scale. The second part of the questionnaire consisted of vignettes. Each vignette contained a hypothesized clinical scenario that covered one of the predefined areas under question along with multiple choice responses of potential actions. For instance, the question of whether family history should be included in the problem list was represented by the following vignette:

> *Donna goes to see her PCP and mentions that she is terrified of getting breast cancer because both her maternal grandmother and mother had breast cancer. Now her sister was recently diagnosed. Should Donna's family history of breast cancer be mentioned on her problem list? (Yes/No)*

Vignettes were used in the survey instrument instead of asking direct questions (for example, "Do you include family history in your problem lists?") because it was thought that practitioners would be challenged to think more deeply about their answers if given a real life scenario.

5.3.3 VALIDATION

To validate that the questionnaire was medically accurate and appropriate, the survey instrument was reviewed by a physician and pre-tested with a focus group. Focus group participants included physicians who were currently students at the Harvard School of Public Health. The survey was conducted through the Turning Technologies Audience Response System (Turning Technologies, Youngstown, OH) where each student anonymously responded to a vignette and the results were then displayed on the screen. The focus group leader then prompted a discussion asking individuals to describe their thought process behind their decision. Overall, the focus group respondents understood the vignettes, were engaged in the exercise, and had definite opinions about their answers.

After the validation process, the survey instrument was further refined to ensure questions were clear and reordered to place compelling questions at the beginning to encourage completion of the instrument.

5.3.4 SAMPLE

The survey instrument was then implemented via the prior described two-pronged approach: in-person interviews and online questionnaire.

For the in-person interviews, practitioners at both Brigham and Women's Hospital (BWH) and Massachusetts General Hospital (MGH) were contacted to participate. A representative sampling method was not feasible and contacted practitioners were selected based on prior participation in a problem list study at the hospitals.

In-person interviews were conducted between December 2010 and February 2011. During the interviews, the interviewer followed the survey instrument. When answering the vignettes, the interviewer followed up with more specific questions to learn how the respondent justified their answer. All interviews were recorded for data tracking purposes. No incentives were provided to respondents. After the interview was conducted, practitioners were given a $5 Starbucks gift card as a thank you token. The practitioners were unaware of the gift card prior to the interview.

For the online questionnaire, the survey instrument was formatted and data collected using REDCap electronic data capture tools [18]. REDCap (Research Electronic Data Capture) is a secure, web-based application designed to support data capture for research studies. To address issues that arose during the in-person interviews, the survey instrument was slightly modified for use in the online questionnaire. Overall, it is not believed that the modifications affected the intent of the questions between the in-person interviews and online questionnaire.

The online questionnaire was hosted from March through June 2011. Physicians (including primary care providers and specialists), physician assistants (PAs), and nurse practitioners (NPs) were included in the sample. The online questionnaires were sent to several departments at BWH and MGH consisting mostly of primary care providers. The respondent pool was determined based on access to department electronic mailing lists which required approval by department directors. All surveyed departments received approval for participation in the study and only one invitation to a division of specialists received no response and thus did not participate in the study. No incentives were provided to respondents.

5.3.5 DATA ANALYSIS

Data collected through the in-person interviews were partially transcribed, partially summarized where appropriate. The same person who conducted the in-person interviews completed the transcription. In creating Additional file 2: Appendix B, the transcriptionist (CH) looked for quotes that represented the different justifications behind decisions towards the problem list in each vignette.

The data from the online interviews were aggregated and analyzed using STATA. The data were then tabulated to observe the proportion of responses to each answer. These proportions were combined with the quotes taken from the in-person interviews in order to create a general analysis of each area of non-standardized practice discussed in the results section [Additional file 2: Appendix B].

Using the responses to the online questionnaire, two summary measures were created using the following methodology:

- Completeness measure: Thirteen of the vignettes specify a situation where a problem is either added or not added to the problem list (Questions #8 - 16, 18, 19, 21, and 24 in Additional File 1: Appendix A). The completeness score displays how many problems the respondent wanted to add to the list across the vignettes. Respondents received one point for every time they selected "yes" to add a potential problem to the problem list. Respondents received zero points for every time they selected "no" to keep a potential problem off the problem list.
- Plurality measure: This measure was designed to see how opinions of individuals differed from the group. Respondents who answered with the relative majority received one point. Respondents who answered with any other response received zero points. For vignette question with more than two responses, respondents received one point if they answered with the response that received the highest percentage of respondents (the plurality) and zero points if they answered with any of response. An aggregate measure was then calculated for each respondent. All vignette questions were analyzed in this measure unless the question responses were evenly split and no plurality existed.

These two summary measures were tabulated and summarized within STATA. We used Student's t test to compare scores based on provider characteristics such as:

- Discipline (MD, PA/NP, Other)
- Role (PCP, Specialist, Other)
- Training status (Resident or Non-Resident)
- Age
- Years of experience practicing medicine
- Importance of the problem list to everyday practice of medicine conducted via a Likert scale of one "not important" to five "very important."

In addition to Student's t test, we also used linear regression models to explore the combined effects of these characteristics in a multivariate setting. P values were used to determine statistical significance measured at the 95% confidence level.

5.4 RESULTS

5.4.1 RESPONSE RATE

Invitations to complete the online questionnaire were sent out to 346 practitioners. The online questionnaire received ninety-seven full responses and fourteen partial responses (response rate: 32%). For the in-person interviews, we contacted fourteen and completed nine interviews (response rate: 64%), ranging in length from eighteen to forty-three minutes (Table 2). One interview had to be excluded from further analysis as the practitioner did not feel confident in his ability to appropriately answer the vignettes. The other eight in-person interviews were completed with practitioners across a variety of disciplines and experience levels (Tables 3 and 4).

TABLE 2: Summary of respondents by data collection type

	n	Sample size	Response rate
In-Person Interviews	9*	14	64.2%
Online Questionnaire	111	346	32.1%

One survey response was excluded from further analysis.

5.4.2 CHARACTERISTICS OF RESPONDENTS

Table 3 describes the characteristics of our online questionnaire respondent base. Most of the respondents were physicians (94%) and the second most frequent respondents were physician assistants/nurse practitioners (5%). The questionnaire was programmed to terminate responses from those who selected other (1%) to ensure that all respondents had a clinical background.

TABLE 3: Online questionnaire respondents, and linear regression and t-test analysis of the completeness and plurality measures

	Online Questionnaire Respondents		Completeness Measure		Plurality Measure	
			Assessment of 13 Yes/No vignettes for inclusion tolerance		Assessment of 20 vignettes for trends in choosing with the plurality	
	N	% Resp	Unadjusted Value	Adjusted P*	Unadjusted Value	Adjusted P*
Role						
MD	105	93.8	9.7	ref	15.1	ref
PA/NP	6	5.4	10.8	0.5	14.6	0.3
Other	1	0.9	NA	NA	NA	NA
Discipline						
PCP	85	76.6	9.7	ref	15.0	ref
Specialist	9	8.1	9.9	0.9	15.3	0.7
Other	17	15.3	10.2	0.2	15.0	0.6
Resident						
No	48	44.0	9.9	ref	15.0	ref
Yes	61	56.0	9.4	0.0	15.0	0.7
Age						
21-30	38	34.9	9.5	ref	15.1	ref
31-40	27	24.8	9.5	1.0	14.6	0.7
41-50	23	21.1	9.9	0.5	15.1	0.1
51-60	13	11.9	10.3	0.7	15.4	0.1
61-70	7	6.4	10.0	0.9	15.3	0.1
greater than 70	1	0.9	12.0	0.0	15.0	0.1
Experience						
less than 1 year	20	18.4	9.9	ref	15.6	ref
1-5	34	31.2	9.3	0.1	14.9	0.3
6-10	10	9.2	9.4	0.1	14.8	0.3
11-20	24	22.0	9.9	0.5	15.0	0.0
21-30	11	10.1	10.5	0.9	14.8	0.1
31-40	7	6.4	10.0	0.4	15.3	0.0

TABLE 3: *Cont.*

	Online Questionnaire Respondents		Completeness Measure		Plurality Measure	
			Assessment of 13 Yes/No vignettes for inclusion tolerance		Assessment of 20 vignettes for trends in choosing with the plurality	
	N	% Resp	Unadjusted Value	Adjusted P*	Unadjusted Value	Adjusted P*
greater than 40 years	3	2.8	11.0	0.6	15.7	0.3
Importance						
1 - not important	2	1.8	10.0	ref	14.5	ref
2	3	2.7	10.5	0.3	17.5	0.0
3	10	9.0	9.5	0.9	14.8	0.5
4	37	33.3	9.7	0.2	15.0	0.1
5 - very important	59	53.2	9.8	0.4	15.0	0.2

Most of the respondents were PCPs (77%), and nearly half of the respondents were residents. The distribution of age closely followed the distribution of experience among respondents. Demographic data sets were not available for non-respondents in departments that agreed to participate or the one department that was invited to participate in the questionnaire, but did not respond to the invitation. Table 4 includes the demographic data of respondents to the in-person interviews. 88% were physicians and among this group, 75% were specialists. Experience varied widely and only one respondent was a resident.

5.4.3 CHARACTER OF RESPONSES

Additional file 2: Appendix B includes select quotes from the in-person interviews. The quotes show some of the logic and opinions behind potential answers to the vignettes. The tabulated data from the online questionnaire are included for convenient reference. Overall, the in-person interviews

TABLE 4: Characteristics of in-person interview respondents

	% Resp	N
Role		
MD	87.5%	7
RN/NP	12.5%	1
Discipline		
PCP	25.0%	2
Specialist	75.0%	6
Resident?		
Yes	12.5%	1
No	87.5%	7
Experience		
1-5	12.5%	1
6-10	12.5%	1
11-20	25.0%	2
21-30	37.5%	3
31-40	12.5%	1

brought out the complexities behind contentious issues in creating the problem list.

Table 5 includes the tabulated answers to each individual vignette from the online questionnaire. Of the thirteen vignettes with a yes or no response, twelve had a meaningful majority answer (statistically significant based on a binomial distribution). The one question that was evenly divided covered whether hospitalizations should be included in the problem list (question4 respectively in Table 5). The other seven questions that contained non-yes/no responses (questions #10, 11, 12, 13, 18, 19, & 20 in Additional File 1: Appendix A) had a range of answers depending on the question.

5.4.4 GENERAL TRENDS AND FINDINGS

The following represents a brief summary of the findings and trends in each category as described in the methodology.

TABLE 5: Tabulated answers to vignettes

What problems should be included (broad)?			
Question 1: Family History	Answers	% Res.	N
Donna goes to see her PCP and mentions that she is terrified of getting breast cancer because both her maternal grandmother and mother had breast cancer. Now her sister was recently diagnosed. Should Donna's family history of breast cancer be mentioned on her problem list?	Yes	76.2	77
	No	23.8	24
Question 2: Social History	Answers	% Res.	N
John comes in to a medical center's urgent care ward with a small facial laceration from playing hockey. John mentions he's a male model to the physician and explains that he wants treatment that will minimize scarring. Should the doctor add John's occupation as a model to the problem list?	Yes	7.9	8
	No	92.1	93
Question 3: Surgeries	Answers	% Res.	N
Ritchie has an appendectomy performed at the local hospital. His PCP gets the medical record from the hospital. Should Ritchie's PCP add 'appendectomy' to Ritchie's problem list?	Yes	73.5	72
	No	26.5	26
Question 4: Hospitalizations	Answers	% Res.	N
Paul is hospitalized due to a heart attack caused by his coronary artery disease. At Paul's PCPs office 'coronary artery disease' is already listed on his problem list. Now Paul's PCP receives Paul's medical information from the hospital. Should Paul's PCP add another item specifically mentioning Paul's recent hospitalization to the problem list?	Yes	50.0	49
	No	50.0	49
What problems should be included (detailed)?			
Question 5: Latent non-transitive diseases	Answers	% Res.	N
Tenesha recently moved to Boston and goes to see her new PCP for an annual physical. Tenesha says that she was diagnosed by a pulmonologist with exercise-induced asthma several years ago. Currently, she takes no medications to treat her asthma, is experiencing no symptoms, and the asthma does not affect her daily life. Should 'exercise-induced asthma' be added to her problem list?	Yes	82.2	83
	No	17.8	18

TABLE 5: *Cont.*

What problems should be included (broad)?			
Question 6: Non-medical conditions	Answers	% Res.	N
Maria is a 52 year old woman and is afraid of doctors. She summons up the courage to go see a doctor for the first time in years because of a persistent cough. Should the doctor add a note about Maria's fear of doctors to her problem list?	Yes	35.6	36
	No	64.4	65
Question 7: Undiagnosed long term symptoms	Answers	% Res.	N
Jorge appears to have ongoing chest pain, but after a full work up the practitioner cannot diagnose the cause. Should the practitioner add an item about chest pain to the Jorge's problem list?	Yes	96.0	97
	No	4.0	4
Question 8: Multiple occurrences of transitive illness	Answers	% Res.	N
Helen is having her third urinary tract infection (UTI) within one year. Should the practitioner add a statement about the Helen's predisposition for urinary tract infections to her problem list?	Yes	92.9	91
	No	7.1	7
Question 9: Sequelae	Answers	% Res.	N
Sally develops coronary artery disease as a result of her Type II diabetes. Should the resultant coronary artery disease be listed on the problem list?	Yes	100.0	97
	No	0.0	0
Terminology			
Question 10: Use of acronyms/Level of detail of problems			
Sally is diagnosed with Type II diabetes. What term should the practitioner use on Sally's problem list?			
Answers	% Res.	N	
DM	1.0	1	
DM II	16.5	16	
Diabetes Type II	17.5	17	
Diabetes	3.1	3	
Diabetes Mellitus	1.0	1	
Diabetes Mellitus Type II	58.8	57	
Other	2.1	2	

TABLE 5: *Cont.*

What problems should be included (broad)?			
Question 11: Listing of sequelae			
If a practitioner wants to list Sally's coronary artery disease, how should coronary artery disease be listed on her problem list?			
Answers		% Res.	N
Diabetes Type II with coronary artery disease		0.0	0
As a separate problem from Diabetes Type II		100.0	97
When to add or delete problems?			
Question 12: Timing (add)	Answers	% Res.	N
Dr. Baker likes to include long term undiagnosed symptoms on his patients' problem lists. Catherine comes in for her first appointment with Dr. Baker complaining of lower back pain. If Catherine keeps coming to see Dr. Baker once a month complaining of lower back pain, at what appointment/month should Dr. Baker add an item about back pain to Catherine's problem list?	1st appointment/month	27.6	27
	2nd	12.2	12
	3rd	25.5	25
	4th	3.1	3
	5th	0.0	0
	6th thru 11th	4.1	4
	> 12th	0.0	0
	It depends	26.5	26
	Never	1.0	1
Question 13: Timing (delete)	Answers	% Res.	N
The practitioner does mention Helen's predisposition for UTI's on her problem list. Three months later, Helen is in for her annual physical and mentions that she has not had any UTIs for the past three months. Helen continues not to experience anymore UTIs. At what point should the item about Helen's predisposition for UTIs be removed from the problem list?	1-3 months	6.1	6
	4-6 months	4.1	4
	6-9 months	5.1	5
	10-11 months	4.1	4
	1-2 years	38.8	38
	3-4 years	6.1	6
	>5 years	2.0	2
	Never	8.2	8
	It Depends	25.5	25

TABLE 5: *Cont.*

What problems should be included (broad)?			
Sensitive Problems			
Question 14: Whether to include sensitive problems?	Answers	% Res.	N
Paul goes to see a psychiatrist and is diagnosed with depression. Should the psychiatrist add 'depression' to Paul's problem list?	Yes	99.0	97
	No	1.0	1
Question 15: To include sensitive problems when other practitioners have access to the same record	Answers	% Res.	N
Janice goes to see a psychiatrist and is diagnosed with anorexia nervosa. She also goes to see a PCP, allergist, gynecologist, and neurologist at the same medical facility. While her psychiatrist's notes are restricted to the mental health department, all of Janice's other doctors are viewing a common problem list through an electronic health record (EHR) system. Under this scenario, should the psychiatrist add 'anorexia nervosa' to Janice's problem list?	Yes	99.0	97
	No	1.0	1
Question 16: To include sensitive problems when a patient disagrees with a diagnosis	Answers	% Res.	N
Dr. Thomas works at a mental health facility that encourages psychiatrists to add mental health problems to the patients' problem lists. During one of Dr. Thomas's patient visits, the patient strongly disagrees with the diagnosis of depression. Should Dr. Thomas still list 'depression' on the patient's problem list?	Yes	75.5	74
	No	24.5	24
Question 17: To include sensitive problems when a patient has access to the problem list through an online patient portal	Answers	% Res.	N
Dr. Brown works at a health center that offers their patients the ability to view their entire electronic health record online through a patient portal. Dr. Brown is with a patient whom he diagnoses with obesity. Dr. Brown knows this patient regularly checks the patient portal to review her medical record. Should Dr. Brown list 'obesity' on this patient's problem list?	Yes	93.9	93
	No	6.1	6
Who can change the problem list across the following roles:			
Question 18: Specialist/PCP			
Toby appears to have an asthma attack during a soccer game. His PCP refers him to a local pulmonologist. The pulmonologist diagnoses him with asthma and has access to the same electronic health record as the PCP. How should the pulmonologist address the problem list?			

TABLE 5: *Cont.*

What problems should be included (broad)?		
Answers	% Res.	N
The pulmonologist should add 'asthma' to Toby's problem list.	77.8	77
The pulmonologist should advise the PCP to add 'asthma' to the problem list in his follow up.	9.1	9
The pulmonologist should perform his regular feedback and assume the PCP will add 'asthma' to Toby's problem list if the PCP feels it is necessary.	12.1	12
Other	1.0	1
Question 19: Nurse practitioner		
John recently moved to Boston and is going for his annual physical exam with a new health center. A nurse practitioner is giving John his physical exam and John tells the nurse practitioner that he was diagnosed with asthma by a pulmonologist. Should the nurse practitioner be able to add problems like John's asthma to the problem list or should only physicians be able to add problems?		
Answers	% Res.	N
The nurse practitioner should be able to add problems to the problem list.	93.8	91
Only physicians should be able to add problems to the problem list.	6.2	6
Other	0.0	0
Question 20: Other RN		
Carlos breaks his leg and goes to the hospital. The nurse is performing her medication rounds when Carlos mentions to her that he forgot to tell the triage nurse that he has hemophilia. What should the nurse do in regards to the problem list?		
Answers	% Res.	N
The nurse should access Carlos's medical record and add 'hemophilia' to the problem list.	22.7	22
The nurse should tell the doctor that Carols has hemophilia and recommend that the doctor add 'hemophilia' to the problem list.	60.8	59
The nurse should tell the doctor that Carols has hemophilia and assume that Carlos's doctor will add 'hemophilia' to Carlos's problem list without specific recommendation.	14.4	14
Other	2.1	2

5.4.4.1 WHAT TO INCLUDE IN A PROBLEM LIST (BROAD CATEGORIES): QUESTIONS #1-4

This category covers whether content such as family history, social history, surgeries, and hospitalizations should be included in the problem list [Table 5 and Additional file 2: Appendix B]. According to the survey responses, a strong majority of practitioners answered for the family history (Question #1, Yes: 76%) and surgeries (Question #3, Yes: 73%) to be included on the problem list. Hospitalizations were contentious at an exact 50/50 split (Question #4). Further, most practitioners (92%) rejected adding an occupation to the problem list (Question #2).

The in-person interviews revealed that practitioners want this information to be easily accessible, but it can be in their own separate list in the medical record or categorized within the problem list. The biggest concern was adding these factors in both locations, creating redundancies across the medical record and extra work for the provider.

A key question that intrigued the interviewed practitioners was Donna's strong family history of breast cancer (Question #1). Some practitioners agreed the family history was important enough to be on the problem list, regardless if it was also included in the family history section of the EHR. For social history, (Question #2) practitioners were concerned that adding an occupation to the problem list would clutter the list as the factor would be unlikely to affect future care or in the specific vignette where the occupation was "male model," perpetuate a negative stigma. One practitioner discussed that she would want to see an occupation listed if it correlated strongly with exposure to a known health hazard.

5.4.4.2 WHAT TO INCLUDE ON A PROBLEM LIST (DETAILED INCLUSIONS): QUESTIONS #5-9

The category covers more finely detailed specifications for inclusion of problems. From the online questionnaire, practitioners showed that they are not limited to the strictest definition of a problem list; namely, chronic diagnoses. Based on the online survey data, practitioners want to include latent chronic diseases (Question #5, Yes: 82%), undiagnosed long term symptoms (Question #7, Yes: 96%), multiple occurrences of transitive illnesses (Question #8, Yes: 93%), and sequelae of problems (Question #9, Yes: 100%). Non-medical conditions (Question #6) or the inclusion of the women's fear of doctors was more controversial (Yes: 36%).

In-person interviews showed that inclusion of these detail specific issues are not as straightforward as the online questionnaire displayed and the action often depends on the patient. For example, in response to question #5 about the woman diagnosed with asthma that was taking no medications and experiencing no symptoms, one practitioner responded that for a young person with few health problems it would not be an issue to add asthma to the problem list. Yet, if the patient was older with multiple health problems and consequently a lengthier problem list, he would be less likely to add the problem. At some point practitioners start editing for length to avoid missing the most crucial facts about the patient the next time they review the problem list.

On question #6 or the vignette about the women's fear of doctors, some interviewed practitioners expressed that their care would remain unaffected by knowing this information and felt its inclusion in the problem list perpetuated a negative stigma. Other practitioners wanted to know such information upfront because it would affect their interpretation of the medical record and they did not want this information buried within the medical note. This example shows how well-meaning practitioners can differ in their action towards the problem list depending on how they wish to practice medicine.

5.4.4.3 TERMINOLOGY: QUESTIONS #10-11

This category covers how problems should be listed in the problem list. It is important to note that the respondents to these questions are allowed to add structured or free text problems to their patient's problem lists in the EHR and therefore have an active choice in their day to day practice of medicine to use personal preferences in listing terminology.

From analysis of the online questionnaire, practitioners indicated that they wished to include more detail in the language used on the problem list than less (Question #10). Only 5% of respondents selected a phrase for diabetes that did not specify type II. Usage of acronyms showed more variability with 16% selecting the equivalent acronym (DM II) and 59% selecting the unabbreviated phrase (Diabetes Mellitus Type II). Finally, respondents unanimously agreed (100%) that sequelae of an initial problem should be listed as a separate problem (Question #11).

Based on the in-person interviews, it appeared that this issue was placed between the ideal world scenario (complete phrases) and reality (practitioners still commonly use acronyms). On sequelae of problems, one practitioner added a notable bit of clarity that once a problem generates its own medical care it should be listed as a separate problem.

5.4.4.4 WHEN TO ADD OR DELETE PROBLEMS: QUESTIONS #12-13

This category covers issues of timing, specifically when practitioners should add problems. The category also includes if practitioners should remove resolved or inactive problems from active status on the problem list and if so, when.

In the online questionnaire, practitioner responses of when to add a transitive problem (Question #12) were clustered around the first three medical visits focused on the health issue (first: 28%, second: 12%, and third: 26%). Opinions on if and when to remove a problem appeared more varied (Questions #13). The highest proportion of responses (39%) was for removing a problem after 1–2 years of non-occurrence. The answer "it depends" received the second highest proportion of responses (26%). Responses were relatively evenly distributed across all other answers which included time periods such as "1-3 months," "4-6 months" and so on up to "Greater than 5 years." Only 8% of respondents selected the option "never."

In general, practitioner responses during the in-person interviews correlated strongly with the online questionnaire (somewhere within the first several visits or months). One practitioner discussed that he was hesitant to add a transitive problem at the first encounter as he found many patients complained of a symptom in the first visit such as back pain and proceeded never to mention it again.

When asked about removing a problem from the list, practitioners explained that it was a complex yet important issue. Answers centered around 1–2 years like the online questionnaire responses, but often came with qualifications. One practitioner mentioned that the lack of specific guidelines and mechanisms for removing cured or latent problems from the list was a key cause of lengthy, cluttered, and unreliable problem lists.

5.4.4.5 SENSITIVE PROBLEMS: QUESTIONS #14-17

This category covers the inclusion of sensitive problems on the problem list such as mental health conditions and HIV status, particularly in scenarios where such information is more easily distributed through information technology.

On inclusion of more sensitive problems (Question #14), practitioners nearly unanimously responded to the online questionnaire that they should be included (Yes: 99%). Further, practitioners did not feel the inclusion of the problem should be affected in situations where the problem list is shared across multiple practitioners (Question #15, Yes: 99%), a patient disagrees with the diagnosis (Question #16, Yes: 76%), or the patient views their record online (Question #17, Yes: 94%).

Some practitioners expressed during in-person interviews that leaving sensitive problems off the problem list would perpetuate negative stigmas and omit crucial information that other practitioners need to know in order to give the best care.

In the vignette where patients were viewing their records online, the interviewed practitioners discussed changing the language to avoid the use of more negative terms. For instance, one practitioner expressed that obesity could be written as a BMI measure. Also, there was a clear concern over maintaining legal privacy of patient health information. One practitioner stated that in an ideal world she would want to have sensitive problems included on the problem list, but she was unaware if the inclusion was in compliance with Health Insurance Portability and Accountability Act (HIPAA) privacy rules. In general, practitioners were aware that special HIPAA standards for treatment of sensitive information existed. Yet, the practitioners were unsure how they would apply to situations where such information was shared through a problem list in the EHR.

5.4.4.6 WHO CAN CHANGE THE PROBLEM LIST?: QUESTIONS #18-20

This category covers the issue of who can add problems to the problem list and also who is ultimately responsible for problem list maintenance such as reviewing, updating, and deleting problems. The issue traditionally is a debate between PCPs and specialists who are both diagnosing new problems and have access to the same problem list.

Among respondents to the online questionnaire, 78% answered that the specialist should put a problem they diagnose on the problem list (Question #18). There appeared to be little issue with nurse practitioners adding problems to the problem list (Question #19, 94%). However, only a minority of respondents endorsed an inpatient nurse adding a problem to the problem list (Question #20), with the majority (61%) preferring that the nurse alert the physician to the problem with a recommendation to add it to the problem list.

Interviewed practitioners discussed that a specialist adding to the list is likely an ideal world scenario not currently met in medical practice at the study sites. Some specialists expressed that adding a problem to the problem list would be an incursion on an area of the medical record owned by the PCP, or that adding to the problem list is extra work that is not strongly relevant to the care they provide. The PCPs interviewed said that they would like to see specialists add to the problem list. For one specialist, he saw this issue as the key to why problem lists are often incomplete and therefore unreliable to use in medical practice.

On the role of nurse practitioners, interviewed practitioners expressed that it was essential for nurse practitioners to make changes to the problem list, particularly if we have the goal to maintain complete and accurate lists. On the inpatient nurse, a medical resident reported that nurses and doctors do not currently add new diagnoses to the problem list during inpatient care, thus is not highly relevant given current behavior. This issue requires more research and a larger sample size to explore the entirety of inpatient care attitudes towards the problem list and the viewpoints on inpatient nurses adding to the list.

5.4.5 ANALYSIS OF THE COMPLETENESS AND PLURALITY MEASURES

Table 6 includes the tabulated results of the completeness and plurality measures. Summary data for the completeness measure ranged from six to twelve with a mean of 9.7 and standard deviation of 1.4. Overall, nearly 50% of respondents received a score of 9 or 10. With a maximum possible completeness score of thirteen, most practitioners voted together on placing more on the problem list than less.

TABLE 6: Tabulation of completeness and plurality measures

	% Resp	N
Completeness Measure		
6	1.1%	1
7	2.1%	2
8	18.1%	17
9	23.4%	22
10	23.4%	22
11	19.2%	18
12	12.8%	12
Plurality Measure		
11	1.1%	1
12	4.3%	4
13	16.0%	15
14	17.0%	16
15	19.2%	18
16	22.3%	21
17	13.8%	13
18	6.4%	6

The plurality measure ranged from eleven to eighteen with a mean of 15 and standard deviation of 1.7. As question four on inclusion of hospitalization history received an exact 50/50 response there was no plurality and data from this question was not included in the analysis of the plurality measure. With a maximum possible score of nineteen, the mean of 15.0 indicates that there is a strong amount of homogeneity in practitioner responses across the questions, but elements of heterogeneity still exist.

Finally, Table 3 includes the results from the univariate and multivariate analysis of the completeness and plurality measures against the demographic data. Only a few significant trends were found among the measures as indicated below.

5.4.6 COMPLETENESS MEASURE

- Non-residents answered with more "yes" responses to adding problems to the problem list than residents (data from the 13 vignette questions with strictly "yes" or "no" responses).
- Practitioners over 70 years of age were more likely to answer "yes" to adding problems to the problem list than practitioners of 21–30 years of age.

Plurality Measure:

- Practitioners with 11–20 years of medical experience were less likely to answer with the plurality than practitioners with less than 1 year of experience.
- Practitioners with 31–40 years of medical experience were less likely to answer with the plurality than practitioners with less than 1 year of experience.
- On the measure of problem list importance, those who selected answer two "less important" were more likely to vote with the plurality than those who selected answer one "not important".

5.5 DISCUSSION

5.5.1 SUPPORT FOR POLICY AND TOOLS

This study confirmed the hypothesis that practitioners differ in their opinions over what should and should not go on the problem list, although many areas of agreement were identified. This difference in opinion is likely a key reason for the variation in the content and structure of current problem lists within and across healthcare organizations. Without consistency across problem lists, patients cannot receive the full benefits problem lists bring to patient care, namely better practitioner compliance with best practices and the complete utilization of clinical decision support and population management tools. The medical community needs to work towards standardization through the development of policies about how the problem list should be used as well as tools built into the EHR that can help practitioners comply with those policies.

Unlike prior research, one valuable component to the study is that the online questionnaire provided quantitative evidence about the size of the disagreement over actions towards the problem list. For instance, all but one vignette question held a statistically significant plurality suggesting that a large portion of practitioners are approaching the problem list in a similar manner. This result implies that it is possible for a majority of practitioners to agree on a common approach to the problem list.

The data also brings attention to possible differences among PCP's and specialists concerning problem list "territory." While specialists believe adding to the problem list would be an incursion on an area of the medical record owned by the PCP, the data indicates that PCP's believe specialists should feel comfortable adding to the problem list.

The findings show that the problem list needs more functionality to help practitioners contribute to the document and also make the list more useful to their work. For instance, one specialist spoke about how when he stages a patient for breast cancer (entering data about the exact size and shape of the tumor) he is frustrated that the EHR cannot follow the logical consequence of automatically generating "breast cancer" on the problem list. Here is an instance where tools could help make the problem list a more integrated part of the practitioner's medical practice and also make it easier to comply with any future policies.

Finally, the summary measures showed a weak correlation between opinions towards the problem list and any common grouping characteristics such as age, medical experience, or opinion on the importance of the problem list. For the completeness measure, the only significant factor with the support of a decent sample size was that residents wanted for less to be included on the problem list than non-residents. Speculation on these differences could be changes to recent training or less experience in the medical field. Although it is important to note that no significant differences were found for the completeness measure amongst the experience and age variables.

The plurality measure contained several more significant measures, specifically within the experience and importance categories. These data indicate that practitioners may approach the problem list differently than their peers based on these characteristics. Yet, with no true dose response and the smaller sample size, this premise is certainly not conclusive and requires further study. In developing a common approach to problem list, these data are not strong enough evidence to suggest value in segmenting opinions by common demographic factors.

5.5.2 RECOMMENDATIONS

Based on the in-person interviews, several issues stood out as greater challenges for practitioners than others. The following recommendations are areas that would benefit the most through the development of policies and EHR tools.

A major cause of unreliable problem lists is the general disagreement in the medical community over "Who is responsible for the problem list?" As discussed in the results section, the debate centers on the roles and responsibilities of the specialist versus the PCP. Due to the disagreement in responsibility, problems diagnosed by specialists do not have a consistent pathway onto the problem list. This process gap could be a primary cause of incomplete problem lists. An official ownership policy would bring clarity to the PCP and specialists relationship towards the problem list. For example, when asked what would need to change for the specialist to start having a more active role in the problem list, an oncologist responded:

> *If the [administration] came out and said everybody owns the problem list...if you are taking care of a problem then you need to make sure that problem is on the problem list, and then I think I would go ahead and do it.*

Another potential cause of clutter and absent problems is the lack of guidelines for when to review the problem list and remove a cured or latent problem. A clarified policy could help specify when and who should be conducting this process and also the role the patient might play in reviewing their own problem list for accuracy. Removing inactive problem would help keep problem lists up-to-date, short, and relevant. Of note, such a policy would likely need to be closely intertwined with an ownership policy.

An additional cause of absent problems (or potentially worse offences) is the potentially murky understanding over how privacy and security regulations apply to the electronic problem list. In response to question #15 about placing sensitive questions on a problem list that can be viewed by many of the patient's practitioners, one specialist commented:

I don't know what the rules are under this, but I think the diagnosis is relevant to everybody else. So the question is I don't know what the legality of mental health records is and how visible they are is, but that is where I would defer to someone and say I don't know. If there's a way where it's not illegal to disclose that, then absolutely.

Concerns towards maintaining compliance with HIPAA and other privacy policies may be keeping practitioners from adding problems. Currently, HIPAA does not restrict what can be placed in the medical health record and instead regulates use and disclosure [19]. Discussions and clarification on how privacy can be maintained in the new digital age where problem lists are more readily accessed and available may help practitioners be more confident in their actions towards the problem list. The need to address this issue will likely become even more important as adoption of health information exchanges and online patient portals increases as well as the sensitivity of information evolves such as questions over listing genetic predispositions on the problem lists based on genetic testing.

Finally, this research gave insight into how restrictive a problem list policy should be towards allowing the addition of a broad range of problem types. As shown by the completeness measure, practitioners were more likely to want to include an item on the problem list than not. Throughout the study, practitioners did not limit themselves to the strictest definition of the problem list, namely only including chronic diagnoses. The results also indicated that any common approach to the problem list will need to leave room for the practitioners' personal judgment. For instance, practitioner reactions during in-person interviews differed greatly to the question about the woman who was highly afraid of doctors. Some practitioners found the information irrelevant to how they would treat her and others wanted it to be the first fact they knew because it could potentially change their analysis of her health history. Variation in how practitioners use the problem list does have policy implication. Based on these findings, practitioners are not looking for a highly restrictive policy that restricts personal judgment on what should be included on the problem list.

Of course, the idea of an unrestrictive policy is not to say that problem lists should include every possible problem without regards to length. An "all inclusive" policy will not create problem lists that are easily scanned and make known the most essential health facts about patients. Further, when and what to include often depends on the patient. As one practitioner responded to the vignette about if a case of asymptomatic asthma should be listed on the problem list:

> *Yeah, that is a grey area, actually. From someone who is... you know... completely well. This is her only issue then I can see why this might make it on to the problem list. Young person. If it's... you know... you're going to be adding on to a list of 10 or 15 problems on a chronically ill person where this is not likely to be a big issue for her, then I could see where you wouldn't put it on the list. The length of a list actually becomes an issue, I think, just like fatigue...attention fatigue.*

Of course, the idea that there needs to be some moderation in the content included in the problem list was known prior to the research, this study showed that practitioners are not looking to be restricted to certain types of information such as only diagnosed diseases. They want the option to include anything, which leaves the greater challenge of how policies and tools can help prioritize information to create the most effective problem lists.

5.5.3 STUDY STRENGTHS AND LIMITATIONS

A key strength of the study was the usage of vignettes to help reveal practitioners' attitudes towards the problem list. While not measured, practitioners appeared to easily comprehend, debate, and find answers to their preferred action and the resulting data did not appear hindered by the vignettes. One downside of the vignettes is that they were narrowly defined to specific clinical situations. Other limitations with the survey instrument included inconsistency of the survey instructions with the vignettes. Specifically, the initial instructions requested that respondents answer in the perspective of a PCP while some of the questions requested the specialist perspective.

The second core strength was the use of the two-pronged implementation method of the survey instrument as it brought out both breadth and depth to analyzing practitioners' opinions towards the problem list. The main weakness was the sample. It was limited to practitioners at two affiliated, well-resourced, academic medical centers in Boston where the EHRs allow great freedom in what can be entered into the problem list (both coded and free text problems). Further weaknesses in the sample were that the respondents came from sources within the healthcare centers that were opportunistic rather than representative. This convenience sample resulted in disproportionate respondent demographics. For instance, the online questionnaire sample consisted mostly of PCPs due to the departments asked to participate, and the in-person interviews consisted mostly of specialists. The results would likely be affected by having a more representative sample of practitioners from across the United States.

In regards to the online questionnaire, it became known after the questionnaire was sent that a limited number of non-clinicians were included in the department mailings lists such as administrative assistants and they likely received emails containing links to the questionnaire. As the survey was designed to screen out non-clinicians based on the response to the first question, the responses were not impacted as long as the non-clinicians answered honestly, but the true response rate is likely slightly lower than reported.

The unavailability of demographic data for non-respondents of the online questionnaire further limited the study sample as it is unknown if the respondents held similar opinions to the non-respondents. Further, lack of significant respondents in the specialist category limited the ability to identify differential response rates based on clinician factors. Increasing the sample size would also further strengthen the findings of this study, and create a more representative collection of data. A larger sample size would also allow for further analysis of differing opinions by various demographic factors, such as clinician specialty, and inpatient versus outpatient practice settings, on clinician attitudes towards the problem list. The results of this study are also specific to the capabilities and design of Partner's Longitudinal Medical Record system used at the study sites. Yet, a core strength of surveying this particular provider population is that the Partner's Longitudinal Medical Record system allows for both structured and free text input. This unique environment means that providers have an active choice in what they list in their problem list on a daily basis and therefore, could readily give feedback on their preferences to this study. Providers who are only allowed structured problems may not have a strong idea of what they would prefer to include or not include on the problem list due to working in a more regulated EHR system.

5.6 CONCLUSIONS

An accurate and reliable problem list could provide great benefits to patient care through ensuring practitioners are aware of the most important health factors about a patient and creating a more refined database from which to identify disease-specific populations. This study showed that practitioners do differ in their judgment towards the problem list overall, but in most situations there is a common approach among a majority. Further, practitioners showed that they do not want to be highly restricted on what information can go on the problem list and that there are areas where they are not meeting their ideal actions towards the problem list. The creation of a policy to help guide a common approach as well as tools to encourage upkeep would be helpful in creating accurate problem lists over time. With a number of more detailed insights into practitioner opinions towards the problem list, this study provided a stronger foundation from which the healthcare community can move forward to improve the problem list to enable better patient care.

REFERENCES

1. Hartung DM, Hunt J, Siemienczuk J, Miller H, Touchette DR: Clinical implications of an accurate problem list on heart failure treatment. J Gen Intern Med 2005, 20(2):143-147.
2. Simborg DW, Starfield BH, Horn SD, Yourtee SA: Information factors affecting problem follow-up in ambulatory care. Med Care 1976, 14(10):848-856.
3. Rabøl LI, Anhøj J, Pedersen A, Pedersen BL, Hellebek AH: Clinical decision support: is the number of medication errors reduced? Ugeskr Laeger 2006, 168(48):4179-4184.
4. Wright A, Goldberg H, Hongsermeier T, Middleton B: A description and functional taxonomy of rule-based decision support content at a large integrated delivery network. J Am Med Inform Assoc 2007, 14(4):489-496.
5. Rothschild AS, Lehmann HP, Hripcsak G: Inter-rater agreement in physician-coded problem lists. AMIA 2005 Symposium Proceedings 2005, 644-648. http://www.ncbi.nlm.nih.gov/pmc/articles/PMC1560827/ .
6. Wright A, Maloney FL, Feblowitz JC: Clinician attitudes toward and use of electronic problem lists: a thematic analysis. BMC Med Inform Decis Mak 2011, 11:36.
7. Szeto HC, Coleman RK, Gholami P, Hoffman BB, Goldstein MK: Accuracy of computerized outpatient diagnoses in a veterans affairs general medicine clinic. Am J Manage Care 2002, 8(1):37-43.
8. AHIMA Best Practices for Problem Lists in an EHR Work Group: Best practices for problem lists in an EHR. J AHIMA 2008, 79(1):73-77.
9. Weed LL: Medical records that guide and teach. N Engl J Med 1968, 278(12):652-657.
10. Holmes C: The problem list beyond meaningful use: part I: the problems with problem lists. J AHIMA 2011, 82(2):30-33.
11. Holmes C: The problem list beyond meaningful use: part 2: fixing the problem list. J AHIMA 2011, 82(3):32-35.
12. Zhou X, Zheng K, Ackerman MS, Hanauer D: Cooperative documentation: patient problem list as a nexus of electronic health records. Proceedings of ACM on computer Supported Cooperative Work 2012, 911-920. http://dl.acm.org/citation.cfm?id=2145340&dl=ACM&coll=DL&CFID=136746389&CFTOKEN=12929118 .
13. Electronic health records and meaningful use. http://healthit.hhs.gov/portal/server.pt?open=512&objID=2996&mode=2 .
14. Health information technology: Initial set of standards, implementation specifications, and certification criteria for electronic health record technology; final rule. http://edocket.access.gpo.gov/2010/pdf/2010-17210.pdf .
15. HL7 EHR system functional model: A major development towards consensus on electronic health record system functionality. http://www.hl7.org/documentcenter/public_temp_02E6E5C2-1C23-BA17-0C8DBE5E1D13ABBD/wg/ehr/EHR-SWhitePaper.pdf .
16. The Joint Commission Resources: Standard RC.02.01.07. Joint Commission E-dition 2011., 3.0

17. Study of an intervention to improve problem list accuracy and use (MAPLE). http://clinicaltrials.gov/ct2/show/NCT01105923 .
18. Harris PA, Taylor R, Thielke R, Payne J, Gonzalez N, Conde JG: Research electronic data capture (REDCap) - A metadata-driven methodology and workflow process for providing translational research informatics support. J Biomed Inform 2009, 42(2):377-381.
19. Understanding health information privacy. http://www.hhs.gov/ocr/privacy/hipaa/understanding/index.html

There are several supplemental files that are not available in this version of the article. To view this additional information, please use the citation on the first page of this chapter.

CHAPTER 6

USE OF AN ELECTRONIC PROBLEM LIST BY PRIMARY CARE PROVIDERS AND SPECIALISTS

ADAM WRIGHT, JOSHUA FEBLOWITZ, FRANCINE L. MALONEY, STANISLAV HENKIN, AND DAVID W. BATES

6.1 INTRODUCTION

The patient problem list comprises an essential part of the modern electronic medical record. Improved problem list documentation has been associated with a higher quality of care and greater adherence to evidence-based guidelines. [1] Effective clinical decision support (CDS) interventions also frequently depend on the problem list, since many CDS rules require accurate, coded problem entries. [2] An electronic problem list can also be a valuable tool for quality and research initiatives as it facilitates the rapid creation of patient registries. [3]

As part of Stage 1 and 2 "meaningful use" guidelines, providers are required to actively "maintain an up-to-date problem list of current and active diagnoses," with 80% of patients having at least one problem recorded

---

With kind permission from Springer Science+Business Media: Journal of General Internal Medicine, *Use of an Electronic Problem List by Primary Care Providers and Specialists, 27(8), 2012, pp. 968-73, Wright A, Feblowitz J, Maloney FL, Henkin S, and Bates DW, Copyright Society of General Internal Medicine 2012.*

or an indication of no known problems. [4,5] However, research has shown that problem lists are frequently inaccurate and out-of-date. [6–10] In a previous study, we demonstrated that common problems were frequently omitted from the problem list at one large hospital network—completeness ranged from 4.7% for renal disease to a maximum of 78.5% for breast cancer. [11] In previous qualitative research, we found that provider attitudes towards appropriate use and content varies widely and problem lists are frequently perceived as inaccurate, incomplete and out-of-date. [9,10]

In order to shape effective problem list policy and meet "meaningful use goals," it will be necessary to gain an improved understanding of current problem list usage patterns. Based on prior research [9,10] we hypothesized that primary care providers (PCPs) would be the primary problem list users while specialists would use the tool much less frequently. For the purposes of this paper, "primary care" is defined to include providers specializing in family medicine, internal medicine (excluding subspecialties), geriatrics and pediatrics. Our goal was to assess the differences in problem list use across specialties and subspecialties and to quantify these differences for the first time.

6.2 METHODS

6.2.1 SETTING

The study was reviewed and approved by the Partners HealthCare Human Subjects Committee. This study was carried out at Brigham & Women's Hospital (BWH) in Boston, MA. All BWH clinicians use the Longitudinal Medical Record (LMR), a self-developed, ONC-ATB-certified outpatient EHR. Care delivered in the outpatient setting (excluding the emergency department) is documented in the LMR—inpatient care is documented in another system. Surgeons use the LMR to document outpatient visits, although surgical records are documented in a different system. Many PCPs affiliated with BWH have used the LMR for a number of years, and the remaining PCPs and specialists have used the LMR since a major initiative to get all providers online in 2007. The LMR includes an electronic problem list tool that allows providers to document patient problems using both coded and uncoded entries. Providers are strongly encouraged to use coded entries they drive clinical decision support features. Problems are coded using a proprietary terminology that is mapped to SNOMED CT. When an uncoded entry is added, the clinician is alerted and is asked to confirm that he or she wishes to make an uncoded entry. The LMR problem list is distinct from the billing system—physicians can bill for any diagnosis regardless of whether it is on the problem list, and billing diagnoses entered do not feed the problem list. The problem list appears on the main summary screen of the LMR (shown in Figure 1). Problem list use is technically required by hospital and Joint Commission policy, [12] but this requirement is not consistently or centrally enforced. Providers receive only basic technical training in how to add problems using the LMR, but no training is provided on what problems

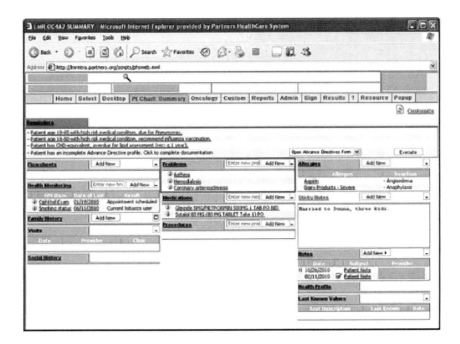

FIGURE 1: The LMR summary screen with the problem list shown in the center.

to add or who should add them. BWH does not have a formal policy on who is responsible for maintaining the problem list or which conditions belong on it. In a previous qualitative study on the use of problem list by clinicians, none reported receiving specific guidance on problem list utilization. [10] When a provider modifies the problem list, the LMR records the identity of the provider and the clinic they are logged into at the time of the change.

6.2.2 SAMPLE

In order to study provider use of the problem list by specialty, we randomly selected 100,000 patient records from the LMR. Participants were drawn from the group of all patients with at least one visit recorded in the LMR from 2007 to 2008 and two or more outpatient notes in their record (n=839,300). Once this sample was defined, we collected all available problem and note data for each of the 100,000 patients dating from 1/1/2002 to 4/30/2010. We limited the note and problem data collected at practices affiliated with the BWH network, which includes hospital-affiliated primary care and specialty clinics, community clinics and two federally-qualified health centers.

The total problem count included all problems recorded on each patient's current problem list and the identity of the provider who added it and the clinic that they were signed into. The total note count for each patient included all available note headers—the descriptive header stored with each note (e.g. Cardiology Note). In addition to progress notes, the note count included letters to patients, "no show" notes and other entries that are recorded in the notes module of the LMR because the LMR does not make a distinction between these note types. Like problem entries, all notes were tagged with the provider and the clinic they were signed into. We selected total note volume as a proxy for visit volume in each specialty. Note volume is an imperfect proxy because some clinics may have different prevalence of non-progress-note storage; however, schedule data were not available for all specialties so it was the best proxy available.

6.2.3 IDENTIFYING SPECIALTY

LMR problem and note records do not contain direct information on the specialty of the recording provider—only the provider's identity and clinic. We initially attempted to link providers directly to specialties using the Partners enterprise master provider file and the National Provider Identifier database. However, this linking proved inexact because some providers were listed under general categories (e.g. "medicine" for a cardiologist) and some providers practice more than one type of medicine. All providers, however, have schedules and see patients in one or more clinics, which are almost always specific to a single specialty in our network and we used the clinic the provider was logged into to classify the data by specialty. Since the provider must log into the proper clinic to view their schedule and properly classify notes, the clinic appears to be a more robust indicator of specialty than the provider themselves.

There was no existing mapping from clinics to specialties, so we mapped the clinics manually, using the Healthcare Provider Taxonomy Code Set [13] to classify each specialty. The Healthcare Provider Taxonomy Code Set defines the type, classification and specialization of health care providers, and is a mandated standard for NPI registration and HIPAA transactions.

Because of issues with legacy data in the LMR, there are many clinic designations which are no longer in current use, or which are used very infrequently. To make the mapping task manageable, we only mapped clinics that had generated at least 50 notes or had added at least five problems to the problem list over the study period.

After mapping all clinics that met our inclusion criteria, we identified 72 separate categories of provider specialty. We combined highly related subspecialties where appropriate (e.g." Anesthesiology" and "Anesthesiology: Pain Medicine" were combined into "Anesthesiology"). In addition, we excluded a small group of notes (n=4,932) that were simply scanned consent forms. A portion of all clinics could not be classified according to the Code Set including: 1) clinics providing a mix of services across specialties, 2) entries without a specific clinic recorded and 3) clinics that did not reasonably map to an existing Code Set term. Additionally, a number of clinics were not classified because they did not meet the threshold inclusion criteria. These groups were combined into the category "Other" which encompassed 0.4% of problems and 6.2% of notes. We were left with 43 distinct categories with total notes counts and problem counts.

6.2.3 ADDITIONAL ANALYSES

In addition to mapping clinics to their associated specialties, we assessed the proportion of patients in our sample that had an assigned PCP at BWH. A patient's PCP can be recorded directly in the LMR but this field is not reliably populated. Instead, to determine which patients had BWH-affiliated assigned PCPs, we examined whether they had any notes recorded by a BWH PCP during the entire study period. This proxy method relied on the following assumptions: 1) patient with notes recorded by a BWH PCP had a very high likelihood of having an assigned PCP (BWH PCPs do not schedule urgent care visits with patients without an assigned PCP) and 2) patient without any notes recorded by a BWH PCP was very unlikely to have an assigned PCP (patients without any primary care notes recorded during the study period most likely do not receive regular care within the system). Consequently, we believe this to be a reasonable method of assessing the proportion of patients with a BWH PCP. Once all patients were classified using this method, we calculated the average total number of problems on patient problem lists for both BWH PCP and non-BWH PCP patients.

For statistical analyses, Student's t-test was used for continuous variables and chi-square test for categorical variables with R Statistical Computing version 2.13.1 (Austria). Statistical significance was set at two-tailed $p < 0.05$.

6.3 RESULTS

A total of 2,264,051 notes and 158,105 problems were recorded in the BWH LMR during the defined study period (approximately 8.3 years). The average number of problems added per note was 0.07. The complete results are shown in Table 1 with the note and problem count for each identified specialty and the rate of problems added per note.

TABLE 1: Note and Problem Counts by Specialty (in Descending Order by Number of Problems Added)

Specialty	Notes	Problems	Problems/Note
Internal Medicine	836,178	121,939	0.146
Obstetrics & Gynecology	227,603	12,879	0.057
Pediatrics	57,089	4,374	0.077
Rheumatology	94,534	3,471	0.037
Cardiology	55,104	2,840	0.052
Geriatric Medicine	2,078	2,015	0.970
Family Medicine	19,514	1,820	0.093
Infectious Disease	19,603	1,682	0.086
Thoracic Surgery	62,848	1,429	0.023
Pulmonary Disease	7,580	933	0.123
Emergency Medicine	83,329	641	0.008
Transplant Surgery	3,247	549	0.169
Endocrinology, Diabetes & Metabolism	41,700	486	0.012
Surgery	53,905	485	0.009
Anesthesiology	53,146	483	0.009
Orthopaedic Surgery	100,049	482	0.005
Hematology & Oncology	3,409	341	0.100
Psychiatry & Neurology	114,352	317	0.003
Nephrology	13,904	75	0.005
Oral & Maxillofacial Surgery	4,657	56	0.012
Radiology	11,924	51	0.004
Allergy & Immunology	20,478	36	0.002
Dermatology	72,933	29	0.000
Gastroenterology	28,217	26	0.001
Hospitalist	2,182	23	0.011
Behavioral Health & Social Service Providers	9,617	10	0.001
Vascular Surgery	3,941	7	0.002
Neurological Surgery	9,923	6	0.001
Other Service Providers	6,208	5	0.001
Otolaryngology	23,812	5	0.000
Plastic Surgery	20,498	5	0.000
Dietary & Nutritional Service Providers	30,924	3	0.000
Surgical Critical Care	991	3	0.003

TABLE 1: *Cont.*

Specialty	Notes	Problems	Problems/Note
Trauma Surgery	417	3	0.007
Urology	21,978	3	0.000
Nursing Service Providers	452	2	0.004
Clinical Pharmacology	1,389	1	0.001
Clinical Genetics	296	1	0.003
Surgical Oncology	2,415	1	0.000
Blood Banking & Transfusion Medicine	548	0	0.000
Podiatrist	196	0	0.000
Speech-Language Pathologist	305	0	0.000
Other	140,578	588	0.004
Grand Total	2,264,051	158,105	0.070

Overall, 49.1% of patients had an assigned PCP affiliated with BWH. The average problem list length at the end of the study period was 4.7 (standard deviation [SD] 5.2) problems for patients with an assigned BWH PCP and 1.5 (SD 3.6) problems for patients without an assigned BWH PCP ($p<0.001$).

PCPs added 82.3% of all problems to problem lists, despite only writing 40.4% of all notes (RR=6.86, 95% Confidence Interval 6.77-6.95, $p<0.001$ compared to specialists). Internal medicine, pediatrics, geriatric medicine and family medicine accounted for 77.1%, 2.8%, 1.3%, 1.2% of total problems added, respectively. With the exception of obstetrics and gynecology, rheumatology, cardiology and infectious disease, all other specialties accounted for less than 1% of problems added. Internal medicine, pediatrics, geriatrics and family medicine also had some of the highest rates of problems added per note: 0.146 problems/note (4th of 43 categories), 0.077 problems/note (9th of 43), 0.970 problems/note (1st of 43) and 0.093 problems/note (7th of 43) respectively. Other specialties with high rates of problems added per note included transplant surgery, pulmonary disease, hematology/oncology, infectious disease, obstetrics and gynecology and cardiology.

As mentioned previously, partners undertook an initiative in 2007 to bring all providers live on the LMR. In order to ensure that our results were not confounded by this initiative we repeated the same analysis using a subsample of data from 1/1/2008 to 4/30/2010. This analysis revealed a similar pattern: PCPs were responsible for 73.4% of problems added but wrote only 35.6% of notes. Specialists' share of problem list use increased slightly, but their volume of care also increased—the ratio of problem and note shares between the two groups remained the same, with PCPs performing slightly more than double the share of problem list documentation after controlling for note volume.

6.4 DISCUSSION

These results show that, at practices affiliated with this hospital in an integrated delivery system in which all providers use the LMR, PCPs document more than four-fifths of all problems, even though they account for less than half of all care provided as measured by note volume. Providers in internal medicine alone documented the vast majority of patient problems on the problem list (~77%). In addition, patients with an assigned PCP had a substantially higher average number of problems at the end of the study period. In contrast, specialists documented very few problems relative to the number of notes they generate. For example, specialists in orthopedic surgery, psychiatry and neurology documented less than 500 total problems during the study period despite generating over 100,000 notes. However, there were some notable exceptions to this pattern, namely obstetrics and gynecology and transplant surgery which generated a relatively large number of problem list entries given their volume.

These results quantify, for the first time, a difference in problem list use between PCPs and specialists and validate previous qualitative findings on problem list documentation patterns. [9,10] It is important to note that PCPs have, in general, used EHR longer than specialists in this network, and that the problem list is integrated so that everyone can see the problems entered by others. This is especially important in light of the substantial financial incentives, which have been invested to increase provider use of EHRs and improve care.

The meaningful use (MU) criteria are intended to encourage both PCPs and specialists to use EHR in ways that will result in tangible improvements in quality, safety, and efficiency, and an accurate problem list is a cornerstone of the EHR. Stage 1 and 2 MU rules stipulate that 80% of all patients must have an up-to-date problem list. Our findings suggest that it may be especially important to track how specialists use problem lists. Dealing with this issue should become easier as problem lists are populated, and data exchange begins to occur, which should decrease the need for multiple individuals to enter problem lists for the same patient across different sites. Furthermore, institutional and national policy on problem list use may need to differ based on provider specialty; a specialist, who is seeing a patient once or twice, should not be required to enter a full problem list, but they should record new problems that they diagnose.

Nonetheless, the difference in problem list use across specialties is concerning given that many specialists are actively involved in diagnosing patient problems, and about half the patients seen by specialists did not have a PCP in the Partners system. While PCPs are probably more likely to diagnose and document common problems, it is unlikely that the observed discrepancy can be explained solely by variations in the problems that each type of specialist deals with. The more likely explanation is that many problems are also going undocumented when diagnosis is carried out by a specialist.

This finding is consistent with our prior qualitative study on problem list utilization by PCPs and specialists. [10] However, there were some notable exceptions to the pattern—obstetrics and gynecology, transplant medicine and oncology all had relatively high use of the problem list compared to other specialties. Some of this difference may be attributable to the fact that providers in these specialties are more likely to have a longitudinal relationship with patients and more incentive or confidence to document problems.

The observed variation between PCP and specialist use of the problem list is likely due to differences in culture and governance with regards to the patient problem list. [9,10] PCPs, who may possess greater awareness of a patient's clinical state over time, may feel more responsibility and ownership of the problem list. In contrast, specialists, who may interact with individual patients in a more condition-focused and time-limited fashion, may believe that the responsibly for maintaining the problem list rests on the shoulders of a patient's PCP. However, the difference may not be entirely cultural. For example, some patients may already have a diagnoses made and entered by the PCP before seeing a specialist for that specific condition, negating the need for the specialist to enter a coded problem. Nevertheless, certain specialties do appear to have a high rate of problem list use, despite the dominant pattern of lower overall specialist problem list usage. Additional research, both quantitative and qualitative, will be needed in order to explore proper problem list policy across specialties and characterize the quality and accuracy of problem documentation.

As MU goals generate increased use of EHRs and problem documentation, we will need to devise policies for problem list use that will improve the value of this shared good for all providers. Even though most clinicians integrate the problem list in their workflow, PCPs tend to shoulder the responsibility for maintaining its accuracy but also believe that specialists should share the responsibility for maintaining the list to make it as accurate as possible. Additionally, problem list usage differs by clinic, where formal or non-formal leadership set expectations for the use and maintenance of the problem list. [10] Although some guidelines for use exist, [14] more specific and consistently applied directives need to be established in order to maximize the utility of this important tool. Specifically, by developing consensus on the optimal use of the problem list by clinicians themselves, specific guidelines could be put into places that govern its use. If the rules were established and the problem list were to be more accurate, more providers may feel responsible for maintaining an accurate and up to date problem list, especially since the MU regulations do not specify what is or is not a problem and who is responsible for maintaining the problem list. Finally, EHR vendors could contribute to improved problem list use via expansion of product functionality. For example, if some orders within a CPOE system require documentation of a specific problem in order to carry out a related order, this may improve documentation of problems dramatically; such requirements could exclude orders for reasons related to prevention or acute, self-limited problems that do not belong on the problem list.

6.4.1 LIMITATIONS

This study has a number of limitations. First, it was more challenging than anticipated to establish the specialty of each provider. We could not identify an adequate method for automatically mapping providers to associated specialties. While we believe that using clinics is an effective method of ascertaining specialty, and that it has the significant advantage of accommodating providers with multiple specialties, the mapping is nevertheless imperfect and resulted in a small number of lost data. In addition, whether a given patient has assigned PCP in the system was also determine via a proxy method. Although we believe our underlying assumptions to be reasonable, a small number of patients may have been misclassified.

Second, this study was conducted at a single academic medical center and thus our results my not generalize to other sites using different EHR. Additionally, clinicians at our site have reported using alternatives to the problem list including past medical history section of the progress notes, discharge summaries, medication lists, relying on their own memory, and asking the patient directly about medical problems. [10] We did not review any progress notes for the presence of the problem list and cannot comment on whether certain subset of clinicians uses this method. Next, to identify the specialty, we looked at clinic level rather than specialty of a specific provider and do not know whether the note was generated by an attending physician or a junior clinician. However, since BWH is a large teaching hospital, we expect that there are trainees in every clinical setting and do not believe that residents in any one clinic significantly influenced the results.

Another limitation is our use of notes as a proxy for volume, whichis twofold: first, clinical volume is an imperfect proxy for the volume of new diagnoses made by providers—it is possible that many visits do not yield any new diagnoses, and that the rate of new diagnoses per visit might differ by specialty, potentially introducing bias. We considered using billing diagnoses to identify potential new clinical diagnoses; however, we previously found that billing codes have a low positive predictive value for clinical problems. [11] Second, notes are an imperfect proxy for visit volume as not all visits result in a note and notes are sometimes written for other purposes. It is possible that the relationship between note volume and visit volume might differ systematically between specialties but we believe that the size of such differences would be insufficient to explain the magnitude of differences seen in problems per note across specialties.

Finally, the specific reasons for the observed differences in problem list use were beyond the scope of this investigation. Additional research is needed in order to determine the factors that drive the differences in problem list use across specialties. Further research might also look into additional behaviors, such as updating or inactivating problems.

6.5 CONCLUSION

Our findings suggest that in this setting PCPs are responsible for the majority of problem documentation and specialists record a disproportionately small number of problems on the problem list. More research is needed to understand what documentation rates are appropriate, especially for specialists. Additionally, specific and consistently applied policies are needed to encourage appropriate use of the problem list across specialties.

REFERENCES

1. Hartung DM, Hunt J, Siemienczuk J, Miller H, Touchette DR. Clinical implications of an accurate problem list on heart failure treatment. J Gen Intern Med. 2005;20:143–7.
2. Wright A, Goldberg H, Hongsermeier T, Middleton B. A description and functional taxonomy of rule-based decision support content at a large integrated delivery network. J Am Med Inform Assoc. 2007;14:489–96.
3. Wright A, McGlinchey EA, Poon EG, Jenter CA, Bates DW, Simon SR. Ability to generate patient registries among practices with and without electronic health records. J Med Internet Res. 2009;11:e31.
4. Poon EG, Wright A, Simon SR, et al. Relationship between use of electronic health record features and health care quality: results of a statewide survey. Med Care. 2010;48:203–9.
5. Meaningful Use Workgroup Presentation to HIT Policy Committee. 2011. Available at: http://healthit.hhs.gov/portal/server.pt/gateway/PTARGS_0_12811_954838_0_0_18/hitpc-mu-recommendations-06-08-11.ppt. Accessed June 8, 2011.
6. Kaplan DM. Clear writing, clear thinking and the disappearing art of the problem list. J Hosp Med. 2007;2:199–202.
7. Szeto HC, Coleman RK, Gholami P, Hoffman BB, Goldstein MK. Accuracy of computerized outpatient diagnoses in a Veterans Affairs general medicine clinic. Am J Manage Care. 2002;8:37–43.

8. Tang PC, LaRosa MP, Gorden SM. Use of computer-based records, completeness of documentation, and appropriateness of documented clinical decisions. J Am Med Inform Assoc. 1999;6:245–51.
9. Feblowitz J, Wright A. The Patient Problem List: An Ethnographic Study of Primary Care Provider Use and Attitudes. AMIA 2011 Annual Symposium. Washington, D.C.; 2011 (under review).
10. Wright A, Maloney F, Feblowitz J. Clinician attitudes toward and use of electronic problem lists: a thematic analysis. BMC Med Inform Decis Mak. 2011;11:36–45.
11. Wright A, Pang J, Feblowitz J, et al. A method and knowledge base for automated inference of patient problems from structured data in an electronic medical record. J Am Med Inform Assoc. 2011;18:859–67.
12. Information Management Processes (Standard IM 6.40): 2008 Comprehensive Accreditation Manual for Hospitals: The Official Handbook. Oakbrook Terrace, Illinois: Joint Commission Resources: 2008.
13. McMullen CK, Ash JS, Sittig DF, et al. Rapid assessment of clinical information systems in the healthcare setting. An efficient method for time-pressed evaluation. Methods Inf Med. 2010;50:299–307.
14. Bonetti R, Castelli J, Childress JL, et al. Best practices for problem lists in an EHR. J AHIMA / Am Health Inf Manag Assoc. 2008;79:73–7.

CHAPTER 7

DISTRIBUTION OF PROBLEMS, MEDICATIONS, AND LAB RESULTS IN ELECTRONIC HEALTH RECORDS: THE PARETO PRINCIPLE AT WORK

ADAM WRIGHT AND DAVID W. BATES

7.1 INTRODUCTION

Many naturally occurring and man-made phenomena demonstrate a non-uniform exponential distribution whereby a small set of common elements in a class represent the bulk of all uses of the class [1]. This phenomenon has variously been referred to as the 80/20 rule [2], the Pareto principle (for continuous data) [3], Zipf's law (for discrete data) [4] and the power-law phenomenon [5]. For example, linguistic researchers studying a large corpus of English language text demonstrated that the word "the" constitutes 7% of all word uses in the corpus, while "to" and "of" each represent another 3%. Indeed, only 135 out of the 50,000 unique observed words are needed to account for half of all word uses, while nearly half of the words in the corpus are used only a single time [6]. This pattern, com-

---

Wright A and Bates DW. Distribution of Problems, Medications and Lab Results in Electronic Health Records: The Pareto Principle at Work. Applied Clinical Informatics 1,1 (2010); doi: 10.4338/ACI-2009-12-RA-0023. Reprinted with permission from the publisher.

monly called Zipf's law, has been observed in a variety of languages including American English, Chinese and the Latin of Plautus [7]. The same phenomenon has been observed in such disparate areas as the population of human settlements [8], distribution of wealth [9], movie rental patterns from Netflix and purchases from Amazon.com [1].

Electronic health records are increasingly widely used in the U.S. [10], although uptake has been limited by a number of issues including ease of use [11]. Improving usability depends on a number of factors, but understanding the distributions of key data elements is likely one of them. Furthermore, clinical data exchange will likely have many clinical benefits, but has been difficult to achieve [12]; enabling this will also require understanding these distributions.

7.1.1 OBJECTIVES

We hypothesized that many forms of clinical data are likely to exhibit these properties as well. Medications, problems and lab results represent central data elements in clinical practice and record keeping and they are also some of the most frequently documented and used elements in electronic health record systems. We tested this hypothesis by analyzing data from a widely deployed electronic health record system and characterizing the distributions of medications, problems and lab results.

7.2 METHODS

We obtained electronic health record data for 100,000 patients seen at least twice in the outpatient setting at the Brigham and Women's Hospital, and with at least one visit between January 1, 2006 and December 31, 2007. The study was approved by the Partners HealthCare Human Subjects Committee. The electronic health record is used for both primary and specialty care, and the underlying sample was drawn from a total population of 839,300 patients (primarily adults, but some neonates). The data were used as recorded in the computer system—no manual validation or aggregation (e.g. into panels or classes) was undertaken.

The data extracted included medications, problems and lab results. We analyzed the data using Microsoft SQL Server and Excel (Microsoft Corporation, Redmond, WA) and used R (the R Foundation, Vienna, Austria) and the zipfR package [13] to characterize their distribution, estimate the distribution's parameters and assess the goodness of fit. For goodness of fit, we used the chi square goodness of fit test with the conservative modifications proposed by Baayen to account for non-constant variance of the distribution elements [14].

7.3 RESULTS

Within this population of 100,000 patients in the electronic health record system, there were a total of 272,749 coded problems, 442,658 medications and 11,736,718 lab results for the 100,000 patients in the electronic health record system during this period.

(Table 1) shows the top ten problems, medications and lab results along with their proportion. Each proportion represents the proportion of total items in that category—i.e. 2.27% of all prescriptions are for ibuprofen. Since each patient may be on multiple medications (an average of 4.42 medications per patient in our dataset), this is distinct from the proportion of patients on ibuprofen (which is 10.1%). It is worth noting that this data is exactly as recorded in the EHR and may reflect imprecisions in coding by users—for example, most of the patients with "diabetes mellitus" on their problem list appear to have diabetes mellitus type 2; however, the recording clinician did not specify the type. Likewise, lab results appear to be a special case: nine of the top ten lab results are components of the complete blood count (results are filed in the EHR independently, even when ordered as part of a panel, which is why these components are presented individually rather than as a group).

(Figure 1) shows the cumulative distribution of the three data types. These distributions show the classic Zipfian form. The observed distributions are even more skewed than the classic 80/20 rule (where 20% of items account for 80% of observations). The 12.5% most frequently used problems account for 80% of all problems, while the top 11.8% of medications account for 80% of all medication orders. The distribution of lab results is even steeper: the top 4.5% of lab tests account for 80% of all lab results.

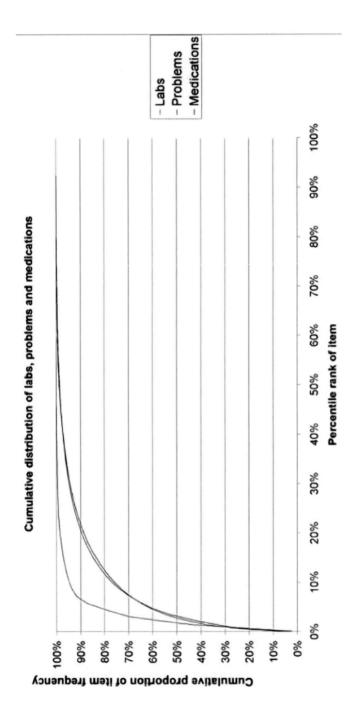

FIGURE 1: Cumulative distribution of item frequency.

TABLE 1: The ten most commonly recorded problems, medications and lab results. There were 272,749 coded problems, 442,658 medications and 11,736,718 lab results recorded for the 100,000 patients in our sample.

Problems		Medications		Lab Results	
Problem	Proportion	Medication	Proportion	Result	Proportion
Hypertension	5.90%	Ibuprofen	2.27%	Hematocrit	2.44%
Elevated Cholesterol	2.52%	Aspirin	2.01%	Potassium	2.40%
Depression	2.31%	Lisinopril	1.87%	Platelets	2.38%
Coronary Artery Disease	2.08%	Multivitamins	1.80%	Hemoglobin	2.37%
Hyperlipidemia	2.00%	Oxycodone	1.60%	White Blood Cell Count	2.37%
Asthma	1.98%	Atorvastatin	1.59%	Mean Corpuscular Volume	2.37%
Gastroesophageal Reflux Disease	1.79%	Albuterol	1.51%	Red Blood Cell Count	2.37%
Breast Cancer	1.58%	Omeprazole	1.49%	Red Blood Cell Distribution Width	2.37%
Diabetes Mellitus Type 2	1.45%	Levothyroxine	1.46%	Mean Corpuscular Hemoglobin Concentration	2.37%
Diabetes Mellitus	1.32%	Simvastatin	1.44%	Mean Corpuscular Hemoglobin	2.37%

We formally fitted the Zipf distribution to these data using the zipfR package in R and assessed the goodness of fit using the Baayen's modified chi square goodness of fit test. The chi square statistic for problems was 100.22, for medications 31.58 and labs 88.02. Lower values of this statistic indicate better fit, but its exact interpretation is controversial. The best norms come from word frequency analysis in linguistics. The chi square goodness of fit measure for a Zipfian fit of the distribution of words in Lewis Carroll's Alice's Adventures in Wonderland is 29.05, while a Zipf distribution fits Arthur Conan Doyle's The Hound of the Baskervilles with $\chi^2 = 227.84$ [14]. The Brown corpus (the source of the word frequency statistics in the introduction) can be fit with Zipf's law with chi square of

819.64. Compared to these sources (considered classically Zipfian), Zipf's law appears to fit our medication, lab and problem data quite well.

7.4 DISCUSSION

As observed in many other areas, the distribution of problems, medications and lab results in our electronic medical record appears to follow a Zipfian distribution with frequently documented or ordered items accounting for a substantial majority of all observations and orders.

The distribution of problems, medications and lab results we have described has a number of implications, particularly in any setting where resources are constrained or space is limited. For example, physicians may want to preferentially stock handouts for common conditions or samples of common medications. It also has implications for designers of electronic health record systems. Screen space is often limited in these systems, so it may make sense to concentrate on displaying the most common choices. Building clinical decision support systems and order entry and documentation templates is time consuming and expensive [15]. System developers may consider focusing their efforts on building top quality interfaces for all of the most common problems, medications and lab results. They may also choose to develop specialized content for items in the less frequently used long tail, particularly where there are quality, safety or risk management issues (e.g. a potentially fatal drug interaction between two uncommonly used medications). For those building clinical data exchanges, this information is also important. If it is possible to begin by ensuring that reliable exchange of the most frequent data types, much of the value may be achieved. However, some infrequently collected data may be especially valuable, for example the results of cardiac catheterizations. In some instances, frequency may even be inversely associated with value (there is low clinical value, for example, of having a long string of MCHC's).

It is worth noting that fitting distributions to data is an inexact and subjective process. In many cases, including ours, a variety of distributions fit our data well, and some more generalized distributions (such as the generalized Gamma distribution) actually fit the data better, although they have more parameters and are generally able to be fit to more kinds of data (indeed the generalized Gamma distribution is the parent of the exponential, chi-square, Erlang and Maxwell-Boltzman distributions, so its ability to fit a variety of data is quite extensive). We preferred the Zipfian distribution because it is relatively parsimonious (having only an exponent and size parameter), because there is a reasonable theoretical basis that suggests why problem, medication and lab result data might follow the distribution, and because it is widely used for assessing the distribution of rank data such as ours. However; even if another distribution were chosen, the implications remain the same: problems, medications and lab results are heavily skewed toward common items.

These results have limitations. They were drawn from a single electronic health record in a single region which has been used for some time, and the results might differ somewhat with a different record or in a different area. Further, the institution under study serves a primarily adult population is a tertiary care center (though it is not a specialty hospital and does provide a full spectrum of medical and surgical care), so the distribution of items used at other sites may differ. For example, an orthopedic hospital might have relatively fewer items in its universe (because of the limited scope of care it provides) but may use some items which are rare in a general hospital more frequently. A direction for future research might be to carry out the same analysis at other hospitals (and with other item types) to see if the pattern holds.

7.5 CONCLUSION

Problems, medications and lab results appear to follow a fairly steep Zipfian distribution, with a relatively small number of items predominating in each class. It may be useful to focus a variety of efforts on these most commonly occurring items when resources are constrained.

7.6 CLINICAL IMPLICATIONS

These results have important implications for both clinical and informatics practitioners. Since a relatively small number of distinct problems, lab results and medications comprise the large majority of usage, practitioners may consider concentrating effort and resources on these common items. This is likely to be particularly true for decision support, where content should be prioritized according to frequency, with content initially targeted at common items before progressing to relatively rarer items.

For example, Lovis et al. described creating an order parser whose knowledge base took into account order frequency [16] and in prior work we described an approach for automated development of order sets and corollary orders based on frequently co-occurring orders [17]. Similar approaches have also been used outside of informatics by, for example, toxicologists making recommendations on antidotes to stock in hospitals based on (among other factors) frequency of use [18] and space planners determining where to store small parts in a warehouse [19].

At the same time; however, focusing solely on common items, though efficient, may lead to unintended consequences, such as poor user experience when performing (or even inability to perform) uncommon actions. Also, for certain types of decision support, users may need the most support when carrying out uncommon and unfamiliar tasks, so rare items should not be entirely neglected. The optimal balance between the efficiency of focusing on common items and the importance of being comprehensive is difficult to strike and has not yet been studied empirically—validating these proposed implications will be an important area for future research.

REFERENCES

1. Anderson C. The long tail. New York: Hyperion; 2008.
2. Trueswell RL. Some Behavioral Patterns of Library Users: The 80/20 Rule. Wilson Libr Bull. 1969;43(5):458-61, 69
3. Bookstein A. Informetric distributions, part I: Unified overview. J Am Soc Inform Sci. 1990;41(5):368-75
4. Reed WJ. The Pareto, Zipf and other power laws. Economics Letters. 2001;74(1):15-9
5. Faloutsos M, Faloutsos P, Faloutsos C. On power-law relationships of the internet topology. Proc Conf on Applications, Technologies, Architectures, and Protocols for Computer Communication. 1999:251-62
6. Kucera H, Francis WN. Computational analysis of present-day American English. Providence: Brown University Press; 1967.
7. Zipf GK. The psycho-biology of language; an introduction to dynamic philology. Boston,: Houghton Mifflin Company; 1935.

8. Gabaix X. Zipf's Law For Cities: An Explanation. Quarterly Journal of Economics. 1999;114(3):739-67
9. Pareto V. Cours d'économie politique. Geneva: Librairie Droz; 1964.
10. DesRoches CM, Campbell EG, Rao SR, et al. Electronic health records in ambulatory care--a national survey of physicians. N Engl J Med. 2008. Jul 3;359(1):50-60
11. Bates DW. Physicians and ambulatory electronic health records. Health Aff (Millwood). 2005. Sep-Oct;24(5):1180-9
12. Adler-Milstein J, McAfee AP, Bates DW, Jha AK. The state of regional health information organizations: current activities and financing. Health Aff (Millwood). 2008. Jan-Feb;27(1):w60-9
13. Evert S, Baroni M. zipfR: Word frequency distributions in R. Proc 45th Ann Meeting of the Association for Computational Linguistics. 2007:29-32
14. Baayen RH. Word frequency distributions. Dordrecht ; Boston: Kluwer Academic; 2001.
15. Johnston D, Pan E, Walker J, Bates DW, Middleton B. Patient Safety in the Physician's Office: Assessing the Value of Ambulatory CPOE. Oakland CA: California Healthcare Foundation; 2004.
16. Lovis C, Chapko MK, Martin DP, et al. Evaluation of a command-line parser-based order entry pathway for the Department of Veterans Affairs electronic patient record. J Am Med Inform Assoc. 2001. Sep-Oct;8(5):486-98
17. Wright A, Sittig DF. Automated development of order sets and corollary orders by data mining in an ambulatory computerized physician order entry system. AMIA Annu Symp Proc. 2006:819-23
18. Dart RC, Borron SW, Caravati EM, et al. Expert consensus guidelines for stocking of antidotes in hospitals that provide emergency care. Ann Emerg Med. 2009. Sep;54(3):386-94e1
19. Bartholdi JJ, Hackman ST. Allocating space in a forward pick area of a distribution center for small parts. Institute of Industrial Engineers Transactions. 2008;40(11):1046-53

PART III

IMPROVING THE PROBLEM LIST

CHAPTER 8

AN AUTOMATED TECHNIQUE FOR IDENTIFYING ASSOCIATIONS BETWEEN MEDICATIONS, LABORATORY RESULTS AND PROBLEMS

ADAM WRIGHT, ELIZABETH S. CHEN, AND FRANCINE L. MALONEY

8.1 INTRODUCTION

Many applications in biomedical informatics require clinical knowledge bases, e.g. relating signs and symptoms to diseases (for automated diagnosis), screening tests and indications (for preventive care decision support) or diseases and medications (for indication-based prescribing). These knowledge bases are often developed and maintained by experts, at significant cost. However, automated methods (usually statistical) for developing such knowledge bases hold promise. In this paper, we describe a set of data mining techniques which can be used to automatically infer (and measure the strength of) relationships between medications, laboratory results and problems, and validate a knowledge base we developed

---

Reprinted from Journal of Biomedical Informatics, *43(6), Wright A, Chenc ES, and Maloney FL, An Automated Technique for Identifying Associations Between Medications, Laboratory Results and Problems, pp. 891–901, Copyright 2010, with permission from Elsevier.*

using the technique against two gold standards. We also describe a particular potential application of this knowledge base: closing "gaps" in patient problem lists.

8.2 BACKGROUND

8.2.1 CLINICAL PROBLEM LISTS

Electronic and paper medical records have long been organized into a variety of sections such as visit notes, medication lists, laboratory results and problem lists. The problem list has been a standard part of the medical record for a considerable period of time, but it began to occupy a central place in the diagnostic reasoning process with Larry Weed's seminal 1968 paper "Medical Records that Guide and Teach," which introduced the concept of the problem-orient medical record (POMR) [1] and the ability to create and maintain a structured, coded problem list is today a requirement of the Certification Commission for Health Information Technology (CCHIT) for all certified electronic health record (EHR) systems [2]

The problem list is important for a variety of reasons. First, having an accurate problem list enables clinicians to see the full spectrum of a patient's problems and is a key input to diagnostic reasoning. The problem list is also a communication tool—when a physician is seeing a patient for the first time (perhaps in a consultation or while providing coverage for the patient's regular physician), the problem list allows him or her to understand the patient's issues. Evidence suggests that patients with complete problems lists may receive higher quality care than patients with gaps in their problem list [3].

In addition to the apparent direct clinical benefits of a complete problem list, the problem list has a number of important ancillary benefits. Clinical decision support systems often depend on coded data elements, and one study found that 22.3% of decision support rules at Partners HealthCare depended on problems [4]. An accurate, complete, coded problem list is also critical for quality measurement and research.

Although the problem list is important, there is also substantial evidence to suggest that it is often woefully incomplete. A study by Szeto et al. found that among patients with coronary artery disease, only 49% had the problem on their problem list (accuracy ranged from 42% for benign prostate hypertrophy to 81% for diabetes) [5]. Szeto also studied the specificity of problems, and found that it was extremely high: 98–100% of patients with a problem on their list actually had the problem, suggesting that false positives are low.

8.2.2 INFERRING CLINICAL PROBLEMS

Because gaps in the problem list are common, researchers have explored methods for automatically inferring problems. These efforts have principally fallen into two categories: proxy methods and natural language processing (NLP)-based methods. Proxy methods attempt to use other clinical data in the EHR to infer problems. Burton and Simonitas described an approach for inferring problems from medications in EHRs based on drug indication data found in the NDF-RT, a standard drug terminology [6]. Carpenter described a similar system which used expert-developed rules to locate potential drug-problem mismatches in diabetes [7]. Lin and Haug described a more sophisticated system based on Bayesian networks [8]; the Lin system focused on five specific diagnoses and used a knowledge base of clinical variable-diagnosis associations derived from internal medicine text books, but tuned the algorithm using Bayesian networks.

Proxy methods that use administrative (e.g., claims) data have also been proposed. Poissant et al. used medication claims from a Canadian provincial insurance system coupled with an expert-developed knowledge base of single-indication drugs to identify problem list gaps with some good success [9].

In addition to proxy methods, a variety of NLP-based methods have also been proposed. Such systems extract candidate problems from unstructured clinical text, such as progress notes. Meystre and Haug described an NLP-based system, using the National Library of Medicine's MetaMap Transfer application [10] and NegEx [11] for negation detection that focused on 80 specific medical problems [12] and [13]. They reported an initial precision of 0.756 and recall of 0.740. By customizing the MetaMap dictionary, they were able to increase their recall to 0.896 with only a slight recall tradeoff. Similar systems have been described using other NLP engines [14].

8.2.3 DEVELOPING A KNOWLEDGE BASE USING AUTOMATED TECHNIQUES

Building on this prior work, we explored and developed data mining techniques to automatically identify associations between problems and structured non-problem data in the EHR (medications and lab results in this analysis). Our goal was to develop a knowledge base of medication-problem and laboratory result-problem associations in an automated fashion using data mining techniques, and to evaluate it. This knowledge base would have a variety of applications, foremost among them inferring clinical problems.

The data mining techniques that we used, frequent item set mining and association rule mining [15] are not themselves novel. The techniques have been developed in computer science for over a decade and have been used in a variety of fields [16], [17] and [18]. Association rule mining underpins Amazon's recommendation feature, which suggests books based on the tastes of others whose past purchase history is similar to yours [19]. We describe frequent item set mining and association rule mining, and our extensions to them, in detail in Section 3.

Association rule mining and related techniques have been used previously in medical informatics. Cao et al. used NLP and co-occurrence statistics to discover disease-finding co-occurrences in discharge summaries with strong results [20]. Wang et al. used similar techniques to locate potentially unknown adverse effects of drugs [21], Mullins et al. used the techniques for public health surveillance [22] and several other applications have also been reported in the literature [23] and [24]. The authors of this paper have also previously used association rule mining to analyze clinical information system log files [25], locate disease-drug associations in the biomedical literature and clinical text [26] and develop order sets and corollary orders in an automated fashion [27].

8.2.4 HYPOTHESIS

We hypothesize that association rule mining will be a feasible technique for analyzing a large clinical data set to successfully identify clinically accurate and meaningful associations between structured data elements (specifically medications and laboratory results) and problems in the EHR. We also hypothesize that the cost of generating such associations through data mining will be less than through manual knowledge base creation and that the volume of rules generated will outstrip existing expert-curated knowledge bases. Finally, we hypothesize that the empiric basis and inherent measurability of the rules developed through these techniques will allow them to be more readily characterized and validated than expert-derived rules without a similar empiric basis.

8.3 METHODS

In our project, we used two related data mining techniques: frequent item set mining and association rule mining. Frequent item set mining is a technique for locating commonly co-occurring items in a transaction database. Association rule mining is an extension of frequent item set mining, which looks at the direction of association in addition to simple co-occurrence. The two techniques are closely related and complementary; in fact, the output of frequent item set mining algorithms can be used as the input to many association rule mining algorithms.

8.3.1 FREQUENT ITEM SET MINING

Frequent item set mining, as introduced in the background Section 2, is an important tool for assessing the co-occurrence of items in a transactional database and, thus, for determining possible associations among them. To describe the technique, we must introduce some formalism. We begin with the set I, which contains all of the items which might appear in the transaction database. In a grocery store example, I would contain all of the items available for purchase in the store; in a clinical example, I might contain all of the medications, procedures and laboratory tests which might be orderable in a hospital. The next concept is the transaction Ti. Each transaction is a set of items that occur together in some logical grouping which we call a transaction. In the grocery example, a transaction might be all the items purchased together by a customer (e.g., the contents of their basket, which is why this frequent item set mining is sometimes called "market basket analysis"). In the clinical example, it might be all the orders for a patient in a particular admission (or perhaps longitudinally). Each Ti ⊆ I . We refer to a database D, which contains all of the transactions $T_0...T_n$.

The concepts introduced thus far (item, transaction and database) are needed to characterize what happened in a particular transactional setting. However, with frequent item set mining, our goal is to determine which items in I naturally occur together within the database D. We call these co-occurring groups of items item sets, and we term candidate item sets X. We define the cover of a candidate item set X to be the set of transactions in D that contain X. The support of X is defined as the number of items in the cover of X (i.e., support(X) = |cover(X)|). We should note that some-

Pt 1: {lisinopril, multivitamin, hypertension}

Pt 2: {insulin, metformin, lisinopril, diabetes, hypertension}

Pt 3: {insulin, diabetes}

Pt 4: {metformin, diabetes}

Pt 5: {metformin, polycystic ovarian syndrome}

FIGURE 1: The medications and problems for 5 sample patients.

times support is alternatively defined as |cover(X)|/|D|, or the proportion of transactions in D that contain X.

8.3.2 AN EXAMPLE

To illustrate these concepts, it is helpful to introduce an example. Consider five patients whom we will characterize only by their medications and problems. These patients are shown in Fig. 1.

In this example, the set I consists of all the unique medications and problems, and contains I = {diabetes, hypertension, insulin, lisinopril, metformin, multivitamin, polycystic ovarian syndrome}. Each patient can be thought of as a transaction Ti in the clinical database D. One can readily observe some frequent item sets that appear to be promising. For example, the item set X = {lisinopril, hypertension} has support of 2 (since two patients have both lisinopril and hypertension in their set transaction). The cover of X is {pt 1, pt 2}. The item set {metformin, diabetes} and {insulin, diabetes} also have support of 2. Patient 5 provides a possible counterexample to this apparent association between metformin and diabetes, however. The statistical measures we use to account for this will be described later.

8.3.3 AN EFFICIENT ALGORITHM

It seems, from this example at least, that frequent item set mining may be a useful technique for determining the relationships between data elements. In the simple example above, one can mentally identify the possible frequent item sets and compute their support. However, when the number of items is high, frequent item set mining poses a substantial computational challenge. Indeed, given a set of items I, there are $2^{|I|}$ candidate item sets. For a small item set, this computation may be tractable. However, it quickly becomes intractable when the size of the item set is large. For example, a two year sample of data from the Brigham and Women's Hospital (BWH) shows a total of 25,848 unique data elements recorded across the medication, laboratory result and problem domains (this includes only coded elements—when uncoded data elements are included the number is much higher). This means the total candidate item set space contains 2^{25848} = 1.055×10^{7781} members, which is computationally intractable.

In 1993, Rakesh Agrawal, of IBM's Almaden Research Center, described an efficient algorithm for computing the complete set of frequent item sets with support greater than a minimum threshold from a database [28]. This algorithm exploits a property of the support metric first described by Agrawal: downward closure. This property states that:

$$X \subseteq Y \Rightarrow \text{support}(Y) \leq \text{support}(X)$$

the property follows trivially from the fact that:

$$\text{cover}(Y) \subseteq \text{cover}(X)$$

In words, it means that, given a candidate item set X, any item set Y which fully contains X must have support less than or equal to the support of X. In other words, if you extend the item set X by adding an item to it, the support must either remain the same or go down, it cannot increase.

The Apriori algorithm has four phases: initiation, joining, pruning and evaluation. The algorithm begins with an initiation phase. In this phase, all 1-item sets with support > minimum support (minsup) are generated. These 1-item sets are frequent (because their support > minsup) so they are added to the result. Next, all of these 1-item sets are joined with each other to produce 2-item sets (the joining phase). Each of these 2-item sets is evaluated to determine whether the item set exceeds the support threshold (the evaluation phase). If it does, it is added to the result. Next, the 2-item sets are combined to form 3-item sets. However, from this point, another step is added: the pruning phase. Each 3-item set is checked to see whether it contains any 2-item sets or 1-item sets that are not in the result set (e.g., non-frequent). The upper bound of the support for any particular 3-item set is, by the downward closure property of support, the support of its least frequent subset. If any subset of the 3-item set is not frequent (e.g., not in the result set), then the 3-item set itself must be non-frequent and does not need to be evaluated. If all subsets of the 3-item set are frequent, then we proceed to the evaluation phase.

Although a naïve algorithm that performed only the initiation, joining and evaluation steps would work correctly, the pruning step has two key advantages over such a naïve algorithm. First, the evaluation space is much smaller, since many candidate item sets are excluded during pruning (and, additionally, all supersets of excluded item sets are also pruned, further limiting the search space). Second, the algorithm naturally terminates when there can be no further joining of k-item sets into k + 1-item sets that are not all pruned. This allows the algorithm to terminate much sooner than the naïve algorithm which must process the entire power set of the item set before terminating.

8.3.4 ASSOCIATION RULE MINING

Frequent item sets, by themselves, are inherently nondirectional. An item set is considered frequent if its support exceeds the support threshold. However, some relationships between items may have a direction. In the example given in Fig. 1, the {insulin, diabetes} relationship is directional. This directionality is fairly obvious clinically: almost everyone who receives insulin has diabetes, but only certain people with diabetes receive insulin.

To account for this directionality, frequent item set mining is often extended to association rule mining. An association rule is an expression $X \rightarrow Y$ where X is an item set, Y is an item set and X and Y are disjoint. Like item sets, association rules can be characterized by their support. We say that support($X \rightarrow Y$)=support($X \cup Y$). This measure, however, is symmetric (i.e., support($X\ Y$) = support($Y \rightarrow X$)). In order to account for directionality, we introduce another measure: confidence. We define confidence($X \rightarrow Y$)=support($X \cup Y$)/support(X). The confidence is the proportion of all transactions containing X that also contain Y. In our example from Fig. 1, confidence({insulin} $\rightarrow$ {diabetes}) = 100% since all patients receiving insulin also have diabetes. However, confidence({diabetes} $\rightarrow$

{insulin}) = 66.7% (because one patient, pt 4, is receiving only metformin for his diabetes).

It is important to note that the directionality inferred by association rule mining is purely correlational. An implication $X \rightarrow Y$, with confidence c, simply means that c% of transactions containing X also contain Y. Such a relationship should not be construed as implying causation without further analysis (typically beyond association rule mining, e.g. an experiment).

8.3.5 MEASURES OF INTERESTINGNESS

Although association rules can be filtered by their support and confidence, there are often many more potential rules produced through these techniques than can be manually reviewed. A variety of measures of "interestingness" have been proposed which can be used to filter these item sets and association rules [29].

In this paper, we concentrate our attention on five commonly used and robust measures: support, confidence, chi square, interest (sometimes called lift) and conviction. The formulas for these statistics are given in Fig. 2. In this figure, for a given rule ($X \rightarrow Y$), a represents the number of transactions in the database containing both X and Y, b the number containing X but not Y, c the number containing Y but not X and d the number containing neither X nor Y.

Support and confidence have already been defined in this section. The chi square statistic has its usual meaning. To compute chisq($X \rightarrow Y$), one conceives of the database D as a two-by-two table. The upper-left cell contains the number of transactions which contain both X and Y, the upper-right the number of transactions which contain X but not Y, the lower-left the number of transactions which contain Y but not X and the lower-right the number of transactions which contain neither X nor Y. The advantage of the chi square statistic is that it accounts for the baseline frequency of X and Y. Support, on the other hand, does not: association rules may score highly simply because their members are very frequent in the database, even if the relationship between X and Y is weak.

Interest (or lift) is another statistic which attempts to correct for this weakness. Confidence tends to rate rules highly where the consequent (Y)

Metric	Formula
Support	a
Confidence	$\dfrac{a}{a+c}$
Chi square	$\dfrac{(a \cdot d - b \cdot c)^2 \cdot (a+b+c+d)}{(a+b) \cdot (c+d) \cdot (b+d) \cdot (a+c)}$
Interest	$\dfrac{\left(\dfrac{a}{a+b}\right)}{\left(\dfrac{a+c}{a+b+c+d}\right)} = \dfrac{a \cdot (a+b+c+d)}{(a+b)^2}$
Conviction	$\dfrac{(a+c) \cdot (b+d)}{(a+b+c+d) \cdot c}$

In this figure, a, b, c and d have their usual meanings in a two-by-two table:

	Y	Y'
X	a	b
X'	c	d

FIGURE 2: Formulation of five measures of interestingness used in the project.

is frequent. For example, if 80% of transactions in a database contain Y, then the expected confidence of any rule X → Y is 80%, even before taking the influence of X on Y into account. The interest(X → Y) is defined as the confidence(X → Y) divided by the proportion of all transactions that contain Y. This scales the confidence to account for the commonality (or rarity) of Y.

The final measure we consider is conviction, described by Brin, Motwani, Ullman and Tsur [30]. Conviction stands out among the other statistics because its derivation is actually grounded in error rates (where an error is a counter example to the rule X → Y, i.e. a transaction where X occurs but Y does not). Conviction, then, is the ratio between the expected error rate assuming independence and the observed error rate. Higher values indicate greater strength of association (indeed conviction has no upper bound, and infinite conviction corresponds to the case where there were no errors observed and every transaction containing X also contains Y).

8.3.6 DATA SET

We hypothesized that association rule mining would be a useful technique for inferring relationships between medications, laboratory results and problems. Such relationships could then be used to identify potential gaps in patient problem lists. In order to explore this, we randomly selected a cohort of 100,000 patients of the Brigham and Women's Hospital. To be included in our cohort, a patient must have been seen at least once during 2007 and 2008 and have two or more outpatient notes in their record. We excluded patients who had fewer than two notes because many of them may have been seen in an acute or consultative setting and have limited documentation.

For each of these patients, we requested and received structured problems, laboratory results and medications as stored in our EHR system. The problems are coded using a proprietary problem terminology that is mapped to SNOMED CT [31]. Laboratory results are coded using LOINC [32] and the result file includes the laboratory test identifier, LOINC code, numeric result, unit of measure, text result, flags and comments. Medications are coded using a propriety medication terminology that is mapped to First Databank and also, indirectly, to RxNorm [33]. The medication file contains the medication, route and dose.

All data were de-identified and encrypted before being analyzed. Our protocol was reviewed and approved by the Partners HealthCare Human Subjects Committee.

After requesting and receiving the problem, medication and laboratory result data files, we prepared them for analysis. Problems were stripped of modifiers and qualifiers, medications were simplified to just the drug product (excluding route and dose) and laboratory results were analyzed three ways: (1) just by unique test (e.g., all CD4 tests would be viewed as identical, regardless of the result), (2) by test and flag (e.g., a high CD4 would be viewed as different from a normal or low CD4) and (3) for tests with qualitative results (which generally lack flags), by test and qualitative result (e.g., a blood smear with the result "2 + sickle cells" would be viewed as different from a smear with the result "normal morphology").

8.3.7 EXTENSIONS TO THE TECHNIQUES

After a preliminary analysis, we noted two problems with conventional approaches to association rule mining that were limiting the accuracy of our results. First, we found that the associations between many anti-HIV agents and the problem HIV was lower than expected. We traced this to the fact that some of the patients had HIV on their problem list while others had AIDS (and some had both). As a result, we developed a set of problem classes, which combined clinically related entities. These classes are described in Appendix 1.

We also found that there were some unexpectedly strong associations between apparently unrelated items which we believed were attributable to comorbidities. For example, the association rule insulin → hypertension scored highly, despite the fact that insulin is used to treat diabetes, not hypertension. However, there is strong comorbidity between the two conditions, so this rule is likely due to transitive association. We were unable to locate any method to control for this in the literature. After significant experimentation, we devised a hold-out method. In this method, significant problem-problem associations (i.e., comorbidities) are first computed. Then, whenever a candidate association is located that meets the support and confidence thresholds (we used a minimum support of 5 and confidence of 10%), we locate the comorbidities for that problem. For each comorbidity, we repeat the analysis of the candidate association is repeated on the subset of patients without the comorbid condition and evaluate the change in statistics.

Prior systems have also used transitive inference in association rule mining; however, they used it to infer additional association rules. For example, Narayanasamy et al. describe a text-mining application mining Medline for associations between diseases and genes [34]. They are interested in the situation where they locate associations A → B and B → C, but do not find an association A → C. In this circumstance, they do an additional round of evaluation to determine if A → C is also a valid association. In other words, they employ transitive association rules as a tool for generating additional candidate associations which are not otherwise found.

We use transitive inference for the reverse problem: pruning spurious candidate associations. Using our diabetes example, we found the rule insulin → hypertension. To validate this candidate association, we reviewed comorbidity data, and found a disease-disease association: diabetes → hypertension, as well as several other disease-disease associations with hypertension. We then iteratively re-evaluated the insulin → hypertension rule once for each disease comorbid with hypertension, and found that the rule fell below our threshold when diabetic patients were excluded. Based on this, we identified diabetes as a transitive mediator for the spurious insulin → hypertension rule and were thus able to automatically reduce the candidate rule set by removing the rule. This is in contrast to the Narayanasamy method, which would apply to a situation where we identified rules insulin → diabetes and diabetes → hypertension but did not identify the rule insulin → hypertension. We would apply the method, which would then propose insulin → hypertension for further study (candidate generation rather than reduction).

8.3.8 ANALYSIS

Several different software packages were tested for computing association rules; however, we found that they were not adequate to perform the analyses needed. Some were unable to handle the large volume of data or required substantial reformatting of the input. Others lacked support for the statistics that we wanted to include in our analysis, and none supported (or could be easily extended to support) our novel iterative transitive reduction technique. As a result, we developed our own analysis software which implements the Apriori algorithm but is tuned specifically for clinical data. It supports all of the statistics of interest, the iterative transitive reduction technique and also provides for on-the-fly encryption and decryption of the datasets. The software was developed in C# and compiled using Microsoft Visual Studio 2008 for the .NET 3.5 Common Language Runtime. All analyses were carried out on a computer with 2 GB of memory and an Intel Core 2 Duo L7500 processor running at 1.60 GHz.

We used the software to generate the top 500 associations for drugs and labs with problems according to each of the five statistics of interest. We limited generation to rules with a single drug or lab in the antecedent set and a single problem in the consequent set in order to enable gold standard evaluation. Because there is significant overlap in the associations selected by each statistic, the total number of associations was less than 2500.

8.4 EVALUATION

After generating the association rules for medications, laboratory results, and problems, we evaluated the rules by comparing them to a gold standard. For medications, we used the Lexi-Comp drug knowledge base (Lexi-Comp, Inc., Hudson, Ohio), which contains information including pharmacology, dosing, administration, use and contraindications of all FDA-approved drug products. For laboratory results, we used Mosby's Diagnostic and Laboratory Test Reference [35] which contains information on common laboratory test results and their uses.

For the evaluation, we identified the top 500 medication-problem and laboratory-problem associations according to each of the five statistics, yielding ten lists of 500 items (e.g., one list for the top 500 medications according to support and another for the top 500 laboratory results using chi square). We then compared each association to the reference sources to determine whether the association was also found in the gold standard reference source. Because the Lexi-Comp database contains all drugs, medication-problem associations were coded as either "indicated" or "not indicated." Mosby's Diagnostic and Laboratory Test Reference, however, did not contain some esoteric laboratory results (the number of unique laboratory tests is much larger than the number of FDA-approved medications, and we were unable to locate any gold standard which was entirely complete). Therefore, for laboratory results, each identified pair was coded as "indicated," "not indicated" or "not found."

Based on these comparisons, we computed an "accuracy" statistic—the proportion of associations found that matched the gold standard. Using a diagnostic testing framework, accuracy is analogous to positive predictive value (or precision in an information retrieval framework). Our gold standards were not necessarily complete (they did not contain all medications, all laboratory tests, all diseases and all associations or indications), so it was not possible to calculate sensitivity and specificity, or to carry out a receiver operating characteristic (ROC) analysis.

8.5 RESULTS

Data were successfully acquired for 100,000 Brigham and Women's Hospital patients. The dataset included 272,749 coded problems, 442,658 coded medications and 11,801,068 coded laboratory results from the EHR system. There were 1756 unique coded problems, 2128 unique medications and 1341 unique coded laboratory results. The total size of the dataset was 762 megabytes (laboratory test results predominated). We ran our programs on the dataset, which took approximately nine minutes to complete (reading the data into efficient in-memory structures predominated—the actual analysis step was very short).

8.5.1 MEDICATION-PROBLEM ASSOCIATIONS

A total of 10,735 medication-problem associations with support of at least 5 and confidence of at least 10% were identified. We characterized all of these pairs with the five statistics described in Section 3: support, confidence, chi square, interest and conviction.

Table 1 shows the top 50 medication-problem associations based on the chi square statistic. A review of the table suggests that all 50 associations are clinically valid when compared to the gold standard, and that many of them are also very specific (for example, a variety of anti-retroviral agents are associated with HIV and/or AIDS—these agents are used only to treat HIV and AIDS). Several rows bear special mention. First, some of the problems (marked with ^) are actually problem classes (described in Section 3 and

TABLE 1: Top 50 medication-problem associations under chi square.

Medication	Problem	Support	Confidence	Chi square	Interest	Conviction
Cyclosporine micro (Neoral)	Cardiac transplant	72	47.37%	15974.05	222.76	1.90
Ritonavir	HIV/AIDS[b]	108	87.10%	13584.49	126.62	7.70
Tenofovir/emtricitabine[a]	HIV/AIDS[b]	117	74.05%	12484.95	107.66	3.83
Multivitamin (vitamins A, D, E, K)	Cystic fibrosis	13	76.47%	12206.84	939.93	4.25
Atazanavir	HIV/AIDS[b]	91	87.50%	11495.76	127.21	7.94
Efavirenz/emtricitabine/tenofovir[a]	HIV/AIDSb[b]	77	95.06%	10576.62	138.20	20.11
Efavirenz/emtricitabine/tenofovir[a]	HIV positive	73	90.12%	10525.03	145.06	10.06
Ritonavir	HIV positive	90	72.58%	10423.49	116.82	3.62
Cyclosporine micro (Neoral)	Stress test	63	41.45%	10390.04	166.04	1.70
Tenofovir/emtricitabine[a]	HIV positive	101	63.92%	10284.74	102.89	2.75
Atazanavir	HIV positive	79	75.96%	9579.52	122.27	4.13
Dornase alfa	Cystic fibrosis	11	68.75%	9283.65	845.03	3.20
Hydroxyurea (non-oncology dose)	Sickle cell anemia	13	44.83%	8502.43	655.23	1.81
Pancrelipase 20,000 units	Cystic fibrosis	16	41.03%	8048.56	504.26	1.69
Cyclosporine micro (Neoral)	Cardiac catheterization	65	42.76%	6597.73	102.79	1.74
Clozapine	Schizophrenia[b]	39	57.35%	6352.86	164.11	2.34
Hydroxychloroquine	Systemic lupus	204	23.26%	5863.47	30.02	1.29
Cyanocobalamin	B12 deficiency	186	18.62%	5815.46	32.48	1.22
Allopurinol	Gout	495	45.50%	5513.09	24.17	1.80
Tiotropium	COPD	223	41.22%	5430.53	25.68	1.67
Abacavir/lamivudine	HIV/AIDS[b]	40	93.02%	5371.03	135.24	14.23
Tiotropium	COPD[b]	224	41.40%	5255.21	24.80	1.68

TABLE 1: *Cont.*

Medication	Problem	Support	Confidence	Chi square	Interest	Conviction
Colchicine	Gout	244	42.00%	5117.07	22.31	1.69
Clozapine	Schizophrenia	31	45.59%	5088.16	165.47	1.83
Latanoprost	Glaucoma	218	57.07%	5044.50	24.40	2.27
Cabergoline	Prolactinoma	20	24.10%	4710.94	236.94	1.32
Pentosan polysulfate	Interstitial cystitis	13	44.83%	4617.13	356.52	1.81
Efavirenz	HIV/AIDS[b]	39	81.25%	4564.53	118.12	5.30
Abacavir/ lamivudine	HIV positive	35	81.40%	4547.55	131.01	5.34
Methotrexate (non-oncology dose)	Rheumatoid arthritis	219	38.76%	4405.36	21.50	1.60
Carbidopa/ levodopa[a]	Parkinson's[b]	47	33.57%	4377.79	94.56	1.50
Mesalamine	Crohns disease	54	45.38%	4373.43	82.35	1.82
Ritonavir	AIDS	20	16.13%	4228.06	212.75	1.19
Griseofulvin	Tinea capitis	5	21.74%	4191.79	839.78	1.28
Glatiramer	Multiple sclerosis	124	34.25%	4166.33	35.02	1.51
Efavirenz	HIV positive	35	72.92%	4066.94	117.37	3.67
Desmopressin nasal	von Willebrand's	7	63.64%	3876.90	555.09	2.75
Pancrelipase 16,000 units	Cystic fibrosis	5	62.50%	3834.74	768.21	2.66
Nephrocaps	End stage renal disease	39	22.16%	3742.90	97.43	1.28
Lopinavir/ Ritonavir	HIV/AIDS[b]	40	63.49%	3641.93	92.31	2.72
Enofovir	HIV/AIDS[b]	32	78.05%	3594.71	113.47	4.52
Carbidopa/ levodopa[a]	Parkinson's disease[b]	40	28.57%	3555.36	90.36	1.40
Carbidopa/ levodopa[a]	Parkinson's disease[b]	40	28.57%	3555.36	90.36	1.40
Tocopherol-dl-alpha	Cardiac transplant	74	10.44%	3539.56	49.08	1.11
Azathioprine	Cardiac transplant	51	14.78%	3473.72	69.52	1.17

TABLE 1: *Cont.*

Medication	Problem	Support	Confidence	Chi square	Interest	Conviction
Pyridostigmine	Myasthenia gravis	10	25.64%	3451.86	346.68	1.34
Lopinavir/ Ritonavir	HIV positive	37	58.73%	3449.47	94.53	2.41
Calcipotriene	Psoriasis	130	38.92%	3303.25	26.85	1.61
Furosemide	Congestive heart failure	351	11.51%	3290.76	10.66	1.12
Tenofovir	HIV positive	29	70.73%	3266.62	113.85	3.40

[a] Combination product. [b] Problem classes.

Appendix 1). In a few cases, this causes duplicate associations: for example, ritonavir is associated both with the HIV/AIDS class and the problem "HIV positive." The HIV/AIDS class association has a higher confidence (87.10%) than the HIV positive problem association (72.58%). This is because some patients have only AIDS and not HIV on their problem list, so when the two are combined the confidence increases. It should be noted that ritonavir is used only to treat HIV (with our without AIDS), so the 12.90% of ritonavir-using patients with neither HIV nor AIDS on their problem list represents an omission (accidental or intentional) from those patients' problem lists.

The pancrelipase, methotrexate and hydroxyurea associations also merit special mention. Although we did not explicitly consider dosing in our analysis, these drugs have doses imbedded in them in the order entry system. This is designed, in the case of methotrexate and hydroxyurea, to enable indication based dosing: these drugs both have oncology uses as well as non-oncology uses (rheumatoid arthritis for methotrexate and sickle cell disease for hydroxyurea) with widely differing doses. Because our system captures the indication and dose range with the order, we can pick out associations between the non-oncology uses and specific problems (we did not find specific associations for these drugs in the domain of oncology problems likely because their use in oncology is so broad).

Fig. 3 shows the results of our gold standard evaluation. We compared the top 500 medication-problem associations according to each of the five

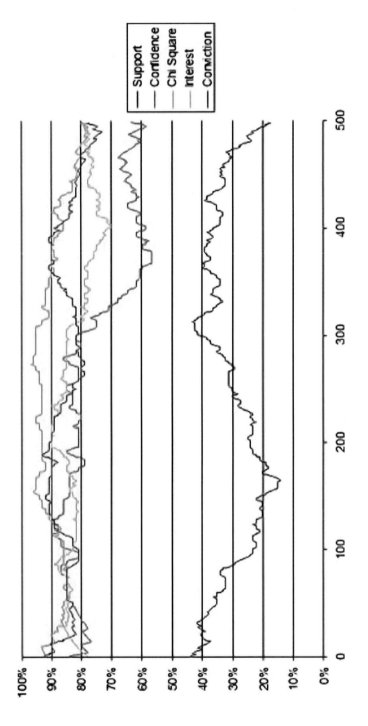

FIGURE 3: Centered moving average accuracy of the top 500 medication-problem associations according to five statistics.

statistics to the gold standard (the Lexi-Comp drug database). Fig. 3 shows how the accuracy of the associations decays as a function of each statistic. Chi square appeared to have the best performance, consistently maintaining accuracy throughout the top 500. Support had the worst accuracy, starting strong but quickly dropping to the 30%-40% accuracy range. Of the top 500 associations, according to the chi square statistic, 89.2% were also found in the gold standard suggesting a high level of accuracy.

We conducted an analysis of the 10.8% associations that were adjudged incorrect. Although not seen in the top 50 medication-problem associations, we found that many of the apparent associations appeared to be transitive. For example, there was an association between insulin lispro 75%/insulin lispro protamine 25% mix (Humalog Mix 75/25) and hypertension. Indeed 60.9% of patients on this insulin preparation also had hypertension on their problem list, and $\chi^2 = 33.20$ for the association ($p < 0.0001$). Although this association is strictly true (indeed, clinically, most diabetic patients on insulin do have hypertension), insulin is not used to treat hypertension. The association is transitive: insulin lispro → diabetes → hypertension.

To control for these transitive associations, we used the novel iterative transitive reduction technique described in Section 3. Our method begins with calculating problem-problem associations to locate statistical comorbidities (we found 17,951 comorbidity rules with support 5 and confidence 10). Then, when we locate a potential association, such as the insulin lispro → hypertension association, we find comorbidities of hypertension (54.52% of diabetic patients in our sample have hypertension) and repeat our analyses holding out these comorbidities one-by-one. When we re-test the insulin lispro → hypertension association excluding all diabetic patients, the support drops to 1 and χ^2 falls from 33.20 to 0.13, strongly suggesting that insulin lispro → hypertension is transitively mediated by diabetes. When other comorbid conditions are used in the hold-out criteria, the chi square statistic changes very little and remains statistically significant.

TABLE 2: Top 50 laboratory-problem associations under interest.

Laboratory Result	Problem	Support	Confidence	Chi Square	Interest	Conviction
Bethesda inhibitor assay	Hemophilia	7	25.00%	5906.03	845.03	1.33
vWF multimers	von Willebrand's disease	8	53.33%	3711.07	465.22	2.14
Fetal hemoglobin	Sickle cell anemia	18	25.35%	6647.50	370.57	1.34
Cotinine	Lung Transplant	9	18.75%	2452.46	274.06	1.23
Cotinine	Cystic Fibrosis	10	20.83%	2545.07	256.07	1.26
Cotinine	Pulmonary Fibrosis	9	27.27%	1997.01	223.48	1.37
Vitamin K	Cystic Fibrosis	8	17.39%	1696.96	213.76	1.21
Cyclosporine level	Cardiac Transplant	101	42.98%	20344.05	202.12	1.75
Tobramycin level	Cystic Fibrosis	10	16.13%	1966.38	198.25	1.19
Cotinine	Pulmonary Fibrosis	11	22.92%	2048.01	187.78	1.30
HHV6 type	Graft vs. host disease	5	10.64%	890.30	179.79	1.12
Voriconazole level	Bone marrow transplant	5	26.32%	870.16	175.71	1.36
HHV6 PCR	Graft vs. host disease	5	10.20%	853.58	172.46	1.11
Respiratory syncytial virus	Lung transplant	14	11.29%	2289.29	165.03	1.13
Cyclosporine level	Stress test	91	38.72%	14031.15	155.13	1.63
HEP C SUPPLEMENTAL	Pulmonary fibrosis	9	18.37%	1339.46	150.51	1.22
Acetylcholine receptor antibodies	Myasthenia gravis	7	11.11%	1039.62	150.23	1.12
Plasma hemoglobin	Cytomegalovirus	5	11.90%	739.84	149.73	1.13
Bone marrow aspirate	Acute myeloblastic leukemia	18	16.51%	2607.68	146.41	1.20

TABLE 2: *Cont.*

Laboratory Result	Problem	Support	Confidence	Chi Square	Interest	Conviction
Vitamin A	Cystic fibrosis	10	11.63%	1412.69	142.92	1.13
Vitamin E	Cystic fibrosis	9	11.54%	1261.32	141.82	1.13
RPR titer	Syphilis	27	17.20%	3709.60	138.82	1.21
HHV6 PCR	Bone marrow transplant	10	20.41%	1345.92	136.26	1.25
HHV6 type	Acute myeloblastic leukemia	7	14.89%	912.19	132.05	1.17
vWF:RCo assay	von Willebrand's disease	23	15.03%	2981.98	131.13	1.18
Factor VIII:C	von Willebrand's disease	23	14.84%	2943.02	129.44	1.17
MHA-TP	Syphilis	27	15.98%	3443.14	128.96	1.19
HHV6 type	Bone marrow transplant	9	19.15%	1135.44	127.85	1.23
HHV6 PCR	Acute myeloblastic leukemia	7	14.29%	874.42	126.66	1.17
vWF antigen	von Willebrand's disease	23	14.29%	2831.95	124.61	1.17
Plasma hgb	Cardiac transplant	11	26.19%	1336.82	123.17	1.35
Coccidioidomycosis	Pulmonary fibrosis	10	14.71%	1188.06	120.50	1.17
HBsAg neutralization assay	Hepatitis B	6	42.86%	592.77	100.34	1.74
Adenovirus PCR	Bone marrow transplant	8	14.81%	777.34	98.92	1.17
BK virus PCR	Kidney transplant	5	12.82%	465.92	94.98	1.15
Cyclosporine level	Cardiac catheterization	92	39.15%	8546.73	94.10	1.64
Rapamycin level	Bone marrow transplant	34	13.99%	3127.36	93.42	1.16

TABLE 2: *Cont.*

Laboratory Result	Problem	Support	Confidence	Chi Square	Interest	Conviction
Blasts	Acute myeloblastic leukemia	21	10.24%	1874.69	90.82	1.11
BK viral load	Kidney transplant	17	12.23%	1512.44	90.61	1.14
Epinephrine-induced plt agg (100 μm)	von Willebrand's disease	5	10.20%	436.00	89.01	1.11
Ristocetin-induced plt agglut	von Willebrand's disease	5	10.20%	436.00	89.01	1.11
Collagen-induced plt agg	von Willebrand's disease	5	10.20%	436.00	89.01	1.11
Epinephrine-induced plt agg	von Willebrand's disease	5	10.20%	436.00	89.01	1.11
Arachiodonate-induced plt agg	von Willebrand's disease	5	10.20%	436.00	89.01	1.11
FMC-7	HIV positive	246	54.67%	21467.36	87.99	2.19
Lymphogranuloma venereum ab	HIV/AIDS[a]	9	60.00%	772.69	87.23	2.48
FMC-7	HIV/AIDS[a]	264	58.67%	22329.93	85.29	2.40
CD4	HIV positive	254	50.50%	20456.20	81.28	2.01
Mycophenolic acid	Cardiac transplant	5	17.24%	396.53	81.08	1.21
CD4	HIV/AIDS^	273	54.27%	21342.46	78.90	2.17

[a] *Problem classes.*

Associations Between Medications, Laboratory Results and Problems

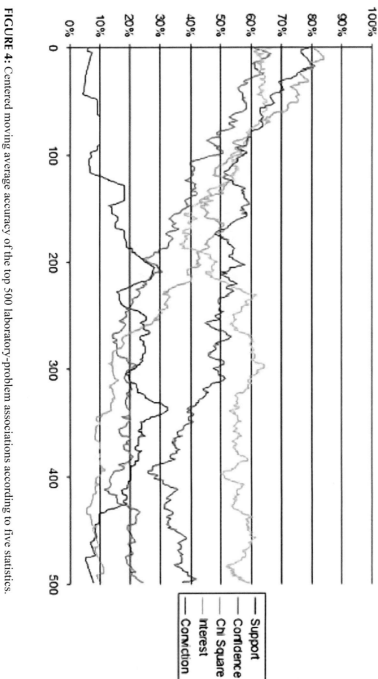

FIGURE 4: Centered moving average accuracy of the top 500 laboratory-problem associations according to five statistics.

8.5.2 LABORATORY-PROBLEM ASSOCIATIONS

As mentioned in the methods, laboratory-problem associations were generated in three different ways: by test, by test with flag and by test with qualitative result. Using a support threshold of 5 and a confidence threshold of 10%, there were 5361 associations with the "by test" method, 8383 with the "by test with flag" method and 5795 with the "by test with qualitative result" method. Each of these methods had its own unique advantages. For example, the mere presence of an HIV screening test means little, but a positive result indicates a high likelihood that the patient has HIV; so in this case, the "test with flag" method would yield the best results.

By contrast, the mere presence of a CD4/CD8 ratio test, regardless of the result, strongly suggests HIV because the test is ordered almost exclusively in this population so the "by test" method may work best. However, for a test with qualitative results (such as a blood smear), there are no flags, so the result itself must be used, making the "by test with qualitative result" superior.

Table 2 shows the top 50 associations using the "by test" method according to the interest statistic. The interest statistic is presented here because it had the highest accuracy (55.6% across the top 500). We focused the analysis on the "by test" method because our gold standard provided clear indications for each test, but interpretation of the test results (either by reference range driven flags or qualitative results) was much more subjective. Like Table 1, the results in Table 2 appear generally accurate based on the gold standard. The table contains a number of drug levels paired with associated conditions, some viral and bacterial antibodies and PCR tests that are highly specific for their associated problems, a number of transplant-related tests and associated transplants as well as a host of tests related to von Willebrand's disease and a substantial number of HIV-related tests.

Fig. 4 shows the results of our gold standard analysis. As mentioned in Section 3, unlike medications, where all medications were listed in our gold standard, not all laboratory tests were listed in our laboratory gold standard. As a result, each association identified by our techniques was coded "indicated," "not indicated" or "not found." The "not found" results were excluded from our analysis. The overall accuracy of the laboratory-problem associations is not as strong as the medication-problem associations and the statistics decay more quickly. However, most of the statistics start out with high accuracy and over the full run of 500, have about 50% accuracy.

8.6 DISCUSSION

Overall, the techniques appear to have worked well and achieved reasonable accuracy. We were able to analyze a large amount of data in a reasonable period of time. We found that the chi square statistic had the best general performance for medications, while the interest statistic was best for laboratory results. The support statistic had the worst performance in both cases. This suggests that there is no clear "best" statistic—instead, statistics should be chosen based on individual data sets and applications—this finding has reported elsewhere in the literature [29]. Indeed, picking the optimal statistic is both an art and a science—some statistics may be heavily biased towards frequently occurring patterns (e.g. support), while others may favor infrequent but strong associations (e.g. interest), and still others try to balance these tradeoffs. Likewise, picking the optimal cut-point for these statistics should also be done with careful reference to both the data and application. For some applications, the cost of a false positive (incorrectly inferring a problem the patient does not have) may be very high (e.g. automated initiation of treatment protocol), while for others, the cost of a false negative (failing to infer a problem that is present) may predominate (e.g. identifying potential patients for a research study, where representativeness is important and the researcher will confirm potential diagnoses).

A potential use of the medication-problem associations and laboratory-problem associations identified by these techniques is identifying and rectifying gaps in problems lists. The fact that the associations were nearly 90% accurate for medications and 50% accurate for problems suggests that, with some appropriate manual review, one could consider implementing them as rules in a clinical information system. In both cases, the results appeared to have reasonable positive predictive value, which would be important for any clinical decision support system.

8.6.1 COMPARISON TO OTHER TECHNIQUES

There are alternatives to using data mining to determine relationships between medications, laboratory results and problems. One alternative is a knowledge-based technique, where human experts determine associations between medications, laboratory results and problem. The techniques used in this study have some advantages over alternative knowledge-based techniques that may be manually intensive and costly.

First, our techniques offer advantages in terms of speed and time. It took about nine minutes to process the entire data set and generate thousands of medication-problem and laboratory-problem associations. Having experts do the same thing would have been much more time-consuming. Our automatically generated associations may require manual review; however, such review is likely to be more efficient than creating rules from scratch.

Second, our technique has advantages in terms of currency: an expert-curated knowledge base must be constantly updated to account for new clinical knowledge and new clinical entities (such as novel drugs); this knowledge management task is very large and perfect currency may be nearly impossible. Our techniques, by contrast, can be repeated as often as is desired, and the incremental cost is negligible.

Third, our techniques may better reflect current practice patterns. For example, some drug knowledge bases (such as the FDA's SPL project [36]) reflect only approved uses of medications, but these techniques can infer both on- and off-label uses.

Fourth, these techniques include inherent metrics. For example, an expert might state that "metformin is used to treat diabetes" but assigning a certainty to this statement is difficult. Our techniques indicate that this association held only 70.6% of the time. Review of the 29.4% of patients on metformin without diabetes also indicates that a greater-than-expected proportion of them have polycystic ovarian syndrome or breast cancer (alternative uses of metformin).

The final advantage of our technique relates to terminologies. Because our techniques operate directly on EHR data, the associations we find are automatically coded using the same terminologies as the EHR. However, implementing an expert statement like "metformin is associated with diabetes" requires manual mapping of the metformin and diabetes concepts.

This mapping is also error prone. In addition to plain metformin, a variety of metformin-containing products are also available (e.g., combined with glyburide or rosiglitazone, or an extended release formulation). All of these products are automatically flagged as related to diabetes by our techniques, but a knowledge engineer would have to know about these products and manually associate them.

Though these advantages are important, there are also some disadvantages of these techniques when compared with knowledge-based techniques. First, these techniques work best for frequently occurring combinations. There are likely many medications, problems and laboratory tests which are used so infrequently that they could not be identified by our methods despite being strongly related. Knowledge-based techniques, given sufficient resources, would be able to identify such relationships (e.g., through substantial literature review).

Second, some of the relationships found in our analysis are only indirect. While it is, for example, strictly true that insulin is strongly associated with hypertension, the association is not direct, and a knowledge base that posited that "insulin is used to treat hypertension" would be incorrect—an error unlikely to be made with a knowledge-based mechanism. This disadvantage may, however, also be an advantage in certain settings: if one were attempting to locate hypertensive patients, it might be reasonable to screen insulin users despite the lack of a direct relationship.

The final disadvantage is the dual of the third advantage: the techniques reflect current practice patterns. To the extent that these practice patterns may be less-than-ideal, or at least not entirely evidence-based, any application of these techniques that tends to perpetuate these patterns may have undesirable results. Knowledge-based techniques, particularly those grounded in evidence, are less likely to perpetuate sub-optimal practice patterns and may, in fact, be useful for correcting such sub-optimal patterns. However, at the same time, these techniques may be powerful tools for identifying and characterizing practice patterns (positive or negative), so that sub-optimal practice might be remediated.

Given this balance of advantages and disadvantages, it is also reasonable to imagine that association rule mining might be used in conjunction with knowledge-based techniques to create maximally effective decision support systems. For example, experts might be presented with automatically inferred association rules, and could validate (or reject them), or simply use them as another input to their knowledge base development process. Alternatively, expert-generated content could be retrospectively validated against association rules and other automatically derived measured, allowing the content to be characterized, and firing rates and accuracy to be predicted before the content goes live. Indeed, all of these approaches could be combined, iteratively, to create a more data-driven, efficient and measurable expert knowledge base development process.

8.7 LIMITATIONS

The techniques used and results have some limitations. First and foremost, this was a single-site study, and our site has fairly advanced clinical systems with good uptake. In a setting with less automation, lower utilization of clinical systems, or less availability of structured data, the techniques might not be as successful. We do, however, believe that the methods are highly generalizable and that similar analyses could be carried out at other sites with similar results.

Second, we limited our analysis to three data types (problems, medications and laboratory results), and only to structured information. There may be additional information available only through other data types that were not included (such as unstructured free text information, or procedure histories) and could be used to validate or complement findings.

Finally, our evaluation compared results to a fixed gold standard. This allows us to measure the accuracy of our techniques but only enables us to speculate about their utility. Since the ultimate goal of these techniques is to identify and help remediate potential gaps in clinical problem lists, an experimental evaluation with an effector arm, such as a system which alerts physicians to probable gaps and invites them to correct them, would allow for more definitive assessment of the techniques' practical utility.

8.8 NEXT STEPS

One obvious next step to extend this work is the addition of further structured data types. For example, procedures may be strong predictors of problems (e.g., CABG for CAD), as might certain visit types or providers (e.g., a patient who visits a mesothelioma clinic likely has mesothelioma, and a patient who visits a urologist who does only TURP likely has BPH). Reliable coded data for these data elements was not readily available to us; however, we hope to acquire and analyze such data in the future.

We also plan to extend our work to consider non-structured data, such as progress notes, radiology reports and operative notes. We believe that these data sources may contain rich predictive information, which is not always available in structured form. For example, the ejection fraction from an echocardiography report may powerfully indicate congestive heart failure, while the indication listed in an operative note might allude to a condition that the patient was treated for but might not be documented on the problem list. We have conducted a small feasibility test of these methods and the results appear intriguing. For example, our association rule mining strategy applied to outpatient notes found that the word "diabetes" in a patient note was not very strongly predictive of having diabetes, largely because of phrases like "will screen for diabetes," "no diabetes" or "family history of diabetes." However, the words "strips," "juice" and "Joslin" (a local diabetes center) were strongly associated with having diabetes. Although these associations make sense in retrospect, we might not have thought of them prospectively.

Further, there may be some value in attempting to locate larger associations rules (i.e., rules with more than one antecedent or consequent). These associations may improve the specificity of rules in ways that are impossible with a single data element. For example, as discussed above, the drug metformin was associated with diabetes in our dataset and this is its primary indication; however, it is also used in the treatment of polycystic ovarian syndrome, so the association between metformin and diabetes is likely to have some false positives. However, adding laboratory information (e.g. the patient's last HbA1c value) to the antecedent set of the association might result in higher confidence (and accuracy under gold standard review). This extension would be quite powerful; however, it is challenging for two reasons: first, it would be considerably harder to find a gold standard—in our evaluation, we used reference sources for medication and laboratory result indications—a similar evaluation of implications involving combinations of multiple drugs or lab results with a single or multiple problems would require a more sophisticated reference source to sue as the gold standard (we are not aware that one exists). Further, when the Apriori algorithm is used to generate rules with large antecedent and consequent sets, the results can be "noisy," containing various trivial combinations and supersets of meaningful rules.

As a further extension of the methods, there likewise may be value in locating unknown associations, such as unexpected problem-medication linkages that could be signs of adverse drug events, or unexpected laboratory-problem associations which may be signs of potential new indications for a test. These are currently counted as "false positives" in our analysis; however, some of them may represent potentially interesting new hypotheses for more detailed investigation.

In addition to these next steps that are focused on extensions of our methods, we have also begun exploring its potential application. We are in the process of developing an intervention within our electronic health record system that will use the rules generated in this study to bring potential problem list gaps to the attention of providers and help them address these gaps. Such an intervention could have the potential to improve quality and safety as well as to enable better decision support and quality measurement.

8.9 CONCLUSION

Overall, the data mining methods described in this paper appeared to produce results with reasonable accuracy. A variety of "interesting" associations between medications and problems and laboratory results and problems were identified and described and the accuracy of these associations was verified through comparison with a gold standard. Further, if these methods can be extended and applied, they may have utility for improving problem list completeness and accuracy which may, in turn, have important benefits for patient care.

REFERENCES

1. L.L. Weed. Medical records that guide and teach. N Engl J Med, 278 (12) (1968), pp. 652–657

2. Certification Commission for Healthcare Information Technology. CCHIT 2009–2010 Ambulatory EHR. 2009 [cited 2009 June 23]; Available from: <http://www.cchit.org/files/certification/09/Ambulatory/CCHITCriteriaAMBULATORY2009-2010Final.pdf/>.
3. D.M. Hartung, J. Hunt, J. Siemienczuk, H. Miller, D.R. Touchette. Clinical implications of an accurate problem list on heart failure treatment. J Gen Intern Med, 20 (2) (2005), pp. 143–147
4. A. Wright, H. Goldberg, T. Hongsermeier, B. Middleton. A description and functional taxonomy of rule-based decision support content at a large integrated delivery network. J Am Med Inform Assoc, 14 (4) (2007), pp. 489–496
5. H.C. Szeto, R.K. Coleman, P. Gholami, B.B. Hoffman, M.K. Goldstein. Accuracy of computerized outpatient diagnoses in a Veterans Affairs general medicine clinic. Am J Manage Care, 8 (1) (2002), pp. 37–43
6. M.M. Burton, L. Simonaitis, G. Schadow. Medication and indication linkage: a practical therapy for the problem list? Proc AMIA Symp (2008), pp. 86–90
7. J.D. Carpenter, P.N. Gorman. Using medication list–problem list mismatches as markers of potential error. Proc AMIA Symp (2002), pp. 106–110
8. J.H. Lin, P.J. Haug. Exploiting missing clinical data in Bayesian network modeling for predicting medical problems. J Biomed Inform, 41 (1) (2008), pp. 1–14
9. L. Poissant, R. Tamblyn, A. Huang. Preliminary validation of an automated health problem list. Proc AMIA Symp (2005), p. 1084
10. A.R. Aronson. Effective mapping of biomedical text to the UMLS metathesaurus: the MetaMap program. Proc AMIA Annu Symp (2001), pp. 17–21
11. W.W. Chapman, W. Bridewell, P. Hanbury, G.F. Cooper, B.G. Buchanan. A simple algorithm for identifying negated findings and diseases in discharge summaries. J Biomed Inform, 34 (5) (2001), pp. 301–310
12. S. Meystre, P.J. Haug. Natural language processing to extract medical problems from electronic clinical documents: performance evaluation. J Biomed Inform, 39 (6) (2006), pp. 589–599
13. S.M. Meystre, P.J. Haug. Randomized controlled trial of an automated problem list with improved sensitivity. Int J Med Inform, 77 (9) (2008), pp. 602–612
14. C. Jao, D. Hier, W. Galanter. Automating the maintenance of problem list documentation using a clinical decision support system. Proc AMIA Symp (2008), p. 989
15. Goethals B. Survey on frequent pattern mining. 2003 [cited 2009 June 15]; Available from: <http://www.cs.helsinki.fi/u/goethals/publications/>.
16. S. Sarawagi, S. Thomas, R. Agrawal. Integrating association rule mining with relational database systems: alternatives and implications. Data Mining Knowledge Discov, 4 (2) (2000), pp. 89–125
17. J. Iskander, V. Pool, W. Zhou, R. English-Bullard. Data mining in the US using the vaccine adverse event reporting system. Drug Saf, 29 (5) (2006), pp. 375–384
18. J.A. Carrino, L. Ohno-Machado. Development of radiology prediction models using feature analysis. Acad Radiol, 12 (4) (2005), pp. 415–421
19. R. Kohavi, L. Mason, R. Parekh, Z. Zheng. Lessons and challenges from mining retail e-commerce data. Mach Learn, 57 (1) (2004), pp. 83–113

20. H. Cao, M. Markatou, G.B. Melton, M.F. Chiang, G. Hripcsak. Mining a clinical data warehouse to discover disease-finding associations using co-occurrence statistics. Proc AMIA Symp (2005), pp. 106–110
21. X. Wang, G. Hripcsak, M. Markatou, C. Friedman. Active computerized pharmacovigilance using natural language processing, statistics, and electronic health records: a feasibility study. J Am Med Inform Assoc, 16 (3) (2009), pp. 328–337
22. I.M. Mullins, M.S. Siadaty, J. Lyman et al. Data mining and clinical data repositories: insights from a 667, 000 patient data set. Comput Biol Med, 36 (12) (2006), pp. 1351–1377
23. S.E. Brossette, A.P. Sprague, J.M. Hardin, K.B. Waites, W.T. Jones, S.A. Moser. Association rules and data mining in hospital infection control and public health surveillance. J Am Med Inform Assoc, 5 (4) (1998), pp. 373–381
24. S. Doddi, A. Marathe, S.S. Ravi, D.C. Torney. Discovery of association rules in medical data. Medical informatics and the Internet in medicine, 26 (1) (2001), pp. 25–33
25. E.S. Chen, J.J. Cimino. Automated discovery of patient-specific clinician information needs using clinical information system log files. Proc AMIA Symp (2003), pp. 145–149
26. E.S. Chen, G. Hripcsak, H. Xu, M. Markatou, C. Friedman. Automated acquisition of disease drug knowledge from biomedical and clinical documents: an initial study. J Am Med Inform Assoc, 15 (1) (2008), pp. 87–98
27. A. Wright, D.F. Sittig. Automated development of order sets and corollary orders by data mining in an ambulatory computerized physician order entry system. Proc AMIA Symp (2006), pp. 819–823
28. R. Agrawal, T. Imielinski. Mining association rules between sets of items in large databases. Proc 20th Int Conf Very Large Data Bases (1993), pp. 688–692
29. P. Tan, V. Kumar, J. Srivastava. Selecting the right interestingness measure for association patterns. Proc Eighth ACM SIGKDD Int Conf Knowledge Discov Data Mining (2002)
30. S. Brin, R. Motwani, J. Ullman, S. Tsur. Dynamic itemset counting and implication rules for market basket data. Proc ACM SIGMOD Int Conf Manage Data (1997), pp. 255–264
31. M.Q. Stearns, C. Price, K.A. Spackman, A.Y. Wang. SNOMED clinical terms: overview of the development process and project status. Proc AMIA Annu Symp (2001), pp. 662–666
32. A.W. Forrey, C.J. McDonald, G. DeMoor et al. Logical observation identifier names and codes (LOINC) database: a public use set of codes and names for electronic reporting of clinical laboratory test results. Clin Chem, 42 (1) (1996), pp. 81–90
33. S. Liu, W. Ma, R. Moore, V. Ganesan, S. Nelson. RxNorm: prescription for electronic drug information exchange. IT Prof, 7 (5) (2005), pp. 17–23
34. V. Narayanasamy, S. Mukhopadhyay, M. Palakal, D.A. Potter. TransMiner: mining transitive associations among biological objects from text. J Biomed Sci, 11 (6) (2004), pp. 864–873
35. K.D. Pagana, T.J. Pagana. Mosby's diagnostic and laboratory test reference. Mosby Elsevier, St. Louis, Mo. (2007)

36. United States Food and Drug Administration. Structured Product Labeling Resources. 2009 [cited 2009 June 15]; Available from: <http://www.fda.gov/ForIndustry/DataStandards/StructuredProductLabeling/default.htm/>.

There a supplemental file that are not available in this version of the article. To view this additional information, please use the citation on the first page of this chapter.

CHAPTER 9

A METHOD AND KNOWLEDGE BASE FOR AUTOMATED INFERENCE OF PATIENT PROBLEMS FROM STRUCTURED DATA IN AN ELECTRONIC MEDICAL RECORD

ADAM WRIGHT, JUSTINE PANG, JOSHUA C. FEBLOWITZ, FRANCINE L. MALONEY, ALLISON R. WILCOX, HARLEY Z. RAMELSON, LOUISE I. SCHNEIDER, AND DAVID W. BATES

9.1 INTRODUCTION AND BACKGROUND

Having a clear picture of a patient's problems and diagnoses is critical for a variety of reasons. First and foremost, knowledge of a patient's problems facilitates optimal clinical decision making—without understanding the full scope of patients' clinical issues, it is very difficult to take good care of them. However, knowledge of problems is also critical for a variety of other activities, such as clinical decision support, [1] quality improvement and measurement, and research.

The most obvious source of information about a patient's problems is the clinical problem list. The concept of a problem list, the central component of the problem-oriented medical record, was first described by Lawrence Weed, MD, in 1968. [2] Weed proposed a new method of organizing medical records with problems at the center and data organized around the problems. Clinical problem lists serve a variety of purposes in facilitating care including: promoting continuity of care, describing active diseases, recording patient risk factor assessments, facilitating diagnostic workups and treatment, and helping providers generate care plans and manage preventive care, among others. [3–5]

Computerized problem lists offer additional advantages over a paper-based list, allowing other patient data such as laboratory results, imaging studies, medications, and allergies to be linked electronically to central problem concepts. [2, 6] Electronic patient problem lists can also be coded using standard terminologies. [7–9] Today, many institutions with electronic health record (EHR) systems utilize either ICD-9, SNOMED, or subsets thereof, as their structured problem vocabulary; and such mappings facilitate automated interpretation of problem data, interoperability, and billing. [10–13] Problem lists in modern EHRs are generally maintained manually; however some methods of augmenting the electronic problem list with clinical knowledge and improving its structure, accuracy, and utility have also been proposed, [9, 14–17] particularly in the area of problem-oriented record visualization and automated knowledge-based linking of problems and data.

An accurate and up-to-date electronic problem list represents the ideal cornerstone of the modern EHR. It provides a succinct clinical picture of the patient, facilitates communication, and enables the electronic record to deliver the appropriate clinical decision support. Clinicians may use the problem list to familiarize themselves with the needs of a patient they are treating for the first time or are covering, as an inventory of conditions that might require management on a particular visit, or as a marker of contraindications for particular therapies. However, despite their importance, patient problem lists are often inaccurate, incomplete, and poorly maintained. [18–20] In addition, inaccurate problem lists have been shown to be associated with lower quality of patient care. [21, 22]

The problem list is perhaps even more important for clinical decision support and quality measurement. For example, at Partners Healthcare, a large integrated academic clinical care network, 22% of clinical decision support rules depend on coded problems in the patient problem list. [1] In many cases, accurately documented patient problems trigger reminders that help clinicians manage chronic diseases, which account for a large proportion of all costs. Consider, for example, a patient with diabetes. If his diabetes is properly documented, his clinician will receive appropriate alerts and reminders to guide care, the patient will be flagged as eligible for special care management programs, and the quality of care provided to him will be measured and tracked. Without diabetes on the problem list, he might receive none of these benefits.

Given that problem lists are often incomplete, researchers and implementers of clinical information systems have turned to a variety of alternative sources for problem information. Several systems have been reported using natural language processing to infer clinical problems. [23–25] Researchers have also used data mining techniques to identify clinical data which can be used as a proxy for problems. [26–28] These proxy methods have been especially fruitful in the case of medications: Carpenter and Gorman used medication information to identify possible problem mismatches [22] and Poissant et al employ a combination of billing codes, single-indication drugs, and prescription indications to infer problems in an electronic prescribing system. [29, 30] In addition, the eMerge group has developed natural language processing, proxy and mixed problem inference methods for the purpose of identifying patient phenotypes and selecting cases and controls for genome-wide association studies. [31–34]

These techniques for inferring patient problems are promising and several have demonstrated positive early results; however, each of the reported systems has one or more limitations. Most use only a single type of data (medications, billing codes, or narrative text) to make their inference, focus on only one clinical problem, or focus on identifying cases (patients who certainly have the disease) and controls (patients who certainly do not have the disease) but leave many patients unclassified. Further, many rely on time consuming manual techniques for generation of their knowledge bases, and none, to our knowledge, have provided their full knowledge base for use or validation by others.

The goal of our project is to describe, in detail, a replicable method for developing problem inference rules, and also to provide a reference knowledge base of these rules for use or validation by other sites.

9.2 METHODS

The methods we used in this project were designed to be easily replicable by other sites interested in developing their own problem inference rules. We describe a six-step process for rule development designed to yield high quality rules with known performance characteristics. The six steps are:

- Automated identification of problem associations with other structured data
- Selection of problems of interest
- Development of preliminary rules
- Characterization of preliminary rules and alternatives
- Selection of a final rule
- Validation of the final rule.

In the following sections, we present the six steps of this process in detail.

9.2.1 STEP 1: AUTOMATED IDENTIFICATION OF PROBLEM ASSOCIATIONS WITH OTHER STRUCTURED DATA

To build inference rules, it is critical to determine what clinical data elements might be useful for predicting problems. Our current project builds on previous work we conducted to identify medication-problem associations and laboratory-problem associations using data mining and co-occurrence statistics. [28] The goal of the Automated Patient Problem List Enhancement (APPLE) project was to develop a database of associations using automated data mining tools. In the APPLE study, we performed association rule mining on coded EHR data for a sample of 100 000 patients who received care at the Brigham and Women's Hospital (BWH), Boston, Massachusetts, USA. This dataset included 272 749 coded problems,

442 658 medications, and 11801068 laboratory results for the sample of 100000 patients.

In the previous study, candidate associations were evaluated using five co-occurrence statistics (support, confidence, χ^2, interest, and conviction). High scoring medication-problem and laboratory-problem associations (the top 500) were then compared to a gold standard clinical reference (*Mosby's Diagnostic and Laboratory Test Reference* for laboratory results and Lexi-Comp drug reference database for medications). For medication-problem associations, χ^2 was found to be the best performing statistic and for laboratory-problem associations, the highest performing statistic was interest. For medication-problem associations, 89.2% were found to be clinically accurate when compared with the gold standard, as were 55.6% of laboratory-problem associations.

The design, implementation, and results of the APPLE project are discussed in detail in a previous publication. [28] The end result of the project was a database of several thousand medication-problem and laboratory-problem associations characterized by multiple co-occurrence statistics. This database was used in the preliminary stages of the current project in the design of inference rules, as described below.

9.2.2 STEP 2: SELECTION OF PROBLEMS OF INTEREST

Given our methods and available resources, we wanted to constrain our knowledge base to no more than 20 problems. In order to identify a final set of conditions for inclusion in this project, we assessed a set of 78 potential 'candidate' problems. This preliminary list of problems was chosen on the basis of several criteria including: (a) recent related pay-for-performance initiatives at BWH, (b) the existence of relevant problem-dependent clinical decision support rules in the hospital's electronic medical records system (LMR), and (c) the strength of related medication-problem and laboratory-problem associations identified during the APPLE project. To guide the selection process, we developed a simple ranking metric which assigned points for each of the three criteria listed. A final list of 17 study problems (box 1) was chosen based on both the results of this analysis and clinician input. Each of the 17 problems was relevant to at least two of the three criteria described above.

BOX 1: TARGET CONDITIONS FOR CREATION OF PROBLEM INFERENCE RULES

Conditions (n=17)

- ADHD
- Asthma/COPD*
- Breast cancer
- CAD
- CHF
- Diabetes
- Glaucoma
- Hemophilia/congenital factor XI/von Willebrand disorder*
- Hypertension
- Hyperthyroidism
- Hypothyroidism
- Myasthenia gravis
- Osteoporosis/osteopenia*
- Renal insufficiency/renal failure*
- Rheumatoid arthritis
- Sickle cell disease
- Stroke

*Multi-condition rules.

ADHD, attention deficit hyperactivity disorder; CAD, coronary artery disease; CHF, congestive heart failure; COPD, chronic obstructive pulmonary disease.

9.2.3 STEP 3: DEVELOPMENT OF PRELIMINARY RULES

Once the list of problems was finalized, we built a preliminary set of inference rules for initial testing. In order to accomplish this task, we first conducted research on each of the selected problems. We began by reviewing the APPLE database to locate all related medication-problem and laboratory-problem associations. Using these automatically-generated inferences as a starting point, we then conducted a thorough review of medical textbooks and online clinical resources, including *Harrison's Principles of Internal Medicine*, eMedicine, and UpToDate, identifying a list of all laboratory tests and medications relevant to each problem. We also identified all related ICD-9 billing codes for each of the conditions and coded problem list concepts relevant to the problem. Finally, because our EHR system allows for free-text problem entries in addition to coded entries, we also carried out a search for common related free-text entries. We identified all free-text (uncoded) problem phrases appearing five or more times in our sample (2441 in all) and manually reviewed each to determine if it matched a coded term for one of our 17 conditions. In the case of diabetes, for example, related free-text entries we found included 'diabetes' (users can enter free-text entries even if they match a coded concept exactly), 'NIDDM,' 'AODM,' 'diabetic nephropathy,' 'diabetic retinopathy,' 'insulin resistance,' 'diabetes type II,' 'diabetic neuropathy,' 'type 2 diabetes,' 'type II diabetes,' 'diabetes mellitus,' 'diet controlled DM,' 'IDDM,' 'diabetic gastroparesis,' 'adult onset diabetes,' and 'diabetic complications.' Many of the benefits of an accurate problem list can only be achieved through the use of coded problem entries. Thus, it was important in the design of our problem inference rules that they be able to identify patients with related free-text problem entries so that a coded entry could be added.

For each of the conditions, we developed a draft condition 'abstract' detailing the relevant information identified from the data sources above (a combination of laboratory-problem and medication-problem associations, literature review, ICD-9 codes, and free-text problem entries), and also developed an initial straw man rule. Each rule is comprised of a series of logic statements such as 'coded or uncoded ADHD entry on problem list OR 1 or more ADHD billing codes OR 1 or more ADHD billing codes AND at least one ADHD medication.'

We presented this set of initial recommendations to an expert panel consisting of three internal medicine physicians (DWB, LIS, HZR). After reviewing the preliminary rules, the committee then recommended changes and proposed alternate rules (eg, additional classes of medications, additional combinations, or modification of thresholds).

In certain cases, the committee had difficulty developing rules that were highly specific for a single condition in our set of interest, particularly when our set of interest contained clinically similar or related diseases. For example, it was feasible to develop a rule that identified patients with either asthma or chronic obstructive pulmonary disease (COPD), but it was difficult to discriminate accurately between the two because of numerous medication overlaps, so the conditions were merged into a rule that predicts asthma or COPD. This strategy was applied in the following final rules: asthma/COPD, osteoporosis/osteopenia, renal insufficiency/renal failure, and hemophilia/congenital factor XI deficiency/von Willebrand disease.

9.2.4 STEP 4: CHARACTERIZATION OF PRELIMINARY RULES AND ALTERNATIVES

Up to this point in the design process, the expert panel was working based on APPLE findings, reference information, and their own expertise, but without the benefit of specific characterization of the candidate rules they developed. In order to further inform their deliberations, we then tested each of the preliminary rules they proposed in step 3 as well as several alternate versions of each rule by applying them to a training set of patient records. The training set consisted of a random sample of 100 000 patient records drawn from a population of 839 300 patients with a progress note recorded in the last 2 years in the electronic medical record system at BWH. For each patient record, rules were automatically checked against coded data present in the electronic medical record system and submitted claims from the BWH inpatient and outpatient billing systems.

Our method of evaluating each rule is summarized in figure 1. Our gold standard, in each case, was the patient having the problem documented by a clinician in their record—we did not attempt to formulate new diagnoses for patients, or to verify the accuracy of existing diagnoses.

Method and Knowledge Base for Inference of Patient Problems

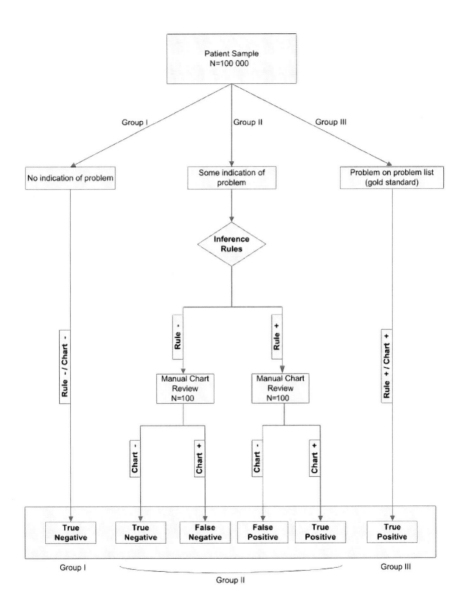

FIGURE 1: Patient flow.

Because we had limited resources for chart review, we also made two assumptions to focus our review. First, we considered the presence of a particular condition on the problem list as a gold standard indicator that the patient had a given problem, and thus these patients were counted among the true positives (group III), since they met the criteria for our rules (by having the problem on their problem list) and since we assumed that the problem list assertion was correct. Our second assumption pertained to a subset of patients who had no relevant data in their record for a given condition. This was assessed by checking for the existence of any data that would inform a rule for a particular condition (but not, of course, checked by using the actual rule). For example, for diabetes, if we encountered a patient where no HbA1c test was ever performed, no diabetes-related billing codes were ever submitted, no related problems were on the problem list, and no related medications were on medication list, we assumed that patient did not have diabetes, and these patients were classified as true negatives (group I). Due to the absence of any relevant data, we determined that there would be extremely low yield in reviewing their charts, and instead focused resources on other groups of patients where there was a more reasonable likelihood of a given patient having the problem.

It is almost certainly the case that some patients with a problem on their problem list do not actually have that problem (despite it having been manually added by a clinician) and that some patients with no documented clinical evidence of a particular problem actually do have the problem. However, we believe that these eventualities are rare and that our assumptions are, thus, reasonable. Indeed, to verify or refute them, we would likely need to bring patients in for additional testing and workup, which would be expensive and likely low yield.

The remaining patients (group II) had at least some indication of the condition in their record (eg, any related laboratory investigation ever performed, any related medication prescribed, any related billing code recorded), but did not have the condition documented on their problem list. To be included in this group, a patient needed to have only a single coded laboratory test, medication, billing code or vital sign entry in their record related to the problem in question. For each of these patients, we applied the candidate rule from step 3 of our process, classifying each patient as either having the problem (rule-positive) or not having the problem (rule-negative).

For each condition, we randomly selected 100 rule-positive patients and 100 rule-negative patients from group II for manual chart review. This review was conducted by a team of research assistants under the supervision of the principal investigator, and included complete review of all data in the record, including problems, with a particular focus on free-text components such as progress notes, admission notes, discharge summaries, and consult notes and letters. If a clinician indicated anywhere in the record that the patient had the relevant condition, they were coded as positive for the condition (chart-positive). If there was no mention of the condition, or if the clinician had affirmatively ruled it out, the patient was counted as negative for the condition (chart-negative).

For the sample of 200 patients, this process left us with two data points: rule inference (rule-positive or rule-negative) and gold standard chart interpretation (chart-positive or chart-negative). Patients who were rule- and chart-positive were counted as true positives. Patients who were rule-positive and chart-negative were counted as false positives. Patients who were rule-negative and chart-negative were counted as true negatives. Patients who were rule-negative and chart-positive were counted as false-negatives (figure 1).

After completion of the manual chart review, each of the 100 000 patients was classified as a true-positive, false-positive, true-negative, or false-negative for each of the 17 conditions and associated candidate rules. We used these classifications to compute the sensitivity, specificity, positive predictive value (PPV), and negative predictive value (NPV) for each rule according to the standard formulas. Because not all charts were manually reviewed, we used inverse probability weights to adjust for our sampling strategy (patients in groups I and III were assigned weights of 1, while patients in group II were divided into rule-positive and rule-negative strata and assigned weights corresponding to the inverse of the stratum sampling fraction).

After computing these quantities for each of the 17 candidate rules, we then evaluated several alternative rules (by varying, for example, laboratory result thresholds, drugs, counts, etc) to determine the performance of each alternative version. For each rule, all versions were tested against the same 200-case set described above.

9.2.5 STEP 5: SELECTION OF A FINAL RULE

After multiple iterations of each rule were analyzed in this manner against the training set, several versions of each rule (ranging from 3 to 8) were then presented to the expert physician panel for a second time along with the sensitivity, specificity, and positive and negative predictive values for each version. The rule versions presented to the panel represented permutations of the original rule. For example, we might modify various thresholds (looking at HbA1c levels of 7% or 9%, or at 1 vs 2 related medications). The rules were selected to cover a variety of performance characteristics, ranging from rules with high sensitivity and lower PPV to rules with high PPV and lower sensitivity. The panel then chose a final rule from the presented options. In designing these rules, we attempted to maximize sensitivity and PPV overall and the options presented to our expert panel reflected this goal. Due to low overall prevalence of each disease, specificities were consistently very high, making it difficult to discriminate between different versions of each rule using this statistic. As a result, we chose to emphasize PPV over specificity in our analysis. In addition, in order to minimize erroneous inferences, we prioritized PPV while accepting some resultant trade-offs in sensitivity.

For example, five separate versions of the diabetes rule were presented to the expert panel with results from training set analysis (figure 2). The rules presented were as follows:

Rule 1

- max A1c ≥ 9 OR
- at least 3 A1c's recorded ≥ 7 OR
- billing codes ≥ 7 OR
- metformin and billing codes ≥ 2 OR
- any insulin OR
- any oral anti-diabetic drug OR
- diabetes on problem list

Method and Knowledge Base for Inference of Patient Problems   195

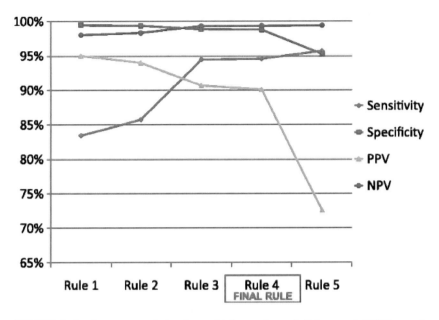

FIGURE 2: Performance statistics for multiple versions of diabetes rule. NPV, negative predictive value; PPV, positive predictive value.

Rule 2

- max A1c ≥9 OR
- at least 3 A1c's recorded ≥7 OR
- billing codes ≥7 OR
- any insulin OR
- any oral anti-diabetic drug OR
- diabetes on problem list

Rule 3

- max A1c ≥9 OR
- at least 3 A1c's recorded ≥7 OR
- billing codes ≥2 OR
- any insulin OR
- any oral anti-diabetic drug OR
- diabetes on problem list

Rule 4 (final rule)

- max A1c ≥7 OR
- billing codes ≥2 OR
- any insulin OR
- any oral anti-diabetic drug OR
- diabetes on problem list

Rule 5

- max A1c ≥5 OR
- billing codes ≥2 OR
- any insulin OR
- any oral anti-diabetic drug OR
- diabetes on problem list.

In the case of diabetes, option 1 (the most conservative and complex rule) achieved a high PPV (>95%) but had lower sensitivity (<85%). At the opposite end of the spectrum, option 5 (the most inclusive and simplest rule) achieved a sensitivity of >95% but a PPV of <80%. On the basis of these trade-offs and after confirmation of the clinical accuracy of each version, the panel recommended option 4 as the final rule in the case of diabetes based on a sensitivity of 94.6% and a PPV of 90.1%. This procedure was repeated for each of the 17 rules.

9.2.6 STEP 6: VALIDATION OF THE FINAL RULE

To validate the final version of each rule and to guard against over-fitting of the rules against the training set, we repeated the analysis of step 4 on an independent validation set. For this analysis, we drew a second random sample of 100 000 patients from the same population as the initial sample, but excluding patients in the initial sample. For each of the final rules, the same classification and chart review process was carried out, and sensitivity, specificity, and positive and negative predictive values were calculated using the same procedure described in the above section.

9.2.7 ADDITIONAL ANALYSIS

After completing the six-step method described here for each problem, we had 17 fully characterized rules. In order to place these rules in context, we also carried out two additional analyses. First, we computed the sensitivity, specificity, PPV, and NPV of using coded problem list entries only using the method and data of step 6 (we did not conduct an additional chart review, but instead retained the results of the step 6 validation chart review). Because we assumed that all patients with a problem on their problem list had the related condition, the PPV of all such rules was necessarily 100%, but the sensitivity varied. We also computed the sensitivity, specificity, PPV, and NPV of using billing data alone to identify patients with the 17 conditions of interest, again using the methods and data of step 6 (and again retaining the step 6 validation chart review results).

In order to more fully characterize the performance of the rules, we also computed F measures according to the method of van Rijsbergen. [35] The F measure is a generalized harmonic mean of the sensitivity and PPV whose parameters can be adjusted to prioritize either variable. We chose to use F0.5 because our goal in developing the rules was to prioritize PPV over sensitivity. The F0.5 measure weights PPV twice as heavily as sensitivity (ie, favoring false negatives over false positives).

9.3 RESULTS

A total of 17 problem inference rules were developed (13 single-problem rules and 4 combined-problem rules). The complete list and description of these rules is provided in online appendix A (available as an online data supplement at www.jamia.org). The number of logic statements comprising each rule ranged from two (hemophilia) to five (hypertension, osteopenia/osteoporosis). Final rules used coded and free-text problem recognition and one or more of the following to infer patient problems: (a) related billing codes, (b) related medications, and/or (c) related laboratory data or vital signs.

The results of analysis on the training set for each rule, including sensitivity, specificity, and positive and negative predictive values, are presented on the left side of table 1. When applied to the training set, the average sensitivity and PPV for all 17 rules were 86.4% and 91.1%, respectively. Twelve of the 17 rules had a PPV of over 90% and all were over 65%. For sensitivity, 14 of the 17 rules were over 75% and all were over 65%.

TABLE 1: Performance analysis of problem inference rules (training and validation)

	Training set				Validation set			
	Sens	Spec	PPV	NPV	Sens	Spec	PPV	NPV
ADHD	67.8	100.0*	99.1	99.7	62.8	100.0*	96.6	99.6
Asthma/COPD	78.1	99.2	92.7	97.0	79.5	99.6	96.7	97.3
Breast cancer	95.1	99.9	99.0	99.7	95.8	100.0*	99.6	99.7
CAD	83.0	99.6	95.7	98.3	86.4	99.9	98.5	98.6
CHF	71.7	99.4	79.1	99.1	70.8	99.4	79.8	99.0
Diabetes	94.6	98.8	90.1	99.4	91.3	99.3	94.9	98.8
Glaucoma	93.8	99.9	95.0	99.9	94.4	99.9	96.2	99.9
Hemophilia	89.7	100.0*	97.7	100.0*	86.5	100.0*	97.8	100.0*
Hypertension	80.6	96.9	92.9	90.8	81.0	96.2	89.0	93.1
Hyperthyroidism	83.6	99.9	87.7	99.9	86.3	99.9	88.1	99.9
Hypothyroidism	91.9	99.8	97.5	99.3	91.0	99.5	93.5	99.3
Myasthenia gravis	87.4	100.0*	89.4	100.0*	82.4	100.0*	85.9	100.0*
Osteoporosis/osteopenia	73.9	99.4	94.0	96.8	70.8	99.2	90.7	97.0
Renal insuf/renal fail	100.0	98.3	69.2	100.0	100.0	99.1	77.5	100.0
Rheumatoid arthritis	94.8	99.8	88.2	99.9	66.5	99.9	91.7	99.3
Sickle cell disease	95.6	100.0*	90.3	100.0*	96.8	100.0*	91.0	100.0*
Stroke	85.8	100.0*	97.4	99.7	87.3	99.9	97.9	99.7

*Actual value slightly less than 100%. Note: CIs were small for each parameter and are thus omitted from the reported results. For example, the CIs for the diabetes rule parameters described above were 86.8% to 94.5% (sensitivity), 98.8% to 99.6% (specificity), 91.0% to 97.3% (PPV), and 98.1% to 99.2% (NPV). ADHD, attention deficit hyperactivity disorder; CAD, coronary artery disease; CHF, congestive heart failure; COPD, chronic obstructive pulmonary disease; fail, failure; insuf, insufficiency; NPV, negative predictive value; PPV, positive predictive value; Sens, sensitivity; Spec, specificity.

The results of validation for each rule, including sensitivity, specificity, and positive and negative predictive values, are presented on the right side of table 1. When applied to the validation set, the average sensitivity and PPV for all 17 rules were 83.9% and 91.7%, respectively. Overall, 12 of the 17 rules had a PPV of over 90% and all were over 75%. Of the 17 rules, 11 had a sensitivity of over 80% and all were greater than 60%.

TABLE 2: Performance of coded problem-only and billing-only rules

	Problem-only				Billing-only			
	Sens	Spec	PPV	NPV	Sens	Spec	PPV	NPV
ADHD	45.0	100.0	100.0	99.4	73.7	99.9	91.3	99.7
Asthma/COPD	44.8	100.0	100.0	92.4	91.5	98.6	89.8	98.8
Breast cancer	78.5	100.0	100.0	98.6	97.9	99.9	97.7	99.9
CAD	58.9	100.0	100.0	95.7	99.2	97.9	83.5	99.9
CHF	9.9	100.0	100.0	91.9	83.3	98.3	70.2	99.2
Diabetes	61.9	100.0	100.0	94.5	89.4	98.5	89.8	98.4
Glaucoma	73.4	100.0	100.0	99.4	90.0	99.9	96.7	99.8
Hemophilia	73.7	100.0	100.0	99.9	100	100.0*	87.2	100
Hypertension	50.7	100.0	100.0	83.2	86.7	95.0	87.5	94.7
Hyperthyroidism	59.3	100.0	100.0	99.5	95.7	99.4	64.4	100.0*
Hypothyroidism	51.8	100.0	100.0	96.7	81.6	98.2	76.4	98.7
Myasthenia gravis	48.6	100.0	100.0	100.0*	97.3	99.9	53.3	100.0*
Osteoporosis/osteopenia	45.1	100.0	100.0	94.2	80.5	98.7	87.4	97.9
Renal insuf/renal fail	4.7	100.0	100.0	83.5	43.3	99.6	86.7	96.4
Rheumatoid arthritis	23.8	100.0	100.0	97.3	90.5	99.6	84.1	99.8
Sickle cell disease	76.2	100.0	100.0	100.0*	98.4	100.0*	67.4	100.0*
Stroke	72.4	100.0	100.0	99.2	100.0	99.6	86.8	100.0

*Actual value slightly less than 100%. ADHD, attention deficit hyperactivity disorder; CAD, coronary artery disease; CHF, congestive heart failure; COPD, chronic obstructive pulmonary disease; fail, failure; insuf, insufficiency; NPV, negative predictive value; PPV, positive predictive value; Sens, sensitivity; Spec, specificity.

TABLE 3: Comparison of problem-only, billing-only, and problem inference rule performance

	F0.5				
	Billing (b)	Rules (r)	Problems (p)	r>b	r>p
ADHD	84.6	81.9	71.1	N	Y
Asthma/COPD	90.4	90.2	70.9	N	Y
Breast cancer	97.8	98.3	91.6	Y	Y
CAD	88.2	94.1	81.1	Y	Y
CHF	74.1	76.6	24.8	Y	Y
Diabetes	89.7	93.7	83.0	Y	Y
Glaucoma	94.4	95.6	89.2	Y	Y
Hemophilia	91.1	93.7	89.4	Y	Y
Hypertension	87.2	86.2	75.5	N	Y
Hyperthyroidism	72.3	87.5	81.4	Y	Y
Hypothyroidism	78.1	92.7	76.3	Y	Y
Myasthenia gravis	62.8	84.7	73.9	Y	Y
Osteoporosis/osteopenia	85.0	82.9	71.1	N	Y
Renal insuf/renal fail	65.0	83.8	12.9	Y	Y
Rheumatoid arthritis	86.1	81.4	48.4	N	Y
Sickle cell disease	75.3	92.9	90.6	Y	Y
Stroke	90.8	94.1	88.7	Y	Y

ADHD, attention deficit hyperactivity disorder; CAD, coronary artery disease; CHF, congestive heart failure; COPD, chronic obstructive pulmonary disease; fail, failure; insuf, insufficiency.

For each problem, we also assessed the accuracy of two simpler classes of rules including (a) problem list-only rules and (b) related billing code-only rules. The results of this analysis (table 2) showed that our inference rules were more sensitive than the problem list alone, and had better PPV than billing codes alone. Notably, all 17 of our rules had better sensitivity than the problem list (ranging from 12.8% better for hemophilia and related disorders to 95.6% better for renal insufficiency/failure). Fifteen of the 17 rules had better PPV than billing codes alone (glaucoma and renal insufficiency/failure had slightly lower PPV), with the greatest improvements being for relatively rare conditions including hyperthyroidism, myasthenia gravis, and sickle cell disease. For those billing-code only rules with a higher PPV, a significant trade-off was observed with disproportionately lower sensitivities.

For each rule, we also computed the F0.5 measure as described in the Methods section. Using F0.5, our inference rules outperformed the problem list alone for all 17 conditions and billing codes alone for 12 of the 17 conditions (table 3).

9.4 DISCUSSION

In this study, we successfully developed and validated a set of rules that identifies patients who are likely to have a particular problem. These rules were shown to have a high sensitivity and specificity and, in our population, a high positive and negative predictive value.

We found that we were able to generate and validate a large number of rules for important conditions with a relatively small team over a period of several months. The rules generally performed quite well, with high sensitivity and PPV. They also withstood validation on an independent sample of records, suggesting that our rules are not over-fitted to our training data. Thus, these methods appear to be both scalable to more conditions and replicable at other sites. Assessing their generalizability, however, will require additional independent validation at other sites.

The performance of the rules varied depending on the condition, and the performance of the renal insufficiency/failure rules deserves special comment. The National Kidney Foundation defines chronic kidney disease as kidney damage or a glomerular filtration rate of less than 60 for at least 3 months. [36] During the chart review, we found many patients meeting these criteria who had no mention of kidney disease anywhere in their record. These patients may have unappreciated renal insufficiency or failure, but were necessarily marked as condition-negative in our analysis (leading to potentially artificially low PPV and specificity). This has two important implications: first, were a different gold standard chosen (eg, evaluation by a nephrologist rather than chart review), the performance of the rules might have been different, although this is more of an issue for some rules like this one than others. Second, although these rules were initially designed to identify problems which are known to providers, they may, in certain instances, also have diagnostic utility in the case of an unappreciated condition. Similar results were reported in another study focusing on renal failure using different methods. [25]

9.4.1 COMPARISON TO OTHER METHODS

The problem list and billing data are often used to infer a patient's problems. However, our analysis indicated that each method had shortcomings. The problem list was extremely accurate (ie, one could have a high degree of confidence that a patient has a problem if it appears on the problem list), but it had very low, and variable, sensitivity. In fact, for most problems, the sensitivity was around 50%, meaning that only about half of patients with the problem had it documented on their problem list. This was higher for some chronic conditions, but was extremely low for renal failure (possibly due to the reasons discussed above) and was also quite low for congestive heart failure (CHF). The CHF finding was surprising; however, it seemed that, in many cases, the patient's CHF was so central to their clinical picture that all providers were aware of it but had simply omitted it from the problem list.

Conversely, billing codes were found to have a considerably lower PPV but a high degree of sensitivity, indicating that in some cases patients are billed for problems that they do not have. A review of these data suggests that, in many cases, patients are billed for screening tests under the related problem code (eg, billing with ICD-9 code 250.00 for a diabetes screening) rather than a screening code, which is not an ideal practice, [37] although the reasons for it are understandable.

Our research shows that the integration of laboratory, medication, billing, problem, and vital sign data can result in robust rules for inferring patient problems, and that such rules, which take advantage of multiple classes of coded data available in the electronic medical record, have superior performance to single-faceted rules.

9.4.2 APPLICATIONS

Our methods and validated knowledge base have a variety of applications. First and foremost, they could be used to alert clinicians to potential gaps in the problem list, and could provide clinicians the opportunity to correct these gaps. Additionally, the rules could be used for any application where it is important to know a patient's diagnoses, such as identification of research cohorts, calculation of quality measures, selection of patients for care management programs, and clinical decision support. To apply the rules, developers of such systems would simply modify their inclusion criteria, replacing their current mechanism of problem identification (problem list or billing data) with inference rules such as these. The use of inference rules for identifying patient problems is also of potential value for meeting meaningful use requirements. The Stage 1 goal requires that providers 'maintain an up-to-date problem list of current and active diagnoses,' with an ambitious 80% of patients having at least one problem recorded or an indication of no known problems. [38] A reliable automated method of increasing problem list use could dramatically improve providers' ability to reach this goal.

One important question for potential users of such rules at other institutions is how to proceed. Ideally, outside sites would utilize our methods to develop and validate their own rules using their own clinical data (and then report the results). However, sites without sufficient clinical data or resources might, instead, choose to use these inference rules (potentially with local modifications). We have provided the complete set of rules in online appendix A. We encourage any site choosing to apply the inference rules to report on their own experience so additional knowledge of the rules' generalizability can be developed.

9.4.3 LIMITATIONS

This investigation has several potential limitations. First, it is possible that our sampling assumptions may have introduced a small amount of bias into our results. As discussed in the Methods section, it is possible that a small proportion of patients in group I or group III, whose charts were not reviewed, may have been incorrectly classified as true negatives and true positives, respectively (because they had a problem on their problem list that they do not actually have, or because they have an undiagnosed problem, or a diagnosed problem without any correlated clinical data). It is important to note that provider awareness of a problem (or lack thereof) was our gold standard, rather than the patient's actual pathophysiologic state—in other words, we did not seek to make new diagnoses. We believe that these assumptions are reasonable given that these rules are designed to infer patient problems based on documented clinical data rather than to yield new diagnoses. Given this gold standard, we suspect that the misclassification rate into groups I and III was low; however, to test this assumption it would be necessary to bring patients in for workups to confirm their diagnoses (or lack thereof)—these workups would likely be expensive and low yield. That said, any misclassification in these groups would introduce a small bias in calculated sensitivity and PPV values (systematically increasing them); however, we believe this potential effect to be very small. Additionally, this bias would have the same effect on the statistics for our comparison groups (the problem-only and billing-only measures) in addition to our rules. As such, our comparison between these rule classes is likely unaffected by any bias introduced (and the magnitude of this bias is still likely to be very small).

Second, problems were selected in part based on the strength of laboratory-problem and medication-problem associations. This potentially limits the generalizability of our results with respect to other conditions that have weaker connections to medications and laboratory results. However, in many cases other data (eg, billing codes) may be available to help with prediction, and there are also a number of data types which we have not yet considered (particularly unstructured data such as images and text, as well as patient-reported data).

Third, as described in the Methods section, for each disease we conducted a chart review of a random sample of 100 rule-positive and 100 rule-negative patients to determine the rule's performance. We then tested a number of alternate versions of each inference rule against the same

200-patient sample for each condition. This may have introduced some bias into the performance characterization of the alternative rules, since their sample was influenced by the initial rule. To mitigate this bias, we attempted to select a 'centrist' initial rule, and then varied the parameters of the initial rule to create the alternatives, hopefully minimizing bias. Further, and more definitively, once the final rule was chosen for each condition (which could have been the initial rule or one of the alternative rules), the final rule was independently validated on a new randomly selected sample of 200 patient charts (100 rule-positive and 100 rule-negative). As such, the performance measures from the validation set were free from this potential bias.

Fourth, we developed and validated the rules at only a single site—as we mentioned above, we believe that the rules are likely generalizable to other sites, but we encourage other researchers to validate them before use, and also to extend them and report on their results.

Finally, because we included all patients with at least a single note in a 2-year period, a small number of patients in our sample had very little data recorded because they had only a single visit or a low number of visits. We chose to include these patients in order to form a more representative sample; however, our rules fired less frequently for these patients because they were less likely to have sufficient data to meet the rule thresholds (eg, multiple visits with a single billing code). Methods for adjusting inference thresholds based on the volume of data available for a patient merit further study.

9.5 CONCLUSIONS

We developed and validated a set of problem inference rules. Our findings show that by using laboratory, medication, problem, billing, and vital sign data, patient problems can be accurately inferred, and that the performance of such multi-source rules exceeds the performance of standard sources, such as the problem list or billing codes, alone. Building an improved problem list has a number of downstream potential benefits for delivering good clinical care, improving quality, and conducting research.

REFERENCES

1. Wright A, Goldberg H, Hongsermeier T, et al. A description and functional taxonomy of rule-based decision support content at a large integrated delivery network. J Am Med Inform Assoc 2007;14:489–96.
2. Weed LL. Medical records that guide and teach. New Engl J Med 1968;278:652–7.
3. Lincoln MJ. Developing and implementing the problem list. In: Kolodner R, ed. Cmputerizing Large Integrated Health Networks: The VA Success. New York: Springer, 1997:349–81.
4. Hurst JW. Ten reasons why Lawrence Weed is right. New Engl J M 1971;284:51–2.
5. Weed LL. The problem-oriented record. In: Hurst JW, Walker HK, eds. The Problem Oriented System. New York: Medcom Press, 1972:23–4.
6. Safran C, Rury C, Rind DM, et al. A computer-based outpatient medical record for a teaching hospital. MD Comput 1991;8:291–9. [
7. Feinstein AR. The problems of the "problem-oriented medical record". Ann Intern Med 1973;78:751–62.
8. Brown SH, Miller RA, Camp HN, et al. Empirical derivation of an electronic clinically useful problem statement system. Ann Intern Med 1999;131:117–26.
9. Wang SJ, Bates DW, Chueh HC, et al. Automated coded ambulatory problem lists: evaluation of a vocabulary and a data entry tool. Intern J Med Inform 2003;72:17–28.
10. Fung KW, McDonald C, Srinivasan S. The UMLS-CORE project: a study of the problem list terminologies used in large healthcare institutions. J Am Med Inform Assoc 2010;17:675–80.
11. Mantena S, Schadow G. Evaluation of the VA/KP problem list subset of SNOMED as a clinical terminology for electronic prescription clinical decision support. AMIA Annu Symp Proc 2007:498–502.
12. Nadkarni PM, Darer JA. Migrating existing clinical content from ICD-9 to SNOMED. J Am Med Inform Assoc 2010;17:602–7.
13. Campbell JR, Payne TH. A comparison of four schemes for codification of problem lists. Proc Annu Symp Comput Appl Med Care 1994:201–5.
14. Weed LL, Zimny NJ. The problem-oriented system, problem-knowledge coupling, and clinical decision making. Phys Ther 1989;69:565–8.
15. Weed LL. Knowledge coupling, medical education and patient care. Crit Rev Med Inform 1986;1:55–79. [
16. Bashyam V, Hsu W, Watt E, et al. Problem-centric organization and visualization of patient imaging and clinical data. Radiographics 2009;29:331–43.
17. Van Vleck TT, Wilcox A, Stetson PD, et al. Content and structure of clinical problem lists: a corpus analysis. AMIA Annu Symp proc 2008:753–7.
18. Kaplan DM. Clear writing, clear thinking and the disappearing art of the problem list. J Hosp Med 2007;2:199–202.
19. Szeto HC, Coleman RK, Gholami P, et al. Accuracy of computerized outpatient diagnoses in a Veterans Affairs general medicine clinic. Am J Manag care 2002;8:37–43.
20. Tang PC, LaRosa MP, Gorden SM. Use of computer-based records, completeness of documentation, and appropriateness of documented clinical decisions. J Am Med Inform Assoc 1999;6:245–51.

21. Hartung DM, Hunt J, Siemienczuk J, et al. Clinical implications of an accurate problem list on heart failure treatment. J Gen Intern Med 2005;20:143–7.
22. Carpenter JD, Gorman PN. Using medication list–problem list mismatches as markers of potential error. Proc AMIA Symp 2002:106–10.
23. Meystre S, Haug PJ. Natural language processing to extract medical problems from electronic clinical documents: performance evaluation. J Biomed Inform 2006;39:589–99.
24. Meystre SM, Haug PJ. Randomized controlled trial of an automated problem list with improved sensitivity. Int J Medical Inform 2008;77:602–12.
25. Chase HS, Radhakrishnan J, Shirazian S, et al. Under-documentation of chronic kidney disease in the electronic health record in outpatients. J Am Med Inform Assoc 2010;17:588–94.
26. Burton MM, Simonaitis L, Schadow G. Medication and indication linkage: A practical therapy for the problem list? AMIA Annu Symp Proc 2008:86–90.
27. Cao H, Markatou M, Melton GB, et al. Mining a clinical data warehouse to discover disease-finding associations using co-occurrence statistics. AMIA Annu Symp Proc 2005:106–10.
28. Wright A, Chen ES, Maloney FL. An automated technique for identifying associations between medications, laboratory results and problems. J Biomed Inform 2010;43:891–901.
29. Poissant L, Tamblyn R, Huang A. Preliminary validation of an automated health problem list. AMIA Annu Symp Proc 2005:1084.
30. Poissant L, Taylor L, Huang A, et al. Assessing the accuracy of an inter-institutional automated patient-specific health problem list. BMC Med Inform Decis Mak 2010;10:10. [
31. Denny JC, Ritchie MD, Basford MA, et al. PheWAS: demonstrating the feasibility of a phenome-wide scan to discover gene-disease associations. Bioinformatics 2010;26:1205–10.
32. Pacheco JA, Avila PC, Thompson JA, et al. A highly specific algorithm for identifying asthma cases and controls for genome-wide association studies. AMIA Annu Symp Proc 2009;2009:497–501. [
33. Denny JC, Ritchie MD, Crawford DC, et al. Identification of genomic predictors of atrioventricular conduction: using electronic medical records as a tool for genome science. Circulation 2010;122:2016–21.
34. Kullo IJ, Fan J, Pathak J, et al. Leveraging informatics for genetic studies: use of the electronic medical record to enable a genome-wide association study of peripheral arterial disease. J Am Med Inform Assoc 2010;17:568–74.
35. van Rijsbergen CJ. Information Retrieval. 2nd edn. London: Butterworths, 1979.
36. KDOQI Clinical Practice Guidelines for Chronic Kidney Disease: Evaluation, Classification, and Stratification, 2002. http://www.kidney.org/professionals/KDOQI/guidelines_ckd/p4_class_g1.htm (accessed 30 Sep 2010).
37. ICD-9-CM Coding for Diagnostic Tests, 2001. http://www.cms.gov/transmittals/downloads/AB01144.pdf (accessed 30 Sep 2010).
38. Comparison of Meaningful Use Objectives Between the Proposed Rule to the Final Rule, 2010. https://www.cms.gov/EHRIncentivePrograms/Downloads/NPRM_vs_FR_Table_Comparison_Final.pdf.

CHAPTER 10

IMPROVING COMPLETENESS OF ELECTRONIC PROBLEM LISTS THROUGH CLINICAL DECISION SUPPORT: A RANDOMIZED, CONTROLLED TRIAL

ADAM WRIGHT, JUSTINE PANG, JOSHUA C. FEBLOWITZ, FRANCINE L. MALONEY, ALLISON R. WILCOX, KAREN SAX MCLOUGHLIN, HARLEY RAMELSON, LOUISE SCHNEIDER, AND DAVID W. BATES

10.1 INTRODUCTION AND BACKGROUND

An accurate and up-to-date patient problem list represents the cornerstone of the problem-oriented medical record, especially in internal medicine. It serves as a valuable tool for providers attempting to familiarize themselves with a patient's clinical status and provides a means of succinctly communicating this information between providers. In addition, an accurate problem list has been associated with higher-quality care. [1] For example, Hartung et al found that patients with 'congestive heart failure' (CHF) on their problem list were more likely to receive ACE inhibitors or angiotensin-II receptor blockers than CHF patients without 'CHF' listed on their problem list. Further, many clinical decision support (CDS) rules use problem list entries to make inferences about patients, [2] so a complete, accurate list may facilitate more effective CDS. Conversely, an incomplete or inaccurate problem list could lead to delayed or inappropriate care. Finally, an accurate and comprehensive problem list would help to correctly identify patient populations and create patient registries conduction of quality improvement activities and research.

Despite these numerous benefits, problems lists are often inaccurate, incomplete, and out of date. [3–5] In previous research, we showed that problem list completeness in one network ranged from 4.7% for renal insufficiency or failure to 50.7% for hypertension, 61.9% for diabetes, to a maximum of 78.5% for breast cancer, [6] and other institutions have found similar results. [3–5] In addition, we have found in previous qualitative studies that provider attitudes toward, and use of, the problem list vary widely. [7, 8]

Beginning in 2011, in order to be considered 'meaningful users' of an electronic health record (EHR) and qualify to receive federal stimulus grants under the HITECH Act, which can total US$44 000 through Medicare and US$63 750 through Medicaid, providers must, among other things, 'maintain an up-to-date problem list of current and active diagnoses,' with 80% of patients having at least one problem recorded or an indication of 'no known problems.' [9–11] Given wide variation in problem list use by providers, [7, 8] new tools are needed to help providers meet this goal.

Researchers have used a variety of strategies in an attempt to detect patient problems and increase problem list use. In general, these methods fall into two broad categories: problem inference (or proxy) rules and natural language processing (NLP) techniques. Problem inference techniques use related clinical information such as laboratory tests, medications, and billing codes to infer problems (eg, a patient receiving metformin who has had multiple abnormal HbA1c tests is likely to have diabetes). In contrast, NLP strategies use algorithms designed to process and code free-text entries such as progress notes. Several groups have used data mining techniques and clinical associations to predict patient problems. [12–14] Others have reported success using NLP techniques to automate the problem list. [15–17] Prior efforts have generally been evaluated in a laboratory setting, and focused on a single or small number of problems.

In this study, we performed a cluster randomized, controlled trial of a clinical alerting system that used inference rules to detect and notify providers of undocumented problems, giving them the opportunity to correct these gaps and increase problem list completeness. Our goal was to assess whether or not this system would improve problem notation for a broad array of patient conditions.

10.2 METHODS

10.2.1 DESIGN OVERVIEW

In a prior study, we presented a novel method for developing and validating problem-inference rules, [6] as well as a knowledge base containing validated rules for 17 clinically important conditions (henceforth referred to as 'study problems'). These rules were based on previous work using data-mining techniques to identify medication-problem associations and laboratory-problem associations. [14] The rules take into account problem list entries (free-text and coded), billing diagnosis codes, laboratory results, medications, and vital signs to identify likely gaps in the problem list. Rule development and validation is described in detail in our previous work. [6] To summarize, rule development occurred in six steps: (1) identification of problem associations with structured data; (2) selection of specific problems; (3) development of preliminary rules; (4) characterization of preliminary rules and alternatives; (5) selection of a final rule; and (6) validation of the final rule. Using these rules, the average sensitivity and positive predictive value (PPV) for the training set were 83.4% and 91.1%, respectively; for the validation set, average sensitivity and PPV were comparable at 83.9% and 91.7%, respectively. Importantly, the inference rules were more sensitive than the problem list itself and had a higher PPV than billing codes. The performance of the rules is fully described in our prior paper, [6] and the contents of the rules are presented in the online appendix. As we developed the rules, we prioritized PPV and specificity in order to minimize the occurrence of false positive alerts, which might annoy users; however, for most conditions, we were able to achieve good performance on all four metrics: PPV, negative predictive value, specificity and sensitivity.

In four cases, we developed rules for groups of clinically similar entities: asthma/chronic obstructive pulmonary disease (COPD), congenital coagulopathy (hemophilia, congenital factor XI deficiency and von Willebrand disorder), osteoporosis/osteopenia, and renal failure/insufficiency. We created these groupings because, although we were able to determine, with a high degree of certainty, that the patient had one of the conditions (eg, asthma or COPD), we could not reliably discriminate between the conditions because of similar diagnostic criteria or treatment approaches. The 17 rules developed were:

- Attention deficit hyperactivity disorder
- Asthma/COPD
- Breast cancer
- Coronary artery disease (CAD)
- Congenital coagulopathy (hemophilia, congenital factor XI deficiency and von Willebrand disorder)
- CHF
- Diabetes mellitus
- Glaucoma
- Hypertension
- Hyperthyroidism
- Hypothyroidism
- Myasthenia gravis
- Osteoporosis/osteopenia
- Rheumatoid arthritis
- Renal failure/insufficiency
- Sickle cell disease
- Stroke

For each condition, problem synonyms were identified (eg, diabetes mellitus, type 2 diabetes, non-insulin-dependent diabetes mellitus). The alert would only fire if neither the problem itself nor any synonyms were present on the patient's problem list. However, hierarchically related problems did not cause suppression of the alert (eg, hyperglycemia on the problem list did not prevent the diabetes mellitus alert from displaying, nor did nephropathy prevent renal insufficiency from being suggested).

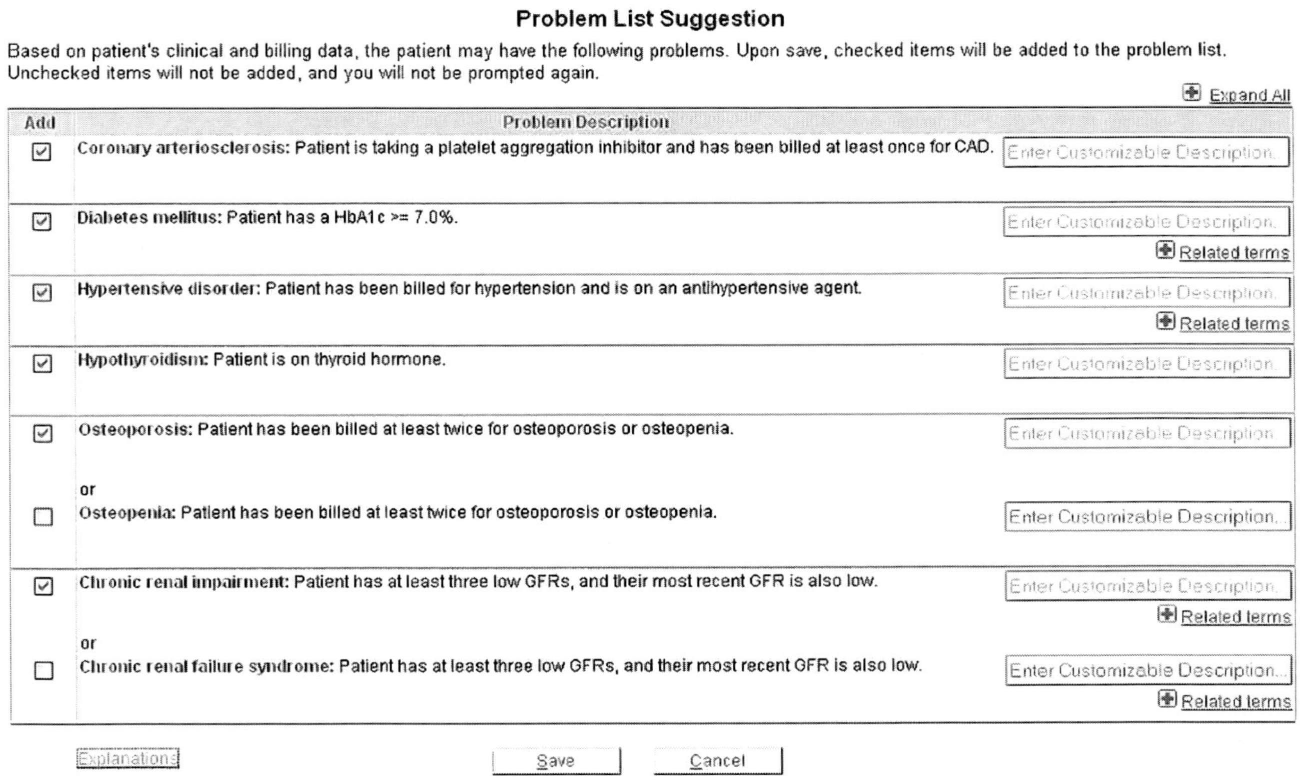

Improving Completeness of Electronic Problem Lists

Problem List Suggestion

Based on patient's clinical and billing data, the patient may have the following problems. Upon save, checked items will be added to the problem list. Unchecked items will not be added, and you will not be prompted again.

Add	Problem Description	
		⊕ Expand All
☑	Coronary arteriosclerosis: Patient is taking a platelet aggregation inhibitor and has been billed at least once for CAD.	Enter Customizable Description
☑	Diabetes mellitus: Patient has a HbA1c >= 7.0%.	Enter Customizable Description
☑	Hypertensive disorder: Patient has been billed for hypertension and is on an antihypertensive agent.	Enter Customizable Description ⊕ Related terms
☑	Hypothyroidism: Patient is on thyroid hormone.	Enter Customizable Description
☑	Osteoporosis: Patient has been billed at least twice for osteoporosis or osteopenia.	Enter Customizable Description
☐	or Osteopenia: Patient has been billed at least twice for osteoporosis or osteopenia.	Enter Customizable Description
☑	Chronic renal impairment: Patient has at least three low GFRs, and their most recent GFR is also low.	Enter Customizable Description ⊕ Related terms
☐	or Chronic renal failure syndrome: Patient has at least three low GFRs, and their most recent GFR is also low.	Enter Customizable Description ⊕ Related terms

[Explanation]   [Save]   [Cancel]

FIGURE 1: Screenshot of problem inference alerts.

The complete set of rules for the study problems is described in detail in the online appendix, which uses standard codes (LOINC, SNOMED and ICD-9) to maximize its usefulness to sites wishing to replicate our study. The longitudinal medical record (LMR), a proprietary, full-featured, outpatient EHR [18] uses proprietary codes for laboratory results and problems, and our internal rules used these codes. However, the proprietary code systems are directly mapped to LOINC and SNOMED, respectively, and we used these pre-existing mappings to create the online appendix, so the description of the rules in the appendix matches the internal logic of our system exactly.

10.2.2 SETTING AND PARTICIPANTS

Participating clinics (n=11) included all primary care practices affiliated with Brigham and Women's Hospital, an academic medical center in Boston, Massachusetts. Each practice used the LMR, which allows providers to record patient problems on an electronic problem list from a database of coded problems or as free-text entries. Participating clinics were divided into a total of 28 'clinical areas' based on pre-existing administrative divisions within the clinics (eg, suites A, B, and C or pediatric vs adult medicine).

Participating practices included both urban and suburban clinics and a diverse mixture of primary care clinics in hospital and community settings across the greater-Boston area. These practices serve a racially and socio-economically diverse population of patients.

10.2.3 RANDOMIZATION AND INTERVENTIONS

We developed an electronic alert in the LMR which notifies providers when there appears to be an undocumented problem. At the time, a provider saves a typed note or reviews a dictation, and our system analyzes the patient's medications, laboratory results, billing codes, and vital signs and uses the knowledge base to determine whether a patient is likely to have any of the 17 study problems. If the system detects one or more potential problems, it reviews the problem list to determine whether the problem is documented, and, if not, an actionable alert is shown onscreen (figure 1). If more than one undocumented problem is detected, alerts for all undocumented problems are displayed in a single window. To the right of each suggested problem is a reason why the alert is appearing. To the left is a check-box, which providers can use to select problems to add. Problems are 'pre-checked' for ease-of-use. Providers can accept the alert (in which case the problem will be added to the problem list), ignore the alert (in which case it will be presented the next time a note is completed for that patient), or over-ride the alert (in which case the alert is suppressed for the duration of the study). When the provider adds a problem, he or she is also given the opportunity to add additional details or select a related term (eg, 'gestational diabetes' or 'diabetes mellitus type 2' instead of simply 'diabetes mellitus').

We conducted a randomized controlled trial of this intervention for a 6-month period, and also collected baseline data before the intervention in order to provide a second control. To reduce the risk of contamination, we used a cluster randomization method.

Clusters (n=28) were designated on the basis of pre-existing administrative divisions within the clinics. For example, one primary care clinic is divided into adult medicine, family medicine, and pediatric medicine, and another is divided into separate suites, A, B, and C. In both cases, these subunits were treated as separate clusters. Clusters were then grouped into three bands: hospital-based, community and federally qualified health center. Once grouped into the three bands, the clusters within each band were randomly allocated to the control or intervention arms, with 14 clinics randomized to the control arm and 14 to the intervention arm.

Providers were not aware to which arm their subclinic group was assigned until the intervention was implemented. Patients were not made aware of the intervention. No pre-intervention orientation or training took place in the intervention arm. Blinding was not possible given the nature of this intervention. Data were collected over a 6-month pre-intervention period and a subsequent 6-month intervention period. The system went live on May 16, 2010 in the intervention group clinics, and post-period data were collected prospectively for 183 days (6 months) for both arms, concluding on November 14, 2010. In addition, 183 days (6 months) of pre-period data from both arms were collected retrospectively to act as a baseline. The study was approved by the Partners HealthCare Human Research Committee and was registered with ClinicalTrials.gov (NCT01105923).

10.2.4 OUTCOMES AND FOLLOW-UP

The primary outcome of this study was the acceptance rate of the alert, defined as number of alerts accepted divided by number of unique alerts presented. In certain instances, providers might see the same alert serially, so we aggregated presentations and acceptances of the same alert for the same patients in our calculation of the acceptance rate.

As a secondary outcome, we measured the number of study problems documented in the two groups during the two time periods, and calculated the unadjusted relative rate of problem notation in the intervention group by comparing the number of problems recorded in the intervention arm during the intervention period to all other groups. The unadjusted relative rate was defined as the ratio $(\text{problems}_{\text{intervention-post}}/\text{problems}_{\text{control-post}})/(\text{problems}_{\text{intervention-pre}}/\text{problems}_{\text{control-pre}})$.

10.2.5 STATISTICAL ANALYSIS

For the primary outcome, we calculated the acceptance rate of the alert for each of the 17 conditions, as well as an overall acceptance rate. For the secondary outcome of problem addition, which consisted of comparisons of count data, we modeled our data as Poisson-distributed counts. The unadjusted relative rate was calculated as described above, and tested for equality with one using a normal approximation.

In addition to this unadjusted relative rate, we used Poisson regression with an interrupted time series approach to control for potential exogenous temporal effects. Specifically, we used five coefficients and a scale parameter to model six features: starting rate, four slopes (pre and post period for the control and intervention arms), and a parameter for effect of the intervention. The effect parameter was an OR for the immediate effect of the intervention. In the case where differences between the control and intervention groups were non-significant, we removed the related terms from our model. This resulted in a new parameter for the intervention, which instead measured the overall effect of the intervention. This parameter has a similar interpretation to our unadjusted relative rate, and was compared for equality with one using a χ^2 test.

Finally, in order to counteract a possible problem of multiple comparisons, we used a Bonferroni correction. This correction maintains the error rate by testing each hypothesis against a lower α value, where the new cut-off for statistical significance is α/n, where n is the number of independent tests. In our case, the new cut-off was calculated to be 0.0029 (0.05/17 rules).

Demographic data were analyzed using a χ^2 test for categorical data and Student t test for continuous variables. Study data were analyzed using SAS V.9.2.

10.2.6 ROLE OF THE FUNDING SOURCE

This work was supported by a grant from the Partners Community HealthCare Incorporated System Improvement Grant Program. Partners Community HealthCare Incorporated was not involved in the design, execution or analysis of the study, or in the preparation of the manuscript.

10.3 RESULTS

10.3.1 PARTICIPANT FLOW

All 28 participating clinics completed the study, and there was no loss to follow-up. Overall, 41,039 patients were seen in the control clinics during the entire study period, and 38,025 patients were seen in the intervention clinics. A small number of patients (n=3,894, 5.2%) were seen in both intervention and control clinics, and thus appear in both arms of the study. Figure 2 shows the flow of subclinics through the study.

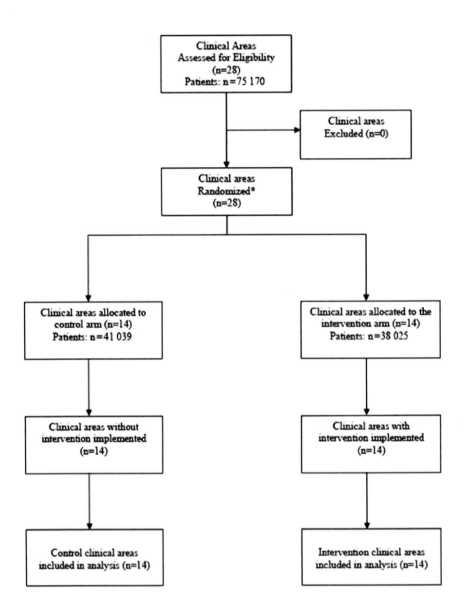

FIGURE 2: Participant flow for study clusters (subclinic randomization). Because randomization was carried out at the subclinical level, a small number of patients (n=3849) appear in both arms of the study.

10.3.2 DEMOGRAPHIC AND BASELINE DATA

Intervention and control groups appeared clinically similar across a range of demographic and clinical variables (table 1). During the 6-month pre-intervention period, greater problem list use was observed in the control group. A total of 3230 study problems (17.8 problems/day) were added in the intervention group, and 3597 study problems (19.8 problems/day) were added in the control group (p<0.001).

TABLE 1: Demographics of patients seen in control and intervention clinics

Demographic characteristic	Control	Intervention	p Value
Age (years), mean (SD)	49.6 (20.0)	47.7 (19.6)	<0.0001
Sex (female)	61.4%	68.0%	<0.0001
Race or ethnicity			
American Indian	0.12%	0.17%	<0.0001
Asian/Pacific Islander/Native Hawaiian	2.4%	3.0%	
Black	14.2%	11.4%	
Hispanic	17.1%	17.6%	
White	57.6%	58.6%	
Other	0.61%	0.55%	
Declined/unknown	7.9%	8.7%	
Language			
English	85.7%	85.3%	<0.0001
Spanish	8.8%	10.0%	
Other	5.5%	4.6%	
Primary insurance			
Commercial	59.6%	64.1%	<0.0001
Medicare	22.3%	17.7%	
Medicaid	14.0%	14.6%	
Other/self pay	4.0%	3.6%	

Income (US$), mean (SD)

10.3.3 PRIMARY OUTCOME: ACCEPTANCE RATE

Problem inference rules fired a total of 17,043 times during the intervention period for a total of 11,508 patients in the intervention arm. The overall acceptance rate for problem inference alerts was 41.1%. The highest acceptance rate of the 17 conditions was 55.7% for glaucoma alerts (table 2). Alerts for myasthenia gravis and sickle cell disease were infrequently presented and infrequently accepted.

TABLE 2: Alert acceptance rates by condition

Disease	Unique rule firings	Number of alerts accepted	Number of alerts over-ridden	Number of alerts ignored	Overall acceptance rate (%)*
Attention deficit hyperactivity disorder	225	102	31	194	45.3
Asthma/chronic obstructive pulmonary disease	2452	842	585	1867	34.3
Breast cancer	245	116	36	209	47.3
Coronary artery disease	1069	439	274	795	41.1
Congenital coagulopathy	45	15	19	26	33.3
Congestive heart failure	914	331	279	635	36.2
Diabetes mellitus	1330	519	324	1006	39.0
Glaucoma	336	187	40	296	55.7
Hypertension	5362	2281	1029	4333	42.5
Hyperthyroidism	141	46	39	102	32.6
Hypothyroidism	1291	639	220	1071	49.5
Myasthenia gravis	15	3	6	9	20.0
Osteoporosis/osteopenia	2285	962	475	1810	42.1
Rheumatoid arthritis	231	61	78	153	26.4
Renal failure/insufficiency	991	413	148	843	41.7
Sickle cell disease	12	1	7	5	8.3
Stroke	99	54	14	85	54.5
Total	17 043	7011	3604	13 439	41.1

* *Overall acceptance rate combines alerts that were accepted after being displayed multiple times (number of alerts accepted/unique rule firings).*

Improving Completeness of Electronic Problem Lists 221

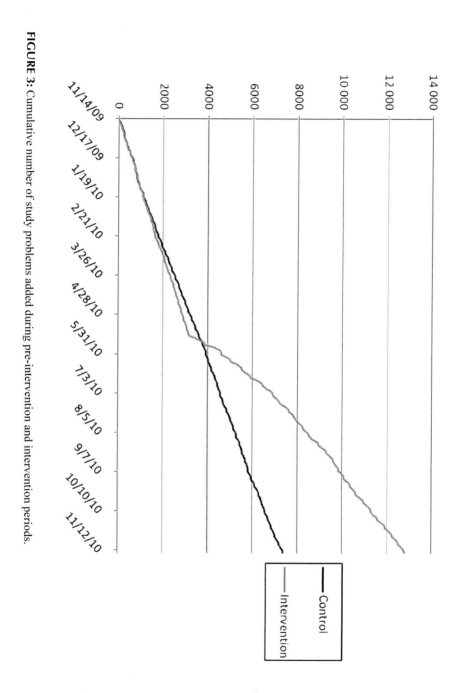

FIGURE 3: Cumulative number of study problems added during pre-intervention and intervention periods.

TABLE 3: Total study problems recorded during pre-intervention and intervention periods with unadjusted and adjusted ORs

Problem	Pre-intervention period		Intervention period		Unadjusted* comparison		Adjusted† comparison	
	Control	Intervention	Control	Intervention	Relative rate	p Value	OR	p Value
Attention deficit hyperactivity disorder	66	72	69	157	2.09	<0.0001	2.23	<0.0001
Asthma/chronic obstructive pulmonary disease	498	503	529	1291	2.42	<0.0001	2.98	<0.0001
Breast cancer	151	123	180	246	1.68	0.0004	1.78	<0.0001
Coronary artery disease	164	134	178	576	3.96	<0.0001	4.66	<0.0001
Congenital coagulopathy	4	4	5	19	3.80	0.0133	2.06	0.0384
Congestive heart failure	64	50	97	373	4.92	<0.0001	7.56	<0.0001
Diabetes mellitus	597	446	535	814	2.04	<0.0001	1.97	<0.0001
Glaucoma	53	74	61	263	3.09	<0.0001	3.78	<0.0001
Hypertension	1019	863	1031	3082	3.53	<0.0001	4.12	<0.0001
Hyperthyroidism	86	96	72	124	1.54	0.0308	1.30	0.2928
Hypothyroidism	207	237	205	823	3.51	<0.0001	3.99	<0.0001
Myasthenia gravis	4	2	3	5	3.33	0.2850	2.10	0.114
Osteoporosis/osteopenia	513	483	582	1521	2.78	<0.0001	3.40	<0.0001
Rheumatoid arthritis	27	21	24	75	4.02	<0.0001	3.97	<0.0001
Renal failure/insufficiency	84	73	87	521	6.89	<0.0001	8.22	<0.0001
Sickle cell disease	9	12	13	23	1.33	0.3538	1.66	0.2897
Stroke	51	37	68	103	2.09	0.0023	2.35	0.0002
Total	3597	3230	3739	10 016	2.98	<0.0001	3.43	<0.0001

* Unadjusted comparison based on unadjusted relative rate of problem list addition, as described in the methods sections. † Adjusted comparison based on Poisson regression model for an interrupted time

10.3.4 PRE-SPECIFIED SECONDARY OUTCOME: PROBLEM NOTATION IN THE PROBLEM LIST

During the intervention period, 10,016 study problems were added in the intervention group compared with 3739 added in the control group—an absolute difference of 6277 problems (compared with 367 fewer problems added in the intervention group during the pre-intervention period, $p<0.0001$). The unadjusted relative rate of study problem addition was 2.98 times more problem notation in the intervention group ($p<0.0001$), and the adjusted OR was 3.43 ($p<0.0001$).

The cumulative number of study problems added over the course of the entire study is shown in figure 3. As reflected in the figure, the rate of study problem notation during the pre-intervention period was slightly lower in the intervention group than in the control group. The inflection point in the intervention group line was coincident with the initiation of the study intervention in that group and, by the completion of the study, the intervention group had added significantly more problems than the control group.

Table 3 shows the rate of problem list addition for each of the 17 study problems. Using the unadjusted differences measure, statistically significant increases in problem notation were seen for 15 of 17 study problems using an uncorrected threshold of $p<0.05$. When the Bonferroni correction was applied to the threshold, two of the 15 problems were no longer statistically significant (congenital coagulopathy and hyperthyroidism). Relative rates of problem notation (for statistically significant conditions) ranged from 1.54 times more notation for hyperthyroidism ($p=0.031$) to 6.89 times more notation for renal failure and insufficiency ($p<0.0001$).

In addition to the unadjusted difference, we used Poisson regression and interrupted time series analysis to control for temporal trends. We began with a model with four slopes (results not shown). Outcomes from this model were similar to unadjusted results; however, the increases for congenital coagulopathy and hyperthyroidism were no longer statistically significant (at either $p<0.05$ or the Bonferroni-corrected threshold of $p<0.0029$). After removal of non-significant model components (yielding a simplified two-slope model shown on the right-hand side of table 3), the difference for congenital coagulopathy was once again statistically significant; however, when the Bonferroni correction was used, this study problem was not statistically significant. ORs from the final model were mostly similar to the unadjusted relative rates, and the overall OR for intervention effect on problem list notation was 3.43 (p<0.0001).

To assess the accuracy of problems added as the result of the intervention, we also conducted an audit of a random selection of accepted alerts (n=1178). In order to form a representative sample, we used a weighting strategy. Each of the 17 may have been suggested on the basis of one or more condition sets (eg, a diabetes suggestion could be triggered by the HbA1c value, medications, billing codes, or a combination of these features). For each condition set, we reviewed the accuracy of up to 30 alerts (less if there were fewer than 30 total accepted alerts for a given condition set). Study staff (FM) conducted a manual chart review, including a review of the notes. The gold standard was free-text documentation of the problem in any stored physician notes. We computed a weighted accuracy score by taking the accuracy for each condition set and weighting it according to how often that condition set triggered an alert. The weighted accuracy of all accepted alerts was found to be 89.8%. The 10.2% of alert acceptances not associated with documentation had a variety of causes, including patients near to diagnosis of a disease (eg, patients with prediabetes or metabolic syndrome on the cusp of diagnosis with diabetes), patients who appeared to actually meet diagnostic criteria for the disease, but for whom the diagnosis was not discussed in the record (eg, patients who met diagnostic criteria for chronic kidney disease based on glomerular filtration rate or hypertension based on serial blood pressure measures but without documentation of the condition in their notes), as well as some potentially erroneous additions.

10.4 DISCUSSION

We found that electronic problem list alerts were often accepted by users, and resulted in a substantial increase in study problem notation. The rate of notation of study problems increased dramatically during the intervention period as a result of this simple alert-based intervention. Overall, study problems were approximately three times more likely to be documented when alerts were shown. This increase is clinically important, since many of these problems are used for quality improvement and CDS.

Importantly, 14 out of 17 study problems were more often recorded in the intervention group than the control group. Only three conditions, myasthenia gravis, sickle cell disease, and hyperthyroidism, had similar rates between the two groups; however, even though the difference for hyperthyroidism was not statistically significant with Bonferroni correction, one could infer that there may be a trend for possible statistical significance with a larger sample size. Since our previous research validated the algorithm for the study problems, [6] it is probable that the overall low prevalence of myasthenia gravis and sickle cell disease is responsible for the lack of any difference in notation between study arms.

Our results suggest that problem inference rules such as these are a valuable tool for improving problem list completeness and thus may be beneficial for improving patient care. A more complete problem list makes it easier for providers to obtain an accurate picture of a patient's issues, which is especially important when an unfamiliar patient is being seen, such as in the case of urgent care or emergency visits, or in inpatient wards. Additionally, since problems are used for CDS, identification of patients for research studies, and quality measurement, these types of rules show great potential for improving quality and reducing costs.

One important question is how the observed increase in the notation of problems would ultimately benefit patients. Assuming that a given alert was correct, there were two potential scenarios for each alert reminder: (1) the alert called attention to an undocumented problem that the provider was not aware of and (2) the alert recommended a problem that the provider was aware of but had not documented in the problem list. Although the first scenario may provide a particular immediate clinical impact (making the provider aware of an unknown diagnosis), it is also likely to be less common. However, both cases provide significant positive clinical benefit, including enabling CDS (such as relevant preventive care reminders), facilitating quality measurement and research, and promoting awareness of a patient's active problems among the entire care team (including providers that may not know the patient well).

An additional implication of this study may be to help providers achieve 'meaningful use' of EHRs, as one of the stage 1 and 2 meaningful use goals is to demonstrate problem list use for 80% of patients over the next few years. [9 ,10] By meeting the meaningful use criteria, clinicians would receive incentive funds that could offset the expenses of implementing and maintaining the LMR. A tool such as that described here may be highly valuable for encouraging problem list use and increasing accuracy in the near term, especially for the large numbers of providers who are just starting with electronic records and are struggling to populate their problem lists.

Given these promising results and diverse potential applications, we hope to dramatically expand the problem inference knowledge base in the future. Ultimately, rules such as these may be used in tandem with provider documentation to increase the accuracy of the problem list, with the potential to improve patient care. However, additional provider engagement will also be required, and some problem list maintenance tasks (such as the removal of resolved problems or consolidation of duplicates) are beyond the scope of our described intervention.

10.4.1 LIMITATIONS

Our investigation has several potential limitations. First, problem inference rules were developed, validated, and tested at a single site. Further research will need to be carried out to assess the generalizability of these results. Additionally, we had the benefit of a self-developed EHR, giving us the ability to extract the necessary data to develop and validate our knowledge base, as well as the ability to design a novel intervention. In contrast, most institutions use commercial EHR systems, which may not have this degree of flexibility. Although we encourage other institutions to develop and validate their own rules when feasible, we have also made our full knowledge base freely available for use by other organizations, including vendors. [6] Another possible limitation of this approach is that imperfect accuracy of the problem inference rules could lead to erroneous alerts, which, if accepted, would result in inaccurate problems being added to the problem list. An audit of a random selection of accepted alerts revealed a global weighted accuracy of 89.8%. Although the accuracy of accepted alerts was very high overall, this finding nevertheless reveals the presence of a number of problems erroneously added to the problem list as a result of the alerts. Many of these instances appeared to be the result of borderline conditions (eg, metabolic syndrome, white-coat hypertension). However, the potential problem of providers accepting erroneous clinical alerts merits further study. Additionally, the overall acceptance rate for the alerts was 41.1%, with the rest of the alerts being either over-ridden or ignored by physicians. Since the accuracy of the accepted alerts was shown to be high in the above-described audit, future research should look into the reasons why alerts are either over-ridden or ignored. Finally, the intervention was limited to primary care providers; extending this tool to specialties may require more focus on the types of alerts presented.

10.5 CONCLUSION

Problem inference alerts appear to be a powerful tool for improving notation of patient problems, and may thus in turn help improve quality of care. The use of problem inference alerts dramatically increased the notation of patient problems in the intervention group. Healthcare providers seeking to increase problem list completeness for meaningful use or other reasons should consider implementing such alerts. Future studies should focus on whether implementing such alerts has a direct effect on patient outcomes.

REFERENCES

1. Hartung DM, Hunt J, Siemienczuk J, et al. Clinical implications of an accurate problem list on heart failure treatment. J Gen Intern Med 2005;20:143–7.
2. Wright A, Goldberg H, Hongsermeier T, et al. A description and functional taxonomy of rule-based decision support content at a large integrated delivery network. J Am Med Inform Assoc 2007;14:489–96.
3. Kaplan DM. Clear writing, clear thinking and the disappearing art of the problem list. J Hosp Med 2007;2:199–202.
4. Szeto HC, Coleman RK, Gholami P, et al. Accuracy of computerized outpatient diagnoses in a Veterans Affairs general medicine clinic. Am J Manag Care 2002;8:37–43.

5. Tang PC, LaRosa MP, Gorden SM. Use of computer-based records, completeness of documentation, and appropriateness of documented clinical decisions. J Am Med Inform Assoc 1999;6:245–51.
6. Wright A, Pang J, Feblowitz JC, et al. A method and knowledge base for automated inference of patient problems from structured data in an electronic medical record. J Am Med Inform Assoc 2011;18:859–67.
7. Feblowitz J, Wright A. The Patient Problem List: an Ethnographic Study of Primary Care Provider Use and Attitudes. Washington, DC: AMIA 2011 Annual Symposium, 2011. under review.
8. Wright A, Maloney FL, Feblowitz JC. Clinician attitudes toward and use of electronic problem lists: a Thematic analysis. BMC Med Inform Decis Mak 2011;11:36.
9. Comparison of Meaningful Use Objectives Between the Proposed Rule to the Final Rule. 2010. https://www.cms.gov/EHRIncentivePrograms/Downloads/NPRM_vs_FR_Table_Comparison_Final.pdf (accessed 13 Jun 2010).
10. Blumenthal D, Tavenner M. The "meaningful use" regulation for electronic health records. N Engl J Med 2010;363:501–4.
11. Jha AK. Meaningful use of electronic health records:the road ahead. JAMA 2010;304:1709–10.
12. Burton MM, Simonaitis L, Schadow G. Medication and indication linkage: a practical therapy for the problem list? AMIA Annu Symp Proc 2008:86–90.
13. Cao H, Markatou M, Melton GB, et al. Mining a clinical data warehouse to discover disease-finding associations using co-occurrence statistics. AMIA Annu Symp Proc 2005:106–10.
14. Wright A, Chen ES, Maloney FL. An automated technique for identifying associations between medications, laboratory results and problems. J Biomed Inform 2010;43:891–901.
15. Chase HS, Radhakrishnan J, Shirazian S, et al. Under-documentation of chronic kidney disease in the electronic health record in outpatients. J Am Med Inform Assoc 2010;17:588–94.
16. Meystre S, Haug P. Improving the sensitivity of the problem list in an intensive care unit by using natural language processing. AMIA Annu Symp Proc 2006:554–8.
17. Meystre SM, Haug PJ. Randomized controlled trial of an automated problem list with improved sensitivity. Int J Med Inform 2008;77:602–12.
18. Poon EG, Wald J, Bates DW, et al. Supporting patient care beyond the clinical encounter: three informatics innovations from partners health care. AMIA Annu Symp Proc 2003:1072.

There are several supplemental files that are not available in this version of the article. To view this additional information, please use the citation on the first page of this chapter.

CHAPTER 11

COMPUTERIZED PHYSICIAN ORDER ENTRY OF MEDICATIONS AND CLINICAL DECISION SUPPORT CAN IMPROVE PROBLEM LIST DOCUMENTATION COMPLIANCE

WILLIAM L. GALANTER, DANIEL B. HIER, CHIANG JAO, AND DAVID SARNE

11.1 INTRODUCTION

The problem list is a key and required [1] element of both the paper record and EMR. Weed [2] and [3] popularized the use of the problem list in an influential book and papers. Benson et al [4] have argued that the "problem list and the medication record are particularly useful for providing an overview of patients' significant diagnoses and treatments. If well-structured, reliable, and consistent, they can also contribute substantially to the quality of patient care." An accurate problem list facilitates automated decision support, clinical research, data mining, and patient care [4], [5] and [6]. The Joint Commission on the Accreditation of Healthcare

---

Reprinted from International Journal of Medical Informatics, *79(5), Galanter WL, Hier DB, Jao C, and Sarne D, Computerized Physician Order Entry of Medications and Clinical Decision Support Can Improve Problem List Documentation Compliance, pp. 332–338, Copyright 2010, with permission from Elsevier.*

Organizations [1] mandates maintenance of a problem list. The problem list can be a useful tool in both paper records and EMRs for organizing physician notes, making patient rounds, and "signing out" patients to covering physicians [7] and [8].

The advent of EMRs could significantly increase the potential power and importance of the problem list. Database links and pointers could make the problem list a true "index" to the EMR as originally conceived by Weed [2] and [3]. For example, selecting a problem off the problem list (e.g. hypertension) could link to all relevant healthcare encounters for hypertension, all relevant laboratory results, and radiology reports that mention the diagnosis of hypertension, or link to all drugs that treat hypertension. Furthermore, detailed electronic problem lists can facilitate the development of CDS, patient registries and research. There is little information on the accuracy of problem list maintenance at either teaching or non-teaching hospitals. A limited study in the adoption of EMRs revealed that users produce more complete problem lists in an EMR than in the paper medical record [9]. However, in a study of the Veterans Administration EMR [10], the sensitivity of the electronic problem list for the diagnosis of hypertension was only 49%. Campbell [11] has attributed poor clinician compliance with the problem list to "minimal rewards for the clinician".

In an audit of 105 outpatients seen in the Neurology Clinic at the University of Illinois Medical Center in 2002, 19% of the medical records had no problems of any kind listed on the electronic problem list and 39% had no problem on the electronic problem list related to the current visit [12]. Furthermore, 47% of the problems were entered as "free text" rather than as codified discrete ICD-9-CM [13], ICD-10 [14], or SNOMED®[15] codes. In an audit of inpatient medical records we compared the problem list as reported in the medical record with the problem list as ascertained by chart review [12]. The number of problems on the problem lists was roughly only a quarter of those found by auditing the chart, while 46% of the charts had an empty problem list. Problem list under documentation is certainly not unique to our institution, a recent study from intermountain health care also reported that their problems lists are "Usually incomplete and inaccurate, and are often totally unused" [16].

One of the potential causes of poor problem list documentation is the use of controlled terminologies; ICD-9-CM [13], ICD-10 [14], or

SNOMED®[15], which may not be ideal for documentation of problems in a problem list [17] and [18]. There are many reasons that problem list use may be underutilized [17] and [18] which may help explain the interest in "free text" problems by users. One of the strategies to improve the use of standardized terminologies has been the development of information technology to convert non-standardized problems into local controlled terminologies [16], [19], [20] and [21] as well as standard terminologies such as SNOMED®[15] and [22].

More accurate problem lists may lead to higher levels of patient safety and lower levels of medical error. Carpenter and Gorman [23] have tested a natural language processor that detects medication errors based upon a mismatch between the drug ordered and problems that reside on the problem list. For example, if a drug does not match up with a problem, either the problem list is deficient and needs to be updated or the drug has been ordered in error and needs to be deleted. A theoretical CDS prototype [24] and [25] has been tested and suggested that integration of problem list maintenance into CPOE workflow may promote better problem list documentation. In this study, we have tested a CDS system that helps maintain the electronic problem list in a real-time clinical environment. The CDS system is triggered by drug orders in CPOE to generate alerts to providers who then have the option to update the electronic problem list by a simple automated process.

11.2 METHODS

11.2.1 EMR, CPOE, CDS AND PROBLEM LIST ENVIRONMENT

The University of Illinois Hospital, a 450-bed teaching hospital, utilizes a commercially available EMR (*Millennium®*, Cerner Corporation, Kansas City, MO) which is used as the primary repository for all results, problem lists, clinical notes, medication lists, and orders. All inpatient medication orders are placed using CPOE. The commercially available CDS (*Discern Expert®*, Cerner Corporation) has been previously described [26], [27] and [28].

Our problem list is multidisciplinary, allowing any clinician to enter problems either codified or as free text. Codified problems could use either ICD-9 CM [13], ICD-10 [14], or SNOMED®[15] codes.

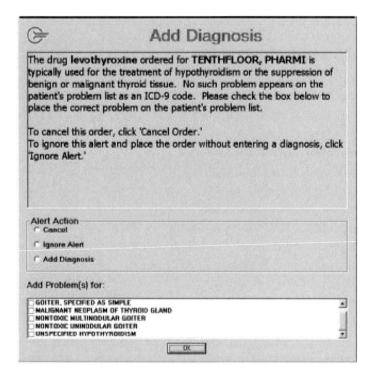

FIGURE 1: Example of a medication-diagnosis link alert. The alert is for an order for levothyroxine in a test patient.

11.2.2 DEVELOPMENT OF ALERTS

A system of alerts are delivered to clinicians during medication CPOE. These alerts prompt clinicans to place a diagnosis on the problem list as a pop-up when the medication order is initiated. For each medication ordered, one or more diagnoses can be proposed. The clinician can place more than one diagnosis if desired. An example alert is triggered by the ordering of levothyroxine (Fig. 1). Placing a diagnosis requires 3 mouse

TABLE 1: Target diagnosis groups and medication triggers used in the CDS intervention

Target diagnosis group name	All ICD-9 diagnoses in group	Medication triggers
Diabetes mellitus (DM)	Diabetes mellitus (250.00)	Exenatide, meglitinides, metformin, pioglitazone, rosiglitazone, sulfonyluria
	polycystic ovarian syndrome (256.4)	
Hypothyroidism	Goiter (240.0)	Levothyroxine
	Hypothyroidism (244.9)	
	Multinodular goiter (241.1)	
	Solitary thyroid nodule (241)	
	thyroid cancer (193)	
Hyperlipidemia, Coronary atherosclerosis	Unspecified hyperlipidemia (272.4)	Niacin, cholestyramine, colesevelam, colestipol, ezetimibe, fenofibrate, gemfibrozil, HMG-CoA reductase inhibitors
	coronary atherosclerosis (414.00)	
Human immunodeficiency virus (HIV)	Human immunodeficiency virus [HIV] disease (042)	Combination medications, fusion inhibitors, nucleoside reverse transcriptase inhibitor, non-nucleoside reverse transcriptase inhibitor, protease inhibitors.
Asthma, chronic obstructive pulmonary disease	Asthma unspecified (493.90)	Fluticasone inhaled, fluticasone/salmeterol inhaled, tiotroprium inhaled
	asthma unspecified with exacerbation (493.92)	
	obstructive chronic bronchitis without exacerbation unspecified (491.20)	
	obstructive chronic bronchitis with exacerbation unspecified (491.21)	
Ischemic stroke, transient ischemic attack (TIA)	Cerebral thrombosis with cerebral infarction (434.01)	Dipyridamole/aspirin (aggrenox)
	cerebral embolism with cerebral infarction (434.11)	
	cerebral thrombosis without mention of cerebral infarction (434.00)	

More then one diagnosis could be proposed for each medication and a diagnosis could be associated with more than one medication.

clicks, while not placing a diagnosis requires 2. This is significantly less than is required to place a diagnosis in this EMR without this type of alert.

The particular combinations of diagnosis to medications associations were chosen based on associations which were likely to yield accurate additions to the problem list. This was determined by choosing medications whose use was limited to a small number of specific indications, whether Food and Drug Authority (FDA) approved or not. Medications with very broad and unpredictable indications, or whose use was not indicative of useful diagnoses were not chosen. An example of an excellent medication would be an oral antidiabetic medication like a sulfonyuria which is almost always used in diabetes mellitus, while a medication that would perform very poorly would be acetaminophen, which is used to treat the pain or fever associated with likely hundreds of diagnoses.

There was a single gender difference in all the alerts, the alert based on an order for metformin allowed for addition of a diagnosis of polycystic ovarian syndrome (ICD-9 256.4) in women, but not in men.

As currently constructed, the CDS system cannot in general produce a complete problem list. Rather, the CDS functions to make a limited number of accurate additions to the problem list based on medication orders. The proposed diagnostic list was reviewed by experts in the relevant clinical domains. If an appropriate problem was already active in the problem list, the logic was constructed so that the alert did not fire. The list of appropriate diagnoses used to prevent the alert from firing was extensive in order to decrease the nuisance of alerts firing when a diagnosis was already in place. The lists were developed by content experts using SNOMED [15] hierarchies and ICD-9 CM [13] three digit codes. The alerts were designed for a limited set of medications that triggered additions of a specific set of six target diagnostic categories (Table 1).

11.2.3 OBSERVATIONAL TRIAL

The alerts were implemented in a staggered manner over a 3-month period. Each alert was analyzed for 2 months after implementation. On occasion, after an alert triggered, clinicians would cancel attempts at ordering and rapidly retry placing the order, we assume in order to see if the alert would appear again. Therefore duplicate alerts that occurred within 1 h of an initial alert triggered by the same clinician were counted as a single alert. For each alert, the medical record was reviewed to determine whether the clinical data supported the addition of a problem to the problem list. Medical record review was completed by a clinician with expertise in the particular clinical domain. Presence of a "free text" problem was not assumed to be proof of a diagnosis, as the presence of a diagnosis was based on the clinical judgment after review of the full chart.

If there were greater than 100 alerts in the 2-month period for a target diagnosis group, a random sample of 100 alerts was selected for analysis. For each of the six alerts (Table 1) the following variables were measured: total number of alerts, alerts in which the diagnosis was confirmed by domain expert review, alerts which led the clinician to add a diagnosis to the problem list, and alerts which led clinician to add a diagnosis which was confirmed by expert review. We defined the following proportions:

Alert Validity = proportion of alerts for which a clinical domain expert confirmed the diagnosis was present.

Problem List Yield = proportion of alerts which led clinicians to add a problem to the problem list.

Problem Addition Accuracy = proportion of clinician problem list additions confirmed by expert review (this is 1 minus the rate of false positive problem list additions).

For each proportion, the standard error of proportion (SEP) was calculated.

11.3 RESULTS

The total number of alerts for all target diagnosis groups in their 2-month sample observation periods was 1011 (Table 2). Of the six categories of alerts, the hyperlipidemia-coronary atherosclerosis alerts fired most often followed by the diabetes alerts. The overall alert validity was 96 ± 1% (Table 2). The highest levels of validity for the alerts were for diabetes and hyperlipidemia, the lowest levels of validity were for ischemic stroke and HIV (Table 2).

TABLE 2: Alert validity, problem list yield, and problem addition accuracy by alert type

Target diagnosis group name	Number of alerts (2-months)	Sample size	Valid alerts (%)	Alert yield (%)	Problem addition accuracy (1 − false positive's) (%)
Hyperlipidemia	442	100	100	72 ± 4a	94 ± 3
Diabetes Mellitus	204	100	99 ± 1	79 ± 4	100
Hypothyroidism	161	100	95 ± 2	84 ± 4	93 ± 3
Asthma/COPD	139	100	93 ± 3	79 ± 5	92 ± 3
HIV	49	49	76 ± 6	69 ± 7	100%
Ischemic stroke	16	16	69 ± 12	62 ± 12	80 ± 13
Total	1011	465	96 ± 1	76 ± 2	95 ± 1

[a]All results are proportion ± SEP. The total proportions are weighted by the number of alerts in each alert type.

When triggered, alerts led to an addition to the problem list in 76 ± 2% of instances, with a range of 62–84% based on the diagnosis group. The average rate of problem list additions over a 2-month period was roughly 13 problems/day for this initial set of alerts.

The accuracy of the problem list additions was determined by expert clinician chart review. Overall the accuracy of problem list additions was 95 ± 1%, or stated another way, the false positive rate was 5%. The target diagnosis groups with the highest problem list accuracy were HIV and diabetes with 100% of the problem list additions considered clinically appropriate. The lowest rate of problem list accuracy was 80% for ischemic stroke and TIA.

11.4 DISCUSSION

We have demonstrated the feasibility of using CDS driven by medication orders from CPOE to assist in the maintenance of the problem list. Problems can be added to the problem list during the routine work of placing medication orders with less clicks than would otherwise be needed in the EMR studied.

We believe that this CDS system has been well received at our institution due to the relatively high compliance rate. This is likely due to the reduction in the labor, or number of screens and clicks involved in adding a problem to the problem list. Although clinician acceptance was not assessed, during the study period there was only one clinician complaint received by Information Services. This complaint was related to a disagreement with the diagnosis prompted by the CDS, rather than with wasted time or annoyance.

The rate of problem list documentation from the alerts was relatively high as compared to other rates of CDS compliance at our institution [27] and [28]. Roughly 75% of the alerts yielded an addition to the problem list. The alerts only required the clinicians to agree with one of the proposed diagnoses by checking a checkbox in the alert. However, as is often the case with alerts, non-compliance can occur even when the actions are clear or simple. In the instance of the hyperlipidemia alerts, 100% of the patients had a valid predefined triggering diagnosis, yet only 72% of the time did clinicians add the problem to the problem list. In this particular case, either a misunderstanding of the alert, or an aversion to complying with the alert reduced the yield of the alert by 28%.

CDS that utilizes the ordering of medications to trigger additions to the problem list has several limitations and cannot fully maintain a problem list. First, this system cannot add problems to the problem list when no specific medication therapy exists for a condition. For example, in the case of cervical myelopathy, there is no specific medication order which would trigger the addition of this diagnosis to the problem list. Second, CDS that depends on medication orders to trigger additions to the problem list will work best with medications that have few indications, while many commonly used medications have numerous indications, both FDA approved and off label. Since we chose a fairly limited set of medications, we did not get involved with decisions regarding medications that may perform only marginally in this type of CDS and produce as much nuisance as benefit. We felt that the medications we chose had clearly limited indications and our data suggest the utility of these choices. Medications that would clearly be problematic would be those that treat common symptoms like inflammation or pain, specifically acetaminophen and ibuprofen, being good examples of medications whose use typically does not clearly indicate a specific diagnosis.

Another reason that a CDS system that depends upon medication orders to drive additions to the problem list will not be able to completely fill a problem list is that some medications are prescribed for unusual indications, even though infrequently. This difficulty is reflected in our observation that the diagnosis offered by the CDS was valid in only 96% of the cases (Table 2) consistent with the fact that medications are not always prescribed for commonly accepted indications.

A last limitation of this type of CDS is that it would trigger in error if the problem list contained problems as "free text". Our logic checked to see if a problem was on the problem list before firing, but only if encoded as SNOMED [15] or ICD-9-CM [13] codes and would fail to catch diagnoses that were simply "free text". In those cases, the CDS would prompt the physician to add the diagnosis even though it was already on the problem list in free text form which would likely be perceived as annoying. This of course could be overcome in future versions of this type of system if capable of natural language processing [16] in real time, or by removal of the option to add problems "free text".

The ability of this type of CDS to more fully maintain a problem list could be increased by driving the CDS off orders other than medications, such as radiology, laboratory, and consultations as well as results from these areas. We are beginning to design such alerts and hope to improve our ability to maintain our problem list, but this needs to be studied.

A major risk of this type of CDS is that it could lead to the addition of erroneous diagnoses to the problem list, thus an important measure of success, as well as safety, of the CDS was how often the diagnosis added by the alert was accurate. Overall, only 5% of the added diagnoses were found to be incorrect after expert review. Errors may occur because the "pick list" of diagnoses is too long and causes clinicians to lose interest or be careless. Errors may also occur if the correct diagnosis was not included as an option. In our case, we did not require the clinician to pick a diagnosis to complete the order (the provider could choose to ignore the "add diagnosis" alert). Requiring the clinician to provide a diagnosis would have produced a system closer to indication based prescribing [29] and [30], but would have likely caused more errors in the additions to the problem list.

Clinicians may also have confusion with regard to which diagnosis to select from the list of diagnoses. For example, clinicians made errors when prompted by alerts from the asthma/chronic obstructive pulmonary disease (COPD) target diagnosis group. While our expert chart reviewers distinguished between COPD (ICD-9 491) and asthma (ICD-9 493), many of our housestaff clinicians chose asthma when the patient had COPD and vice-versa. This also occurred for the hyperlipidemia/coronary atherosclerosis alert where the problem addition accuracy was lower than the alert validity, meaning that some clinicians added the problem of coronary atherosclerosis (414.00) to the problem list when the patient instead only had hyperlipidemia (272.4). It would be interesting in the future to see if this type of information could be used to measure and correct knowledge gaps.

One potential benefit of this form of CDS is the ability to prevent inappropriate drug use. Though this study was not powered to examine this effect, analysis of the triggers and charts showed that on some occasions the prompt to add a diagnosis led to the cancellation of the medication order without any attempt to re-order it. It is very possible that these were either attempts at erroneous orders or non-indicated usages. It will be of interest to study this system further to try to obtain a quantitative measure of its ability to prevent inappropriate medication orders by linking medication orders to the problem list. Such an effect might help diminish potential medication errors [31] as well as inappropriate off label prescribing [32] being executed.

This system does not behave as mandated indication based prescribing as once a diagnosis is documented, the alerts for that diagnosis will not fire again in the future even if the drug is reordered. This design was based in our interest in decreasing the intrusiveness and annoyance of the system.

Our goal was improving problem list documentation rather than creating a system of mandatory indication-based prescribing. It is likely in the future that CDS systems can accomplish both functions by prompting for diagnostic indication when not documented, but then saving the association between the noted indication and the medication so that clinicians will not be required to have to respond to the CDS with each medication order. The final mechanism for this type of system will be based on both software development as well as any future regulatory guidelines for prescribing. It is possible that in the future, "ordering by indication" will become mandatory due to patient safety purposes [29] and [30] and regulations, similar to the indication-based mandate for laboratory testing for Medicare reimbursement [33]. CDS similar to our system may prove useful in expediting the process of matching medications to indications on the problem list.

11.5 LIMITATIONS

This analysis was limited to inpatient order entry with CPOE. Although we use the same EMR in the ambulatory environment, electronic prescribing was not fully implemented in the ambulatory setting to test whether outpatient prescribing would be similarly successful in generating additions to the problem list. In addition, our institution is a public teaching hospital with the majority of orders placed by housestaff physicians using CPOE. While the CDS could be implemented regardless of the type of clinicians placing the medication orders, it is not clear that our efficacy findings would be generalizable to non-university hospital settings where orders are placed more commonly by providers such as attending physicians or advanced practice nurses.

While problem list documentation is a JCAHO requirement and has theoretical promise in research and clinical care, this study did not directly make any measurements on the actual quality, safety or cost of care. It is important that future studies are conducted to answer whether improvements in discrete problem list maintenance will translate into clinically important outcomes.

Another limitation of this study is that our institution, like others, struggled with problem list documentation in part due to the difficulties of using ICD-9-CM [13] with no mapping to the more clinically expressive SNOMED®[15] until after this study was completed. A lower than typical level of problem list documentation would probably tend to make this type of decision support more robust, though the tool should be useful in any institution that has less than perfect native problem list documentation.

11.6 CONCLUSIONS

In summary, this novel CDS worked within the process of medication ordering at our institution. It was successful in improving problem list documentation with minimal diagnostic inaccuracies. Future work should be focused on expanding this work to more medications as well as for use in all forms of clinician orders to increase the scope of problems that can be added to the problem list through this type of CDS coupled to CPOE.

REFERENCES

1. Comprehensive Accreditation Manual for Hospitals, The Joint Commission on Accreditation of Healthcare Organizations, Oakbrook Terrace, IL, 1996.
2. L.L. Weed. Medical records that guide and teach. N. Engl. J. Med., 278 (1968), pp. 593–600
3. L.L. Weed. Medical Records, Medical Education, and Patient Care. Yearbook Medical Publishers, Chicago (1969)
4. D.S. Benson, W. Van Osdol, P. Townes. Quality ambulatory care: the role of the diagnostic and medication summary lists. Qual. Rev. Bull., 14 (6) (1988), pp. 192–197
5. M.E. Johnston, K.B. Langton, R.B. Haynes, A. Mathieu. Effects of computer-based clinical decision support systems on clinician performance and patient outcome: a critical appraisal of research. Ann. Intern. Med., 120 (2) (1994), pp. 135–142
6. A. Rothschild, D.B. Hier, A. LeMaistre, J. Keeler. Enthusiastic Adopter and Reluctant Users: Faculty Physician Attitude towards an Electronic Health Record One-Year after Implementation. University of Illinois Hospital Internal Document (2000)
7. U. Sarkar, J.T. Carter, T.A. Omachi, A.R. Vidyarthi, R. Cucina, S. Bokser et al.. Synopsis: integrating physician sign-out with the electronic medical record. J. Hosp. Med., 2 (5) (2007), pp. 336–342
8. G. Frank, S.T. Lawless, T.H. Steinberg. Improving physician communication through an automated, integrated sign-out system. J. Healthc. Inf. Manag., 19 (4) (2005), pp. 68–74
9. P.C. Tang, M.P. LaRosa, S.M. Gorden. Use of computer-based records, completeness of documentation, and appropriateness of documented clinical decisions. J. Am. Med. Inform. Assoc., 6 (1999), pp. 245–251

10. H.C. Szeto, R.K. Coleman, P. Gholami, B.B. Hoffman, M.K. Goldstein. Accuracy of computerized outpatient diagnoses in a Veterans Affairs general medicine clinic. Am. J. Manag. Care, 8 (2002), pp. 37–43
11. J.R. Campbell. Strategies for problem list implementation in a complex clinical enterprise. AMIA Annu. Symp. Proc. (1998), pp. 285–289
12. D.B. Hier, Unpublished Audit of Medical Records at the University of Illinois Hospital, 2002.
13. ICD-9-CM, International Classification of Diseases, ninth revision, Clinical Modification, http://www.cdc.gov/nchs/about/otheract/icd9/abticd9.htm (accessed December 17, 2007).
14. ICD-10, The International Statistical Classification of Diseases and Related Health Problems, tenth revision, http://www.who.int/classifications/icd/en/ (accessed December 17, 2007).
15. SNOMED®, Systematized Nomenclature of Medicine, http://www.cap.org/apps/cap.portal?_nfpb=true&_pageLabel=snomed_page (accessed December 17, 2007).
16. S.M. Meystre, P.J. Haug, Randomized controlled trial of an automated problem list with improved sensitivity, Int. J. Med. Inform. (2008), in press.
17. P. Fabry, R. Baud, P. Ruch, C. Despont-Gros, C. Lovis. Methodology to ease the construction of a terminology of problems. Int. J. Med. Inform., 75 (August (8)) (2006), pp. 624–632
18. P.L. Elkin, A.P. Ruggieri, S.H. Brown, J. Buntrock, B.A. Bauer, D. Wahner-Roedler et al. A randomized controlled trial of the accuracy of clinical record retrieval using SNOMED-RT as compared with ICD9-CM. Proc. AMIA Symp. (2001), pp. 159–163
19. S.J. Wang, D.W. Bates, H.C. Chueh, A.S. Karson, S.M. Maviglia, J.A. Greim et al.. Automated coded ambulatory problem lists: evaluation of a vocabulary and a data entry tool. Int. J. Med. Inform., 72 (December (1–3)) (2003), pp. 17–28
20. J. Zelingher, D.M. Rind, E. Caraballo, M.S. Tuttle, N.E. Olson, C. Safran. Categorization of free-text problem lists: an effective method of capturing clinical data. Proc. Annu. Symp. Comput. Appl. Med. Care (1995), pp. 416–420
21. J.J. Warren, J. Collins, C. Sorrentino, J.R. Campbell. Just-in-time coding of the problem list in a clinical environment. Proc. AMIA Symp. (1998), pp. 280–284
22. H. Wasserman, J. Wang. An applied evaluation of SNOMED CT as a clinical vocabulary for the computerized diagnosis and problem list. AMIA Annu. Symp. Proc. (2003), pp. 699–703
23. J.D. Carpenter, P.N. Gorman. Using medication list - problem list mismatches as markers of potential error. AMIA Annu. Symp. Proc. (2002), pp. 106–110
24. C. Jao, D.B. Hier, W. Wei. Simulating a problem list decision support system: can CPOE help maintain the problem list?. Medinfo (2004), p. 1666
25. C.S. Jao, D.B. Hier. Overcoming limitations of data entry for the semi-automated detection of drug orphans in the EMR. AMIA Annu. Symp. Proc. (2006), p. 967
26. R.A. Raschke, B. Gollihare, T.A. Wunderlich, J.R. Guidry, A.I. Leibowitz, J.C. Peirce et al. A computer alert system to prevent injury from adverse drug events. JAMA, 280 (15) (1998), pp. 1317–1320
27. W.L. Galanter, R. Didomenico, A. Polikaitis. A trial of automated safety alerts for inpatient digoxin use with computerized physician order entry. J. Am. Med. Inform. Assoc., 11 (July–August (4)) (2004), pp. 270–277

28. W.L. Galanter, R. Didomenico, A. Polikaitis. A trial of automated decision support alerts for contraindicated medications using computerized physician order entry. J. Am. Med. Inform. Assoc., 12 (3) (2005), pp. 269–274
29. A.G. Kennedy, B. Littenberg. A modified outpatient prescription form to reduce prescription errors. J. Comm. J. Qual. Saf., 30 (9) (2004), pp. 480–487
30. M.S. Leonard, M. Cimino, S. Shaha, S. McDougal, J. Pilliod, L. Brodsky. Risk reduction for adverse drug events through sequential implementation of patient safety initiatives in a children's hospital. Pediatrics, 118 (4) (2006), pp. e1124–e1129
31. R. Kaushal, K.G. Shojania, D.W. Bates. Effects of computerized physician order entry and clinical decision support systems on medication safety: a systematic review. Arch. Intern. Med., 163 (12) (2003), pp. 1409–1416
32. D.C. Radley, S.N. Finkelstein, R.S. Stafford. Off-label prescribing among office-based physicians. Arch. Intern. Med., 166 (May (9)) (2006), pp. 1021–1026
33. D.M. Wolman, A.L. Kalfoglou, L. LeRoy. Medicare Laboratory Payment Policy: Now and in the Future. Institute of Medicine, National Academy Press, Washington, D.C. (2000) p. 81

CHAPTER 12

RANDOMIZED CONTROLLED TRIAL OF AN AUTOMATED PROBLEM LIST WITH IMPROVED SENSITIVITY

STÉPHANE M. MEYSTRE AND PETER J. HAUG

12.1 INTRODUCTION

The last decade has witnessed a substantial growth in the amount of medical data recorded for a given patient, along with an increasing pressure to improve the quality of healthcare and reduce medical errors. The problem-oriented, Electronic Health Record (EHR), centered on the problem list, is seen by many as a possible answer to these growing challenges. The problem list is a central place for clinicians to have a concise view of all of a patient's medical problems. The problem list also encourages an orderly process of clinical problem solving, prevents redundant actions [1], and supports the clear documentation of patient condition and clinical decision-making and improves communication among caregivers.

At Intermountain Health Care (IHC), a health maintenance organization serving Utah, the problem list is an important piece of the medical record, and a central component of the clinical information system called

---

Reprinted from International Journal of Medical Informatics, *77(9), Meystre SM and Haug PJ, Randomized Controlled Trial of an Automated Problem List with Improved Sensitivity, pp. 602–612, Copyright 2008, with permission from Elsevier.*

HELP2 [2]. To enable its potential benefits, the problem list has to be as accurate, complete and timely as possible. Unfortunately, problem lists are usually incomplete and inaccurate, and are often totally unused. To address this deficiency, we have created an application using Natural Language Processing (NLP) to harvest potential problem list entries from the multiple free-text electronic documents available in a patient's EHR [3] and [4]. The medical problems identified are then proposed to the physicians for addition to the official problem list. This system, referred to as the Automatic Problem List (APL) system, is evaluated here. We hypothesize that the use of NLP to automatically provide potential medical problems will improve the completeness, accuracy and timeliness (decreased time between problems identification and their addition to the list) of this Automated Problem List.

12.2 BACKGROUND

The problem list in a Problem-Oriented Medical Record (POMR) was proposed more than three decades ago by Weed [5] and [6] as an answer to the complexity of medical knowledge and clinical data, and to address weaknesses in the documentation of medical care. In recent years, the problem-oriented, Computer-based Patient Record (CPR) and the problem list have seen renewed interest as an organizational tool [1], [7], [8], [9], [10], [11], [12] and [13]. Advantages to this approach are that the problem list provides a central place for clinicians to obtain a concise view of each patient's problems. This approach also facilitates associating clinical information in the record to a specific problem, and encourages an orderly process of clinical problem solving and clinical judgment. The problem list in a problem-oriented patient record also provides a context in which continuity of care is supported, preventing redundant actions [1]. The problem list reminds clinicians of issues often forgotten, helps reduce errors [14], and improves communication between healthcare providers [15]. The Institute of Medicine [16] recommends that the CPR contain a problem list that specifies the patient's clinical problems and the status of each. Also, convinced of the benefits of the problem list, the Joint Commission for the

Accreditation of Hospitals (JCAHO [17]) has established the problem list as a required feature of hospital records.

To enable many of the potential advantages of a computerized problem list, problem list entries must be coded, which means that each problem entered will have a corresponding code in a controlled vocabulary. Advantages of coded data are that data are classified and standardized, facilitating storage and retrieval, clinical research, and administrative functions like billing. Coded data are also desirable to enable exchange and sharing of data [18]. Medical vocabularies used in problem lists are numerous, ranging from ICD-9-CM [19] and [20], to SNOMED [21], the Unified Medical Language System (UMLS®) [11] and [22], and locally developed vocabularies [23], sometimes mapped to multiple medical vocabularies, like the University of Nebraska Medical Center's multidisciplinary problem list [24]. Coding of problems may be achieved by manually assigning a code when the problem is entered, or by using NLP techniques to map free-text problem list entries to appropriate codes. The process of manual coding is usually eased by the use of pick lists or search engines [25]; both of these features are available in our institution's application for management of the problem list. NLP techniques, where available, allow users of the problem list to use natural language, still the most user-friendly and expressive way of recording information.

The patient record contains a large amount of information captured as narrative text. These free-text documents represent the majority of the information used for medical care [26] and have the advantage of relating findings, interpretations, and decisions as a part of the documentation process. Decision-support, research, and quality improvement activities create a need for structured and coded data instead. As a possible answer to this issue, NLP can be used to convert free-text into coded data [27].

At Intermountain Health Care, a web-based clinical information system has been developed and is in use. This system is called HELP2 [2] and offers secured access to clinical data through specialized modules like "Patient search," "Labs," "Medications," and "Problems." The "Problems" module allows viewing, modifying, and adding medical problems along with their status (active, inactive, resolved, or error) and other information. The records created include the user entering the problem, the date it was entered, and relevant comments. Filters control the display of problems based on their status and other personal preferences. Active problems can also be assigned a priority order. Access to medical knowledge specific to each problem is provided through the "Infobutton" [28]. This problem list features most of the attributes recommended by Campbell [7]: it is clinically focused, with coded problems, modifiable problems' status, and, to a degree, allows tailoring its presentation to the users' needs. The only missing feature is an audit trail of the problems modifications that is easily accessible by the users. This electronic problem list has been used regularly in the outpatient setting, but was in limited use for hospitalized patients. Only one of the wards that participated in our study, the medical and surgical ICU, had significant experience with this application. This site was piloting the inpatient use of the problem list.

A second ward, the cardiovascular surgery unit was not using an electronic problem list but expressed a willingness to begin using it and to help test our system. All other inpatient wards were using a paper-based problem list, or no problem list at all. We should also mention that, except the "Infobutton" cited above, this electronic problem list has limited integration with other computer-based clinical activities. In the future, order sets, physician documentation, and nursing intervention and documentation will be linked with the problem list and provide far more incentives to use it.

12.3 METHODS

As mentioned earlier, the Automated Problem List system extracts potential medical problems from free-text medical documents, and uses NLP to achieve this task. The two main components comprising the system are a background application for problem discovery and the problem list management application mentioned above. The background application is responsible for the text processing and analysis and stores extracted problems in the central clinical database. These problems can then be accessed by the problem list management application integrated into HELP2. For the study described here, we developed the background application to recognize 80 different diagnosis problems, which were selected based on their frequency in the clinical environments chosen for our evaluation (the cardiovascular surgery unit and the intensive care unit). Those 80 problems represented about 64% of all coded medical problem instances in our EHR in 2003. The NLP tools used in this experiment were based on the Java™ version of MetaMap [29] and [30] called MMTx (MetaMap Transfer) and on a negation detection algorithm called NegEx2 [31], and are described in another publication [4]. The problem list management application was based on the "Problems" module described above, and was enhanced to take advantage of the problems automatically detected by the background application. These problems were listed with a new proposed status, and included a link back to the source document(s) and the sentence(s) that each problem was extracted from, as seen in Fig. 1.

12.3.1 STUDY DESIGN

We evaluated the Automated Problem List system with a prospective study in a clinical environment. The APL system includes a human intervention to accept or reject problems proposed by the background application. The evaluation of this intervention therefore requires a prospective study. Patients were included if they met the following criteria: inpatient in one of the two inpatient wards for a duration of at least 48 h (cardiovascular surgery or medical and surgical ICU at the LDS Hospital, Salt Lake City, Utah), older than 18 years, and not already enrolled in a previous phase of this study.

The study started with an initial control phase with all patients assigned to a control group, followed by a Randomized Controlled Trial (RCT) phase with patients randomly assigned to a control or to an intervention group. In the control group, patients received care from physicians using the standard electronic problem list (without proposed problems). In the intervention group, patients were treated by physicians with access to the Automated Problem List system. Their documents were analyzed by the background application, and medical problems extracted were proposed for inclusion into their electronic problem list.

This study was single blinded. The information used was that routinely collected as part of the patient work-up, and patients were not aware of

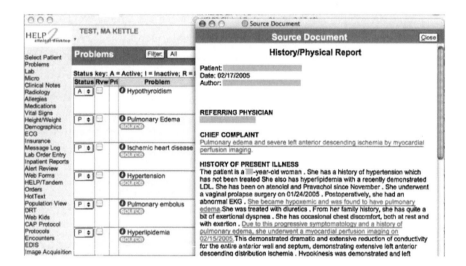

FIGURE 1: Screen capture of the "Problems" module in the HELP2 system. The source document for the problem pulmonary edema is displayed, with the source sentence highlighted in red (underlined in this grayscale figure). (For interpretation of the references to color in this figure legend, the reader is referred to the web version of the article.)

the study. Users of the problem list were physicians and they could not be blinded, since the difference in content of the problem list between the two groups was obvious. All measurements and calculations are described in the following sections and are detailed in Table 1.

12.3.2 PROBLEM LIST COMPLETENESS AND ACCURACY

Three different problem lists were considered for each patient: the reference standard (i.e., what should be in the problem list), the "official" problem list (i.e., problems manually entered and listed as active, inactive, or resolved and problems proposed by the APL system and changed to active, inactive, or resolved by the user), and the "potential" problem list (i.e., problems listed in the "official" list, combined with the problems that had remained proposed at patient discharge) as seen in Fig. 2. We compared the content of each patient's official and potential problem list with the relevant reference standard. We counted and categorized each problem list entry as true positive, false negative, false positive, or true negative. Only our 80-targeted problems were considered in this study.

TABLE 1: Study measurements

Measurement	Abbreviation	Definition
True positive	TP	Problem recorded in the patient's documents and in the problem list
False negative	FN	Problem recorded in the patient's documents but absent from the problem list
False positive	FP	Problem not recorded but listed in the problem list
True negative	TN	Problem not recorded and not listed in the problem list
Sensitivity		TP/(TP + FN)
Specificity		TN/(TN + FP)
Positive predictive value	PPV	TP/(TP + FP)
Negative predictive value	NPV	TN/(TN + FN)
Likelihood ratio for a positive test	LR+	Sensitivity/(1 − specificity)
Likelihood ratio for a negative test	LR−	(1 − sensitivity)/specificity

We then calculated different standard measurements listed in Table 1 to assess the quality of the problem list's content. These calculations were made for each patient, and then averaged across the group or subgroup of patients analyzed. Statistical analysis was executed using a nonparametric test (Mann–Whitney test) for non-normality reasons.

12.3.3 REFERENCE STANDARD

We created the "gold" standard for our 80-targeted problems using an electronic chart review. Two physicians reviewed each electronic document independently using a web-based review application described in another publication [3]. They were asked to detect all mentions of any of the 80-targeted problems that were present (i.e., not negated), in the present or in the past. When the two reviewers disagreed, a third physician determined the presence or absence of the disputed problem. The documents analyzed were all clinical documents (radiology reports, consultation reports, progress notes, H&Ps, discharge summaries, etc.) stored for each patient during his hospital stay, plus a maximum of five older documents of specific types including discharge summaries and consultation reports from previous hospital stays or outpatient care episodes. The reviewers also reviewed the patients' electronic problem list, to map problems manually entered as free-text (not coded) with a relevant coded problem, and also to map "children" of our targeted problems to the relevant "parent" problem (e.g. adhesive pericarditis to pericarditis). To reduce disagreement between reviewers, we used a medical record review technique called explicit review, that directs the reviewers' attention to specific issues (our list of targeted problems) on which judgment is to be based [32]. The explicit review technique is associated with higher inter-rater reliability than implicit review, where reviewers use only their knowledge or beliefs to make judgments. We implemented the explicit review technique in the web-based review application by displaying the document to review beside a checklist of the 80-targeted medical problems. The resulting list of problems provided a reference standard against which other listing of problems could be compared.

12.3.4 PROBLEM LIST TIMELINESS

For all problem list entries, we measured the time elapsed between the first mention of the medical problem in a clinical document (i.e., the date/time when the document was stored) and its addition to the "official" problem list (i.e., the date/time when the status was changed from proposed to active, inactive, or resolved or when the problem was manually added). If a problem was manually added before being detected in a document, this time was equal to zero. This value is one representation of the timeliness of problem recording and was compared between the control and the intervention groups.

Randomized Controlled Trial of an Automated Problem List 253

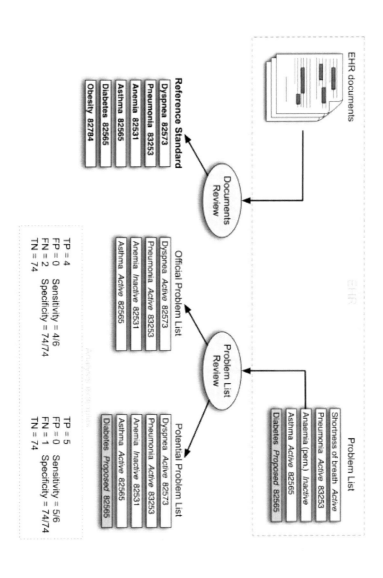

FIGURE 2: Documents and problem list review process with analysis examples.

This timeliness does not represent the real time elapsed between a problem's "appearance" (i.e., the first moment that a medical expert could recognize the problem from the patient's data) and its addition to the problem list. The timeliness does, within the limitations of the study design, allow us to calculate an interval from the first mention in clinical documentation and the addition to the problem list.

12.4 RESULTS

Ten different reviewers, all physicians, reviewed clinical documents to create the reference standard. Eight were board-certified physicians (most of them in internal medicine), and two were residents with at least 2 years of training. Each reviewer examined an average of 686 different documents with the web-based application described above. The time spent for a review was between 48 and 216 s per document. Reviewers' overall agreement was very good, with a Finn's R of 0.897 when reviewing documents and 0.995 when reviewing problem lists. We used Finn's R instead of Cohen's kappa, because the agreement table was strongly skewed, with far more true negatives than true positives.

During the study, 247 patients were enrolled: 76 during the initial control phase, and 171 during the RCT phase (Table 2). Enrollment of patients and data collection lasted 69 days (23 days for the initial control phase; 46 days for the RCT phase), between December 2004 and February 2005.

A total of 2943 clinical documents of various types (Table 3) were analyzed by our system (893 during the initial control phase, 2050 during the RCT phase).

TABLE 2: Number and distribution of patients enrolled in the study

	All patients	ICU patients	CVS patients
Initial controls	76	44	32
RCT: tests	88	54	34
RCT: controls	83	51	32
Total	247	149	98

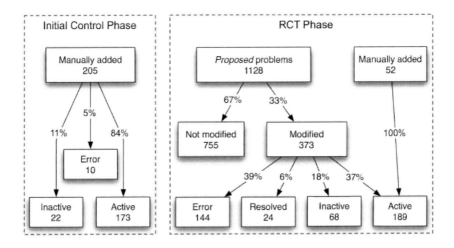

FIGURE 3: Number and proportion of manually added or proposed and subsequently modified medical problems.

TABLE 3: Clinical documents analyzed during the study

Document types	Initial control phase	RCT phase
Radiology reports	395	861
Cardiac catheterization/angiographies	36	57
Progress notes	48	165
Consultation reports	68	168
Operative and procedure notes	64	152
History and physicals	94	200
Discharge summaries	56	118
Emergency department reports	68	132
Surgical pathology/cytology reports	24	71
Letters and other reports	40	126
Total	893	2050

During the whole study, 1385 medical problems were added to problem lists: 205 during the initial control phase and 1180 during the RCT phase (Fig. 3). During the latter, 1128 medical problems were automatically extracted and proposed. These problems were eligible to have their proposed status changed by users of the problem list (i.e. physicians taking care of enrolled patients) to another status, either active, inactive, or resolved when adding them to the "official" problem list, or to error when rejecting them as erroneous.

12.4.1 PROBLEM LIST COMPLETENESS AND ACCURACY

Mean and 0.95 confidence intervals were computed for the sensitivity, specificity, positive predictive value, negative predictive value, and likelihood ratios (Table 4). These calculations were done using the data from all patients enrolled and also using data from subgroups of those patients.

During the initial control phase, results showed a sensitivity of about 6% in the subgroup of patients from the ICU, but this result was significantly higher than in the cardiovascular surgery patient subgroup where sensitivity was only 1.4%. Those results mean that the electronic problem list was barely used during the initial control phase.

When comparing the initial control phase and the RCT phase, and only considering ICU patients, no significant differences were observed between the control groups. When only considering cardiovascular surgery control patients, we measured a significantly higher sensitivity during the RCT phase, rising to 12% (about 1.4% in the initial control phase).

Patients in the intervention group had a significantly higher sensitivity than in both control groups (initial control phase and RCT phase). It reached 41% in the subgroup of patients from the ICU, and about 26% when considering all patients. Likelihood ratios were also very significantly different, and the negative predictive value was significantly higher in the intervention group.

During the RCT phase, when evaluating all patients, the results showed a sensitivity and a likelihood ratio for a positive test (LR+) that were significantly higher in the intervention group (Fig. 4). The likelihood ratio for a negative test (LR−) was significantly lower in the intervention group, dropping from 0.90 to 0.737. Sensitivity in the intervention group was 26.6%. When evaluating the potential problem list (i.e., with proposed problems included), the sensitivity increased even more in the intervention group, but specificity and positive predictive value were reduced.

TABLE 4: Measurements during the study, in all patients, in the ICU patient subgroup, and in the cardiovascular surgery patient subgroup (tests + prop. corresponds to the potential problem list)

	Initial control phase			Randomized controlled trial phase								
	All patients	ICU patients	CV surgery patients	All patients			ICU patients			CV surgery patients		
	Controls	Controls	Controls	Controls	Tests	Tests + prop.	Controls	Tests	Tests + prop.	Controls	Tests	Tests + prop.
Sensitivity	0.042 (0.022–0.062)	0.062 (0.032–0.093)	0.014 (0–0.035)	0.102 (0.069–0.135)	0.266 (0.192–0.34)	0.815 (0.771–0.859)	0.089 (0.049–0.129)	0.41 (0.308–0.512)	0.774 (0.714–0.835)	0.123 (0.063–0.182)	0.037 (0.013–0.063)	0.88 (0.823–0.938)
Specificity	0.998 (0.996–0.999)	0.997 (0.994–0.999)	0.999 (0.997–1)	0.998 (0.995–0.999)	0.993 (0.988–0.999)	0.957 (0.947–0.966)	0.999 (0.998–1)	0.989 (0.98–0.998)	0.963 (0.95–0.976)	0.995 (0.989–1)	1	0.947 (0.933–0.96)
PPV	0.649 (0.462–0.836)	0.652 (0.45–0.854)	0.625 (−0.729 to 1.98)	0.886 (0.795–0.976)	0.924 (0.88–0.967)	0.784 (0.744–0.825)	0.919 (0.81–1)	0.905 (0.852–0.958)	0.811 (0.758–0.865)	0.839 (0.671–1)	1	0.743 (0.681–0.804)
NPV	0.85 (0.829–0.87)	0.87 (0.846–0.894)	0.821 (0.785–0.857)	0.864 (0.848–0.879)	0.88 (0.861–0.899)	0.965 (0.955–0.974)	0.863 (0.842–0.884)	0.898 (0.874–0.923)	0.956 (0.942–0.97)	0.865 (0.842–0.889)	0.851 (0.824–0.878)	0.978 (0.969–0.987)
LR+	2.9 (−1.15 to 6.95)	1.49 (−1.17 to 4.16)	9.23 (−108 to 126)	8.103 (1.047–15.16)	38.291 (25.307–51.275)	24.319 (19.652–28.987)	12.565 (0–92.514)	38.291 (25.307–51.275)	27.902 (20.374–35.43)	5.872 (0–12.333)	N/A	19.9 (15.127–24.675)
LR−	0.961 (0.94–0.981)	0.941 (0.91–0.972)	0.987 (0.967–1.01)	0.9 (0.867–0.933)	0.737 (0.663–0.81)	0.191 (0.146–0.236)	0.912 (0.872–0.952)	0.595 (0.492–0.697)	0.233 (0.171–0.294)	0.881 (0.822–0.94)	0.963 (0.937–0.989)	0.125 (0.066–0.183)

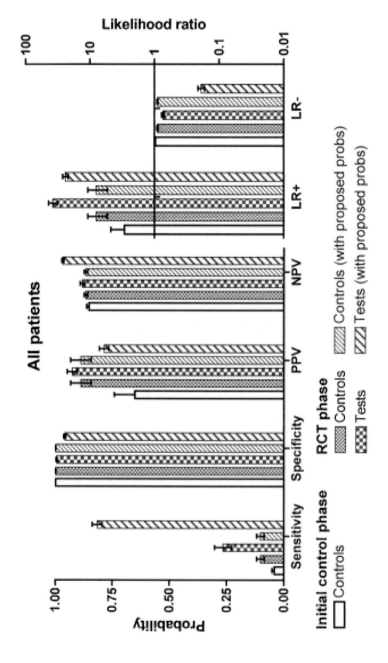

Figure 4: Measurements in all patients, with means and 95% confidence intervals. Results of potential problem lists (i.e., problems that remained proposed included) are also displayed.

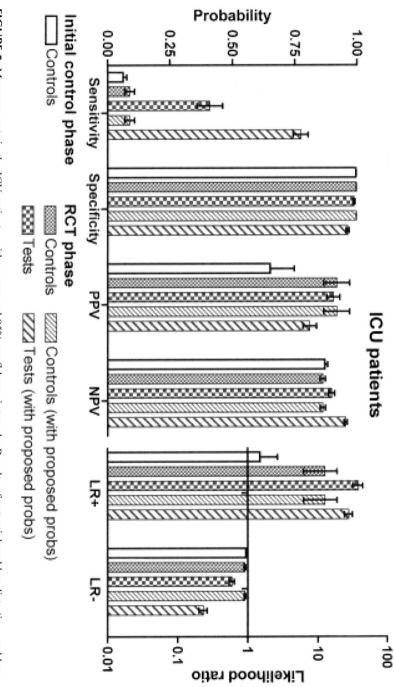

FIGURE 5: Measurements in the ICU patients, with means and 95% confidence intervals. Results of potential problem lists (i.e., problems that remained proposed included) are also displayed.

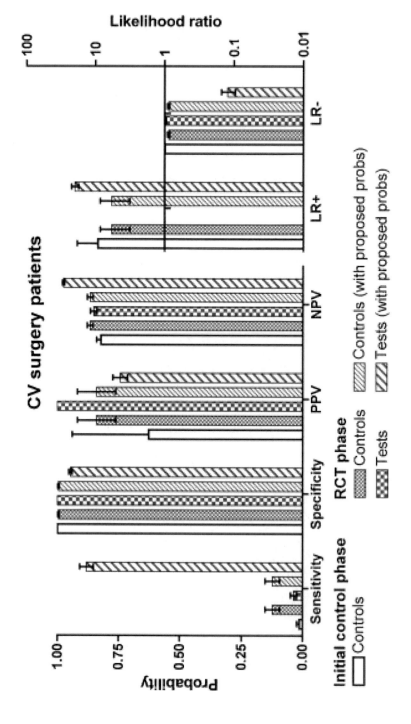

FIGURE 6: Measurements in the cardiovascular surgery patients, with means and 95% confidence intervals. Results of potential problem lists (i.e., problems that remained proposed included) are also displayed.

Analysis of the subgroup of patients from the ICU showed greater differences between control and intervention groups (Fig. 5). The sensitivity in the intervention group reached 41%, and even 77.4% when analyzing the potential problem list. The LR+ was not significantly different.

In the cardiovascular surgery patient subgroup, no significant difference between the control and the intervention groups were observed (Fig. 6). Even though physicians in this unit expressed their interest and willingness to use the electronic problem list, we were not able to find an incentive compelling enough to cause them to edit the problem list.

These results mean that the electronic problem list was used minimally in the cardiovascular surgery unit, but was well used in the ICU, where it grew to be more complete and more timely in the intervention group than in the control group.

12.4.2 PROBLEM LIST TIMELINESS

Finally, during the RCT phase, the timeliness of the addition of problems to the problem list was significantly different between the control and the intervention groups. We also executed the statistical analysis using a nonparametric test (Mann–Whitney test) because of non-normality of the groups. In the control group, the distribution was especially skewed, as seen in Fig. 7. In the intervention group, the mean time until a problem, mentioned in clinical documents, was confirmed by a physician was 44 h 27 min and 39 s. This time was significantly longer ($p = 0.0413$) in the control group: 144 h 28 min 39 s (after excluding a few outliers at up to 58 days).

12.5 DISCUSSION

This evaluation of our Automated Problem List system suggests that the addition of NLP to improve accuracy and timeliness of the problem list was successful. We measured a significantly increased sensitivity. Clearly, enhancing the problem list management application with NLP made the problem list more complete. We also measured a significantly improved timeliness of the problem list, with an average time difference between a medical problem's first mention in text and its addition to the problem list that was reduced from about 6 to 2 days.

12.5.1 COMPLETENESS, ACCURACY AND TIMELINESS OF THE PROBLEM LIST

Within all patients (ICU and cardiovascular surgery patients), the sensitivity of the problem list was increased from about 10% to 25% in the intervention group. The problem list was more complete in this group. The specificity of the problem list was high before the intervention and remained high (i.e. proposing problems for inclusion did not significantly increase the presence of false positive problems in the list). The positive

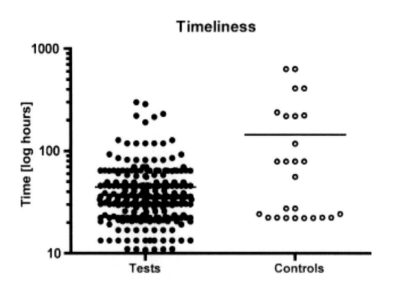

FIGURE 7: Logarithmic plot of the distribution of timeliness (in h).

predictive value was also high, and was not altered by our intervention. The likelihood ratios were improved by the intervention. The LR+ increased from about 8 to 38, meaning that this Automated Problem List could be used to "rule in" a patient's medical problem when present in the problem list. These results support using the problem list as an alerting tool for medical problems present in the patient's text documents.

Analysis of the ICU patients separately showed results similar to the whole patient group, but with accentuated differences: the sensitivity grew to almost 80%, but the specificity was slightly lower ($p = 0.0238$), and the negative predictive value was increased in this subgroup.

The results of the cardiovascular surgery patients were very different, showing no significant difference between the control and intervention group. These results reduced the effect of our system when considering all patients. They were due to a lack of use of the problem list in this clinical environment during the study, even after multiple presentations and discussions with potential users there, and positive feedback from them. This part of the EHR was simply not used there, and our study was not a sufficient motivation to users to start using it. This issue is discussed further below.

12.5.2 EVALUATION OF THE POTENTIAL PROBLEM LIST

When analyzing the potential problem list (i.e., including problems that remained proposed), the sensitivity increased as in the example depicted in Fig. 2 (where Diabetes remained proposed but was a true positive). When considering all patients, we measured a sensitivity of more than 80%. However, in the absence of review by users of the problem list (i.e. accepting or rejecting problems proposed by our system), a few errors were introduced, reducing the specificity of the problem list from about 100% to 96%. We could have inserted proposed problems directly into the "official" problem list, and this would have added only about one false positive medical problem in three problem lists, but the final human review was considered important in this first evaluation of such a system in a clinical setting, to eliminate the false positives introduced by the system.

12.5.3 AGREEMENT BETWEEN REVIEWERS

The excellent inter-reviewer agreement in this study allowed a high quality reference standard, therefore giving reliable results. This was made possible by the use of explicit review techniques: the list of targeted problems was always provided beside the document or problem list to review.

12.5.4 COMPARISON WITH OTHER SIMILAR STUDIES

Our results are difficult to compare to other published results because very few similar studies have been published. A rare example is an evaluation by Szeto et al., measuring the accuracy of an outpatient problem list for nine different diagnoses [33]. A sensitivity of 49% and a specificity of 98–100% were measured. Our study targeted 80 different diagnoses, and gave very similar specificity results, but the sensitivity without intervention was much lower. The effect of our Automated Problem List system increased the sensitivity to a similar degree.

12.5.5 LIMITATIONS

A first important issue that was striking in the cardiovascular patient subgroup is the use of the problem list by physicians. The application suite in which these tools were embedded originated in the outpatient setting and is in the process of moving into the hospital environment. The study described here was the first introduction for most of the physicians to any electronic means of maintaining a problem list. As mentioned in the background section of this paper, the problem list currently used in this environment is paper-based and is usually incomplete and is seldom timely. In fact, it is often totally unused. There is good reason for this: very few of the therapeutic or documentation functions that are done by the physicians are tied, in any way to the problem list. Maintaining a dynamic list on paper is also quite difficult. The frequent resetting of statuses, movement of problems to new positions to show relationships, subsumption or replacement of problems, etc. do not lend themselves to paper-based management.

In the electronic record that is evolving at our institution, the problem list will be integrated into the care process. Electronic order entry, documentation, and a variety of decision support tools will be tied to the problem list. However, currently, the single function currently mediated through the problem list is the "infobutton" [28], a tool that provides problem-specific electronic information to the user. Therefore, this study is best seen as an effort to explore the possibilities offered by NLP to support the problem list. Efforts to secure the general adoption of the problem list await its further integration into the clinical workflow.

Another issue with this system is the scalability of the list of targeted medical problems and the performance of our NLP module. Our system is currently designed to extract 80 different medical problems, but more will need to be added to allow this system to be used in other settings. A very simple solution is to use the default full UMLS® data set provided with MMTx instead of a custom data subset, but this reduces the NLP module performances (decreased recall and slower processing).

The speed of our NLP module may be an issue. During the 46 days this study lasted, 2050 text documents were analyzed and the average time required to analyze a document was about 50 s. This means that a maximum of about 79,000 documents could be analyzed during the same period. Each patient had an average of 12 documents analyzed. The maximum number of patients that could be analyzed by our system would therefore be about 6600, or 140 each day. This gives room for extension to other settings, but the need to include additional problems will reduce this ability to expand.

Finally, study design issues are related to blinding and potential biases. The blinding issue has already been discussed as a part of the study design. In a study of this sort, many different biases are possible. Blinding the data collectors and reviewers eliminated the assessment bias. Recruitment and allocation biases were excluded by clearly defining the inclusion and exclusion criteria, randomizing as late as possible, and concealing the allocation until the recruitment was irreversible. Data collection biases were avoided by collecting the same data the same way in all groups. Within our study design, some biases were still possible and should be taken into consideration. These include contamination, learning effect, and a global Hawthorne effect. Contamination was of special concern and motivated the provision of an initial control phase. The goal was to be able to compare the initial control phase with the control group during the RCT phase and use the initial controls if we could not identify significant differences during the RCT phase. Biases of these sorts would tend to underestimate the differences between groups. We have shown significant differences between the control group and the intervention group, but these differences could therefore be even more important since some of those biases may have been present in this study.

12.5.6 POTENTIAL BENEFITS OF OUR SYSTEM

The medical problem list figures prominently in our plans for computerized physician order entry and medical documentation in the new Electronic Health Record currently under development at IHC. A well-maintained problem list will significantly enhance this Electronic Health Record. The Automated Problem List system improved the quality of the problem list, a central component for our electronic health record. This could be beneficial for many reasons: A better problem list could potentially improve patient outcomes and reduce costs by reducing omissions and delays, improving the organization of care, and reducing adverse events. It could enhance decision-support for applications requiring knowledge of patient medical problems. A timely and accurate problem list could improve patient safety, an important and timely issue that has received substantial attention since the 1999 Institute of Medicine report [34].

12.6 CONCLUSION

The Automated Problem List system that we developed to extract potential medical problems from free-text documents in a patient's EHR has shown satisfying results. This system's goal to improve the problem list's quality by increasing its completeness and timeliness was met, showing higher sensitivity and better timeliness in the intervention group. This was achieved only when the problem list was used. By encouraging the use of a problem list of better quality, this system could potentially improve patient outcomes and security, improve care organization, reduce costs, and diminish adverse events.

REFERENCES

1. E. Bayegan, S. Tu. The helpful patient record system: problem oriented and knowledge based. Proc. AMIA Symp. (2002), pp. 36–40
2. P.D. Clayton, S.P. Narus, S.M. Huff, T.A. Pryor, P.J. Haug, T. Larkin et al.. Building a comprehensive clinical information system from components. The approach at Intermountain Health Care. Methods Inf. Med., 42 (1) (2003), pp. 1–7
3. S. Meystre, P.J. Haug. Natural language processing to extract medical problems from electronic clinical documents: performance evaluation. J Biomed. Inform., 39 (6) (2006), pp. 589–599 Epub Dec 5, 2005
4. S. Meystre, P.J. Haug. Automation of a problem list using natural language processing. BMC Med. Inform. Decis. Mak., 5 (2005), p. 30
5. L.L. Weed. Medical records that guide and teach. N. Engl. J. Med., 278 (11) (1968), pp. 593–600
6. L.L. Weed. Medical records that guide and teach. N. Engl. J. Med., 278 (12) (1968), pp. 652–657 concl
7. J.R. Campbell. Strategies for problem list implementation in a complex clinical enterprise. Proc. AMIA Symp. (1998), pp. 285–289
8. J.R. Campbell, T.H. Payne. A comparison of four schemes for codification of problem lists. Proc. Annu. Symp. Comput. Appl. Med. Care (1994), pp. 201–205
9. M.S. Donaldson, G.J. Povar. Improving the master problem list: a case study in changing clinician behavior. QRB Qual. Rev. Bull., 11 (11) (1985), pp. 327–333
10. P.L. Elkin, D.N. Mohr, M.S. Tuttle, W.G. Cole, G.E. Atkin, K. Keck et al. Standardized problem list generation, utilizing the Mayo canonical vocabulary embedded within the Unified Medical Language System. Proc. AMIA Annu. Fall Symp. (1997), pp. 500–504
11. H. Goldberg, D. Goldsmith, V. Law, K. Keck, M. Tuttle, C. Safran. An evaluation of UMLS as a controlled terminology for the Problem List Toolkit. Medinfo, 9 (Pt 1) (1998), pp. 609–612
12. J.W. Hales, K.M. Schoeffler, D.P. Kessler. Extracting medical knowledge for a coded problem list vocabulary from the UMLS Knowledge Sources. Proc. AMIA Symp. (1998), pp. 275–279
13. J. Starmer, R. Miller, S. Brown. Development of a structured problem list management system at vanderbilt. Proc. AMIA Annu. Fall Symp. (1998), p. 1083
14. D.W. Simborg, B.H. Starfield, S.D. Horn, S.A. Yourtee. Information factors affecting problem follow-up in ambulatory care. Med. Care, 14 (10) (1976), pp. 848–856

15. B. Starfield, D. Steinwachs, I. Morris, G. Bause, S. Siebert, C. Westin. Concordance between medical records and observations regarding information on coordination of care. Med. Care, 17 (7) (1979), pp. 758–766
16. Institute of Medicine (U.S.), Committee on Improving the Patient Record, R.S. Dick, E.B. Steen, D.E. Detmer, The Computer-based Patient Record: An Essential Technology for Health Care, Rev. ed., National Academy Press, Washington, DC, 1997.
17. Joint Commission on Accreditation of Healthcare Organizations (JCAHO), Available from http://www.jcaho.org.
18. A.M. van Ginneken. The computerized patient record: balancing effort and benefit. Int. J. Med. Inform., 65 (2) (2002), pp. 97–119
19. A.A. Bui, R.K. Taira, S. El-Saden, A. Dordoni, D.R. Aberle, Automated medical problem list generation: towards a patient timeline, Medinfo, San Francisco, CA, 2004, pp. 587–591.
20. H.J. Scherpbier, R.S. Abrams, D.H. Roth, J.J. Hail. A simple approach to physician entry of patient problem list. Proc. Annu. Symp. Comput. Appl. Med. Care (1994), pp. 206–210
21. H. Wasserman, J. Wang. An applied evaluation of SNOMED CT as a clinical vocabulary for the computerized diagnosis and problem list. Proc. AMIA Symp. (2003), pp. 699–703
22. T. Payne, D.R. Martin. How useful is the UMLS metathesaurus in developing a controlled vocabulary for an automated problem list?. Proc. Annu. Symp. Comput. Appl. Med. Care (1993), pp. 705–709
23. J. Zelingher, D.M. Rind, E. Caraballo, M. Tuttle, N. Olson, C. Safran. Categorization of free-text problem lists: an effective method of capturing clinical data. Proc. Annu. Symp. Comput. Appl. Med. Care (1995), pp. 416–420
24. J.J. Warren, J. Collins, C. Sorrentino, J.R. Campbell. Just-in-time coding of the problem list in a clinical environment. Proc. AMIA Symp. (1998), pp. 280–284
25. S.J. Wang, D.W. Bates, H.C. Chueh, A.S. Karson, S.M. Maviglia, J.A. Greim et al. Automated coded ambulatory problem lists: evaluation of a vocabulary and a data entry tool. Int. J. Med. Inform., 72 (1–3) (2003), pp. 17–28
26. A.W. Pratt. Medicine, computers, and linguistics. Adv. Biomed. Eng., 3 (1973), pp. 97–140
27. P. Spyns. Natural language processing in medicine: an overview. Methods Inf. Med., 35 (4/5) (1996), pp. 285–301
28. J.C. Reichert, M. Glasgow, S.P. Narus, P.D. Clayton. Using LOINC to link an EMR to the pertinent paragraph in a structured reference knowledge base. Proc. AMIA Symp. (2002), pp. 652–656
29. A.R. Aronson. Effective mapping of biomedical text to the UMLS Metathesaurus: the MetaMap program. Proc. AMIA Symp. (2001), pp. 17–21
30. A.R. Aronson, O. Bodenreider, H.F. Chang, S.M. Humphrey, J.G. Mork, S.J. Nelson ea. The NLM indexing initiative. Proc. AMIA Symp. (2000), pp. 17–21
31. W.W. Chapman, NegEx 2, Available at: http://web.cbmi.pitt.edu/chapman/NegEx.html.
32. C.M. Ashton, D.H. Kuykendall, M.L. Johnson, N.P. Wray. An empirical assessment of the validity of explicit and implicit process-of-care criteria for quality assessment. Med. Care, 37 (8) (1999), pp. 798–808

33. H.C. Szeto, R.K. Coleman, P. Gholami, B.B. Hoffman, M.K. Goldstein. Accuracy of computerized outpatient diagnoses in a Veterans Affairs general medicine clinic. Am. J. Manage. Care, 8 (1) (2002), pp. 37–43
34. Institute of Medicine, C.o.Q.o.H.C.i.A., L.T. Kohn, J.M. Corrigan, M.S. Donaldson, To Err is Human: Building A Safer Health System, 1999.

PART IV

APPLICATIONS OF THE PROBLEM LIST

CHAPTER 13

INCOMPLETE CARE: ON THE TRAIL OF FLAWS IN THE SYSTEM

TEJAL K. GANDHI, GIANNA ZUCCOTTI, AND THOMAS H. LEE

It was no one's fault, but it was everyone's fault. The 53-year-old woman had presented with pneumococcal sepsis with disseminated intravascular coagulation and had barely survived but had lost multiple digits. Ten years earlier, she had undergone splenectomy after a motor vehicle accident. There was no evidence that she had received pneumococcal vaccination at any time since the operation. After she recovered, she filed suit against her primary care physician, a doctor in our integrated delivery system. We settled the case and began the work of trying to prevent similar omissions in the future. We discovered that although information technology offers apparently simple tools for solving such problems in care delivery and improving quality and patient safety, it can be surprisingly complex to redesign systems and processes of care—including their human components—to prevent common errors.

The clinical issues involved were familiar and noncontroversial. Surgical splenectomy, a common result of trauma, leads to a 0.9-to-4.4% incidence

---

From Gandhi TK, Zuccotti G, and Lee TH. Incomplete Care—On the Trail of Flaws in the System. The New England Journal of Medicine 365,6 (2011), pp. 486–488; DOI: 10.1056/NEJMp1106313. Copyright © 2011 Massachusetts Medical Society. Medicine. http://www.nejm.org/doi/full/10.1056/NEJMp1106313 Reprinted with permission from the authors from The New England Journal of Medicine.

of sepsis. [1] Asplenic persons are susceptible to severe infection from many pathogens, *Streptococcus pneumoniae* being the most common. Post-splenectomy sepsis often progresses rapidly to overwhelming sepsis, disseminated intravascular coagulation, shock, and frequently death. Hence, the Centers for Disease Control and Prevention and the Advisory Committee on Immunization Practices recommend that asplenic adults receive two doses, 5 years apart, of the 23-valent purified pneumococcal polysaccharide vaccine (Pneumovax). [2]

An investigation by our Patient Safety Team revealed that the patient had received her care for the past 10 years, including her splenectomy surgery, within our system. Our electronic medical record (EMR) issues reminders recommending pneumococcal vaccination every 5 years for patients who have undergone splenectomy. This patient, however, did not have "splenectomy" on her EMR "problem list."

Moreover, even if it had been on that list, she might not have received the vaccine: analysis of our EMR data revealed that only 60% of patients with splenectomy on their problem list had a documented pneumococcal vaccination, a rate consistent with those in published data [1]—but discouraging evidence that our computerized reminders weren't being followed in 40% of cases. In fact, most studies of the impact of computerized reminders have demonstrated only small-to-moderate improvement, [3] not rates approaching high reliability (>95%).

We realized that other approaches were needed. For instance, protocols or checklists could be integrated into the workflow so that whenever patients are booked for elective splenectomy, clinicians are prompted to order vaccines 2 weeks in advance. For patients who can't or don't get vaccines preoperatively, a more effective, targeted postoperative strategy is needed. Reminders that appear on the screen when physicians log on to a patient's record are evidently not enough, but active interruptive prompts might work better.

The Patient Safety Team began exploring tactics that don't rely on clinicians' logging into an electronic record and immediately responding to a reminder. Reports could be sent to practices or providers routinely, identifying (through the EMR problem list) patients who had undergone splenectomy but whose data suggested they were unvaccinated and asking the practice to send letters to those patients.

Further investigation of our case revealed that the EMR had been adopted by the patient's primary care physician 1 year after her motor vehicle accident, so splenectomy could not have been included in her electronic problem list at the time and was not added subsequently. Analysis of outpatient records of more than 1.7 million patients who had recently received care within our system revealed that 7125 had the word "splenectomy" somewhere in their office notes, but 5028 (71%) of them didn't have it on their problem list. Among these patients, the pneumococcal vaccination rate was 17%, as compared with 54% among patients whose splenectomy was included on the problem list. [4]

So there were at least two EMR-related problems contributing to incomplete care: many patients had splenectomy on their problem lists, but the appropriate reminders had not been followed; and many had undergone a splenectomy that had never been entered in their problem list. Both errors exposed patients to gaps in appropriate care that left them vulnerable to complications.

How could we increase problem lists' accuracy? One option was creating reports listing patients with the word "splenectomy" in their notes and not on their problem list and distributing those reports to providers and practices, who could review the records and update the lists. Practical problems with this approach included uncertainty about which provider should receive such reports (e.g., the primary care physician, the surgeon, a nurse, or a physician assistant). Alternatively, the task could be performed centrally with health system resources. In this instance, moonlighting residents were paid to review the records and update problem lists for patients seen in the health system during the previous 3 years; this approach could address much of the at-risk population while using reasonable amounts of resources. The residents reviewed charts of 4324 patients and added splenectomy to 2880 patients' problem lists (67%), at a cost of $6,250 ($1.45 per record).

This one-time intervention probably reduced the risk of a repeat of the patient's scenario among people who've already had a splenectomy, but the risk of similar gaps in care remains for patients who undergo splenectomy in the future. One option might be educating and training surgeons, hematologists, primary care physicians, and other clinicians about the importance of both maintaining accurate problem lists and adhering to vaccination recommendations. However, education alone is not a highly reliable intervention.

Some potential additional solutions include creating linkages between surgical operative notes and EMR problem lists—for example, automatically populating the list with the procedure from the operative note. Another possibility is to generate a prompt for physicians to update the problem list at subsequent visits; natural language processing or billing data could be used to identify patients who have undergone splenectomy and then prompt the physician to enter the information into the problem list and facilitate entry. [5]

Before the patient-safety movement and EMRs, the system response to cases such as ours would have been virtually nil. Physicians would have been exhorted to be more vigilant and try harder to comply with guidelines. Today, effective organizations try to learn from such cases and redesign systems and care processes to prevent future errors. Our case demonstrates the complexity of system redesign—and its potential value for a population. Its lessons regarding creating methods for identifying a patient population and providing it with safe, high-quality care can be applied broadly. For example, the ability to target for appropriate monitoring all patients receiving anticoagulation therapy or all diabetic patients requires accurate identification of patients through the EMR and the use of population-management tools such as reminders and patient-level reports about guideline compliance.

As we discovered, a task that seems relatively simple can quickly become complicated. Was it worth the time and effort for a health system to delve into this issue to prevent a rare complication that causes terrible outcomes? Preventing one malpractice case might make such efforts worthwhile financially. But the real argument for studying these cases is to improve our understanding of how clinicians need to work with each other and their information systems to improve quality and safety in general. A key lesson is that to achieve reliable care, multiple approaches—such as checklists, reminders, practice-level reports, and alerts—are required, and clinicians' workflow should be a key consideration in applying any approach. Interventions should make it easy to do the right thing and hard to do the wrong thing. Finally, the responsibility for ensuring compliance with key recommendations needn't always fall on the physician—and indeed would probably be better handled by a team approach to care. These implications are relevant well beyond the population of patients who have undergone splenectomy.

REFERENCES

1. Sumaraju V, Smith LG, Smith SM. Infectious complications in asplenic hosts. Infect Dis Clin North Am 2001;15:551-565
2. Updated recommendations for prevention of invasive pneumococcal disease among adults using the 23-valent pneumococcal polysaccharide vaccine (PPSV23). MMWR Morb Mortal Wkly Rep 2010;59:1102-1106
3. Shojania KG, Jennings A, Ramsay C, Eccles M, Grimshaw J. Effect of point of care reminders on physician behaviour: a systematic review. CMAJ 2010;182:E216-E225
4. Turchin A, Shubina M, Gandhi T. NLP for patient safety: splenectomy and Pneumovax. In: Proceedings of the AMIA 2010 Annual Symposium, Washington, DC, November 13–17, 2010:1282.
5. Pang JE, Wright A, Ramelson H, et al. Accurately identifying diabetic patients with problem list gaps. J Gen Intern Med 2010;25:Suppl 3:216-216

CHAPTER 14

LEVERAGING ELECTRONIC HEALTH RECORDS TO SUPPORT CHRONIC DISEASE MANAGEMENT: THE NEED FOR TEMPORAL DATA VIEWS

LIPIKA SAMAL, ADAM WRIGHT, BANG T. WONG, JEFFREY A. LINDER, AND DAVID W. BATES

14.1 INTRODUCTION

Chronic diseases such as diabetes, coronary artery disease, hypertension, cerebrovascular disease, congestive heart failure (CHF) and chronic obstructive pulmonary disease account for as much as 75% of US healthcare costs and will eventually outpace infectious diseases in terms of costs worldwide. [1,2] Management of diabetes alone cost $116 billion in 2007 in the USA, and diabetes is now epidemic in south Asia. [3] However, our current healthcare system manages chronic diseases poorly in the outpatient setting. For example, up to two-thirds of the money spent on diabetes hospitalisations could be saved with improved primary care management. [4]

Leveraging Electronic Health Records to Support Chronic Disease Management: The Need for Temporal Data Views. Samal L, Wright A, Wong BT, Linder JA, and DW. Informatics in Primary Care *2011,19 (20011), pp. 65–74. Licensed under Creative Commons Attribution 4.0 International License, http://creativecommons.org/licenses/by/4.0/.*

Electronic health records (EHRs) may improve primary care management and care co-ordination. However, studies have failed to consistently show improved quality with EHRs in chronic disease care. For example, diabetes disease management programmes using physician reminders, performance feedback and nursedriven structured care have been shown to improve process outcomes such as rates of haemoglobin A1c testing, but not intermediate clinical outcomes, such as glycaemic control [5] Recent reviews show positive results fromabout two-thirds of trials of clinical decision support, but absolute changes in clinical outcomes are small; a Cochrane systematic review of point-of-care reminders for hypertension management reported a median reduction in systolic blood pressure of only 1.0 mmHg in intervention groups. [6–9] Finally, some studies have shown that EHRs have failed to improve care when implemented as part of a disease management programme, when clinical decision support is incorporated, or when used for care co-ordination across settings. [10–13]

EHRs may have failed to improve chronic disease care in these studies in part because most EHRs in use today do not facilitate longitudinal data management. [14] We believe that the contribution of health information technology has been limited because EHRs are largely visit oriented and clinicians need contextual information for each data point. For example, a provider treating a patient for hypertension needs not only the medication list, but also context about how the patient's blood pressure has responded to each medication that the patient has tried in the past. [15] To attempt to provide context, systems designed for clinical care have attempted to display all patient data on one screen, but this causes cognitive overload from the presence of extraneous data. [16] Chronic disease management requires filtering pertinent diagnosisoriented information. For this reason, we propose the term 'temporal data views' to mean both an improved interface and a filtered view of patient data. Chronic disease management requires numerical data, best displayed using visualisation, as well as nonnumerical data, best displayed using diagnosis-oriented text summaries. Neither data visualisation nor diagnosisoriented text summaries have been widely adopted into the EHRs commonly used in primary care practices today.

Currently, patient data are organised in EHRs by source, i.e. clinic notes, phone notes, laboratory results, radiology results, medication lists and problem lists. While providers used to flip back and forth between sections of a paper chart in order to recognise trends or create a mental timeline, they now must click on multiple screens to accomplish the same goal. In the Methods section we use clinical scenarios to explain how temporal data views can aid providers in this goal and we define two types of temporal data views: visualisation and diagnosis-oriented summaries. In the Outputs section we illustrate the potential of visualisations and diagnosis-oriented summaries in chronic disease management. In the Discussion section we summarise our argument for improved longitudinal data management and review prior literature.

14.2 METHODS

14.2.1 DATA VISUALISATION AND CHRONIC DISEASE MANAGEMENT

A data visualisation, which may be as simple as a graph of a patient's creatinine, is more efficient than reviewing a series of laboratory reports. As opposed to flowsheets in which there is little visual association between the individual values, graphs reveal connections between data points. Using graphs, the visual detection and assembly of data points to recognise a trend can be exceedingly fast. Many EHRs offer the ability to graph laboratory results over time, but this tool is not commonly used by primary care providers (PCPs) because of usability issues. For example, some systems do not automatically adjust the y-axis to the range of values. Other systems do not indicate the normal range, which leaves interpretation to the memory of the provider. These graphs should be improved in EHRs that are currently widely used. More advanced designs could be added, such as Sparklines, small information graphics embedded in the context of text to show temporal data in a condensed way. [17] Previously evaluated in an intensive care setting, they should be available to primary care clinicians to display numerical data intuitively and compactly. [18] Another study reported a visualisation which used stacked timelines of information from different sources such as medications and subjective complaints, which allows clinicians to recognise correlations between disparate information, such as initiation of a new drug and development of an adverse drug reaction. [19] The clinical scenarios below describe common problems encountered by PCPs which may be improved by data visualisation.

14.2.1.1 SCENARIO 1: EMERGENCY ROOM VISIT FOR GOUT FLARE

Dr Phair's patient, Mr Taylor, calls the office after an emergency room visit for a gout flare. She reviews his electronic chart, but does not notice that his last flare had occurred a number of years ago and that it was related to a medication change. Nor does she realise that he was recently started on Ibuprofen.

In the Outputs section, we explain how data visualisation could improve the efficiency of this task and help the PCP to discover a likely cause of Mr Taylor's gout flare. When assessing a gradual decline in status, data visualisations may aid physicians in recognising subtle changes over time as described in the following scenario.

14.2.1.2 SCENARIO 2: EARLY CHRONIC KIDNEY DISEASE

One year later, Dr Phair sees Mr Taylor for his annual physical. She reviews his past notes and health-monitoring flowsheet, but fails to notice that he is slowly developing worsening chronic kidney disease.

In the Outputs section, we explain how a data visualisation may improve quality of care in this scenario by raising awareness of a change from baseline and providing clues to potential causes. We also suggest how data visualisation tools may increase use of clinical decision support of electronic reminders.

14.2.1.3 SCENARIO 3: WEIGHT LOSS IN END-STAGE CANCER

An 87-year-old man, Mr Radley, comes in for a followup visit with his longtime PCP, Dr Holtzman. Mr Radley has end-stage cancer and has failed multiple treatment regimens. In past discussions, he has asked that Dr Holtzman refer him to an inpatient hospice 'close to the end' because his wife's arthritis will make it hard for her to care for him at home. Dr Holtzman reviews the patient's symptoms and determines that his clinical condition is stable. He schedules a followup visit in two months. Unfortunately, he fails to note that Mr Radley has been losing weight rapidly and that his last routine blood test showed a decrease in albumin level. Two weeks later, Mr Radley acutely decompensates and is hospitalised rather than being admitted to an inpatient hospice.

The addition of a patient-specific data visualisation would make it easier for this busy PCP to recognise a crucial turning point in this patient's course and to make recommendations that are consistent with the patient's previously stated wishes. We present an example of such data visualisation in the Outputs section.

The next section describes the opportunities for text summaries and how a diagnosis-oriented text summary may be superior to data visualisations when narrative information is present in notes, labs, radiology, problem lists and medication lists.

14.2.2 DISEASE-ORIENTED TEXT SUMMARIES FOR CHRONIC DISEASE MANAGEMENT

When assessing time intervals between events or observing a trend in numeric data, visualisation is superior to other approaches. By contrast, in situations where narrative information is dispersed throughout the record, diagnosis-oriented text summaries are superior. [20]

The following scenario describes a common situation in which a PCP is searching for pertinent diagnosis-oriented data in narrative documents.

14.2.2.1 SCENARIO 4: SOURCE-ORIENTED REVIEW OF LOW BACK PAIN DATA

Mrs Hyatt is a 31-year-old woman who has been seen by her PCP Dr Mackay for a number of years. Recently, she began to complain of low back pain. Today she leaves a message for Dr Mackay requesting a referral for an MRI. Dr Mackay begins to search through her chart in order to find data from radiology, notes and referrals. After scrolling up and down through multiple screens, he sees a phone note where he noted that Mrs Hyatt was having so much pain that she could no longer do heavy housework. He opens the referral section and sees a referral to neurology. He decides to order an MRI because it is reasonable, because it may be a requirement for a neurology assessment and because gathering more information would be too time-consuming.

Dr Mackay should be able to access all data pertinent to low back pain with one click as described in the revised scenario in the Outputs section.

14.2.3 COMBINED VISUALISATION AND DISEASEORIENTED TEXT SUMMARIES FOR CHRONIC DISEASE MANAGEMENT

A temporal patient data view, as we have described it, differs from a disease registry or dashboard in that it is not a cross-sectional data view. Since the most recent LDL value and current dose of medication is often all that is needed for lipid management decisions, a crosssectional view for lipid management may increase quality and efficiency of medical decision making. [21] However, the management of complex chronic diseases requires more context than the most recent value. [22] For example, CHF management may require recent and distant data about medication changes, symptoms, diagnostic test results and vital signs, as illustrated in the next scenario.

14.2.3.1 SCENARIO 5: SOURCE-ORIENTED REVIEW OF CHF DATA

Mr Davis is a 76-year-old man who has been hospitalised multiple times and has coronary artery disease and CHF. Dr Floyd, who is covering for his PCP, is called by a visiting nurse for a blood pressure of 78/42. Dr Floyd clicks onmultiple screens to reviewMr Davis's medical problems

Leveraging Electronic Health Records to Support Disease Management   285

and medications, but soon decides to send him to the emergency department where he is admitted.

In order to avoid an unnecessary emergency department visit and hospitalisation, Dr Floyd needs to feel confident that the low blood pressure is not due to worsening CHF. Ideally, she would be able to read a text summary of his CHF course and open a visualisation of medications, clinical assessments of New York Heart Association (NYHA) functional class, weight, blood pressure and gain access to reports of non-invasive diagnostic studies such as echocardiograms. We illustrate a combined data visualisation and CHF-based text summary in the Outputs section.

These five clinical scenarios illustrate common situations in primary care. Unlike intensive care settings, in which physicians review dense, uniform data over short periods, primary care physicians must review sparse, incongruous data spanning many years.

14.2.4 OUTPUTS

In this section, we review the current method of longitudinal data review in each scenario and provide a figure illustrating an innovative temporal data view.

14.2.4.1 SCENARIO 1: DIAGNOSING THE CAUSE OF GOUT FLARE USING A VISUALISATION OF CREATININE PEAKS

Mr Taylor's gout flare could be related to renal function. Knowing this, his PCP decides to examine how Mr Taylor's serum creatinine has changed over time. The EHR displays a flowsheet of results from basic metabolic panels. She must scroll through multiple screens to find his last high creatinine value. She then must close the lab results section of the chart in order to open his medication list and display all of his past medication changes. She is not able to quickly determine that his last creatinine rise was related to medication changes and also does not notice that he has recently been started on a new nephrotoxic medication.

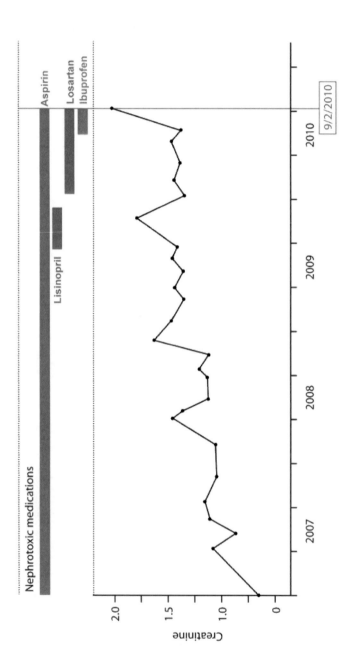

FIGURE 1: Visualisation of serum creatinine and nephrotoxic medications. A graph overlaid with nephrotoxic medications allows Dr Phair to implicate the Ibuprofen as the cause of Mr Taylor's gout flare

With a temporal data view, Dr Phair would be aided in the task of finding pertinent information. Using the data visualisation in Figure 1, she realises that Mr Taylor's last creatinine peak coincided with the addition of Lisinopril in 2009 and that his creatinine improved when Lisinopril was stopped. She also realises that his current spike in creatinine coincides with the addition of Ibuprofen. She concludes that this new medication may be contributing to his problem by reducing his creatinine clearance. She discontinues it and substitutes Acetaminophen.

Reviewing this data visualisation is more efficient than chart review because the graph condenses more data onto one screen compared with a flowsheet and juxtaposes nephrotoxic medications with laboratory data.

Our proposed improvement in Scenario 2 includes both a data visualisation and actionable clinical decision support to remind the PCP of an appropriate next step.

14.2.4.2 SCENARIO 2: DIAGNOSING CHRONIC KIDNEY DISEASE USING A VISUALISATION OF CHANGE IN RATE OF GLOMERULAR FILTRATION DECLINE

When Mr Taylor returns for his physical, Dr Phair checks under the lab results tab to make sure that his creatinine improved after the gout flare. She does not notice that he is rapidly approaching chronic kidney disease.

With an improved temporal data view, Dr Phair would be able to synthesise data about his mild chronic kidney disease. This data visualisation plots his trend in estimated glomerular filtration rate alongside a plot of expected change due to rising age alone, which is derived from population data (Figure 2). Although he has not yet crossed a predefined threshold for stage 3 chronic kidney disease, she sees that his renal function has declined substantially from his own baseline and from the population trend. In this case, the interface not only shows her the pertinent information, but also provides a link to an actionable order to check for proteinuria. A positive proteinuria test classifies him as having chronic kidney disease, she institutes measures to delay progression of chronic kidney disease, and his condition stabilises.

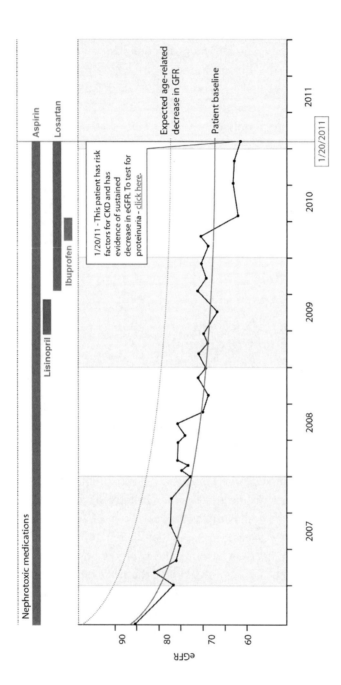

FIGURE 2: Visualisation of rate change, benchmark data, nephrotoxic medications, actionable order. The benchmark data of expected age-related change in glomerular filtration rate makes it clear that not only has there has been a gradual decline in renal function, but it is greater than that expected due to age alone. A stacked timeline infers that the Ibuprofen was likely the inciting event. Clinical decision support with an actionable order is embedded directly into the visualisation

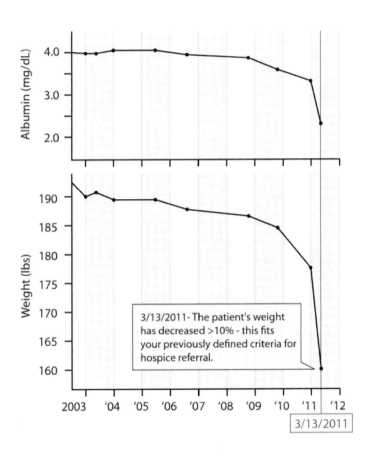

FIGURE 3: Visualisation of weight loss. An individualised display alerts Dr Holtzman to the fact that the rate of weight loss has accelerated

This type of data visualisation raises the awareness of a change from baseline, provides clues to potential causes, and may make providers more likely to use clinical decision support, which has been cited as a barrier to quality improvement. [11]

Similar to Scenario 2, the outcome of Scenario 3 would be improved with a data visualisation and illustrates the potential for patient-specific alerts.

14.2.4.3 SCENARIO 3: RESPECTING PATIENT END-OF-LIFE WISHES USING A VISUALISATION OF WEIGHT LOSS

Dr Holtzman was unable to follow Mr Radley's wishes because it was difficult to detect a change in status. A temporal data display could be customised to include the data he needs to recognise a change in status, for example, with a graph of weight loss including a prespecified alert (Figure 3). The data visualisation makes it is clear to Dr Holtzman that Mr Radley is declining rapidly and, after checking for reversible causes, he refers him to hospice.

Scenario 4 illustrates how inefficient source-oriented review is when a provider is searching for data from different sources over a long period of time. Unlike the preceding scenarios, Scenario 4 does not lend itself to data visualisation because the information is not numeric. A potential improvement is a diagnosis-oriented text summary.

14.2.4.4 SCENARIO 4: USING A DISEASE-ORIENTED TEXT SUMMARY OF LOW BACK PAIN DATA TO APPROVE A REQUEST FOR AN MRI

In most EHRs in use today, Dr Mackay would need to open the radiology section to review previous back imaging. He would then check the notes section and go to multiple notes searching for mention of low back pain. Eventually he would see that he has referred Mrs Hyatt to physical therapy and then neurology.

Leveraging Electronic Health Records to Support Disease Management 291

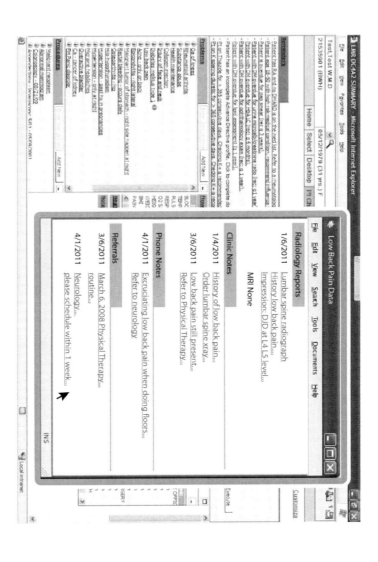

FIGURE 4: Disease-oriented text summary. Dr Mackay may access diverse data using hyperlinks to the original document. The temporal data view improves efficiency of navigation and may impact MRI utilisation

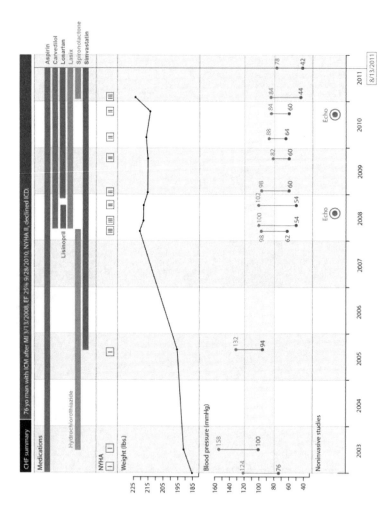

FIGURE 5: Visualisation and disease-oriented text summary. A CHF temporal data view brings together diverse data in anticipation of changes in patient status so that Dr Floyd is able to manage the patient as if she were his PCP. She is aided by a succinct one-line text summary at the top of the display and links to pertinent information such as echocardiogram reports

In an EHR with improved temporal data views, Dr Mackay would be able to click on 'low back pain' from her problem list. All information pertinent to an evidence-based work-up of low back pain would be included in one temporal data view. He would be able to see excerpts of text by rolling over each note and quickly determine that an MRI is indicated (Figure 4).

Dr Mackay may come to the same decision in this case, but since he is able to locate information more efficiently, this tool may also help him to decrease unnecessary utilisation. Also, another member of the team could use this tool to gather appropriate information for him or for a prior authorisation request to an insurance company.

Currently, the design and implementation of such a summary would require free text searching, but in the future, EHRs could be designed to produce diagnosis-oriented data displays by tagging all patient data with diagnosis-oriented metadata.

Another opportunity to reduce healthcare costs and improve quality of care is illustrated in the following scenario with a data visualisation and a CHF-oriented text summary.

14.2.4.5 SCENARIO 5: DETERMINING THE CAUSE OF HYPOTENSION USING A VISUALISATION AND TEXT SUMMARY FOR CHF

Although the visiting nurse reports that Mr Davis is not symptomatic with his low blood pressure, Dr Floyd is too unfamiliar with his case to feel comfortable waiting for a routine follow-up visit. The situation would be improved with a temporal data view specific to CHF (Figure 5). Dr Floyd would be able to open the temporal data view while speaking to the nurse. The brief text summary at the top of the figure tells her that, 'This is a 76-year-old man with ischemic cardiomyopathy resulting from a myocardial infarction on March 13, 2008. His most recent systolic ejection fraction was 25% as measured by echocardiogram on September 28, 2010. He isNYHA Class II. He has declined an implantable cardioverter defibrillator'. She would quickly note that his NYHA class has recently increased, which indicates a recent decompensation, and that hewas subsequently started on Spironolactone. She believes that this contributed to his current low blood pressure. She stops this new medication, he does not go to the emergency department, is not readmitted, and is able to attend his next scheduled clinic visit with his PCP as planned.

In this case of an abrupt change in patient status, the temporal data view helped the physician to identify a potential cause. We propose that EHRs should be designed to produce such disease-oriented text summaries for all chronic diseases.

If we solve the problem of data overload in primary care, we may be able to provide real value to the healthcare system and society. Temporal data views such as the ones we have illustrated are appropriate to the task, but are not yet commonplace in primary care settings.

14.3 DISCUSSION

14.3.1 PRINCIPAL FINDINGS

We have explained that the management of chronic diseases can be complex using five clinical scenarios. We have illustrated five temporal data views that can assist physicians by providing pertinent information. In these scenarios, improvements in the representation of longitudinal data led to improvements in healthcare costs, efficiency and quality. EHRs can be used as tools for analysis and we should leverage these capabilities in clinical care.

14.3.2 IMPLICATIONS OF FINDINGS

Poorly designed EHRs have unintended consequences including cognitive overload during clinic visits and increased workload for PCPs. In the USA, the meaningful use criteria promote patient-centredness and the ability to produce chart summaries, both of which depend on the ability of EHRs to not only retrieve vast quantities of data, but also to synthesise it in ways that make it useful for physicians and patients. [23] Diagnosis-oriented text summaries could be a key platform for co-management in accountable care organisations so that the responsibility for appropriate test utilisation may be shared between primary care and specialist providers. Such a tool could also be designed to anchor the patient data to a clinical algorithm, thereby driving practice improvement.

14.3.3 COMPARISONS WITH THE PRIOR LITERATURE

Medical informatics studies have established that current human–computer interfaces adversely impact provider efficiency while reviewing patient data. [24–26] A seminal work in the area of temporal data representation was the LifeLines project which was first reported over a decade ago and was the first to present data visualisation as a solution to longitudinal data needs. [19] This system and others were designed for clinical research informatics and have not been widely adopted in clinical care settings. [27–29] Only two systems have been designed to display longitudinal data filtered by diagnosis; both display anti-hypertensive medications alongside blood pressure measurements. [30,31] A tool for reviewing laboratory results has been developed at Regenstrief Institute and presents information such as historical test results, medication-dispensing events, visit information and clinical reminders. [32] However, there is not yet widespread implementation of such tools.

14.3.4 LIMITATIONS OF THE METHOD

Our theory has not been tested with empirical research. There may be other conditions that are more costly or more profoundly impact a patient's quality of life than those we have used to illustrate temporal data views. A time–motion study may identify other management scenarios that are time-consuming and would benefit from such views. A qualitative research study might identify different provider preferences for temporal data views.

14.3.5 CALL FOR FURTHER RESEARCH

Academic researchers should pursue research to improve longitudinal data management. EHR vendors for primary care EHRs may not have the capacity or market to develop highly innovative solutions. Both clinical decision support and population disease registry functions may improve care and they will likely be accompanied by team-based care and payment reform. If accountable care organisations are to be successful, they will need to improve co-ordination of chronic disease management across settings, perhaps through care redesign efforts such as patient-centred medical homes.33,34 Accountable care organisations would represent an ideal environment for trials of such tools in chronic disease management. A variety of approaches should be evaluated and the most valuable ones should be incorporated in new EHRs.

14.4 CONCLUSIONS

PCPs need better tools in order to improve longitudinal chronic disease management. We propose that incorporating temporal patient data views into EHRs will reduce costs and improve efficiency and quality of care.

REFERENCES

1. Hoffman C, Rice D and Sung HY. Persons with chronic conditions. Their prevalence and costs. JAMA 1996; 276(18):1473–9.
2. Yach D, Hawkes C, Gould CL and Hofman KJ. The global burden of chronic diseases: overcoming impediments to prevention and control. JAMA 2004;291(21): 2616–22.
3. American Diabetes Association. Economic costs of diabetes in the U.S. in 2007. Diabetes Care 2008;31(3):596–615.
4. Agency for Healthcare Research and Quality. Economic and Health Costs of Diabetes: HCUP highlight 1. Rockville, MD: Agency for Healthcare Research and Quality, 2005. Report No.: AHRQ Publication No. 05–0034.
5. Mangione CM, Gerzoff RB, Williamson DF et al. The association between quality of care and the intensity of diabetes disease management programs. Annals of Internal Medicine 2006;145(2):107–16.

6. Garg AX, Adhikari NK, McDonald H et al. Effects of computerized clinical decision support systems on practitioner performance and patient outcomes: a systematic review. JAMA 2005;293(10):1223–38.
7. Kawamoto K, Houlihan CA, Balas EA and Lobach DF. Improving clinical practice using clinical decision support systems: a systematic review of trials to identify features critical to success. BMJ 2005;330(7494):765.
8. Buntin MB, Burke MF, Hoaglin MC and Blumenthal D. The benefits of health information technology: a review of the recent literature shows predominantly positive results. Health Affairs (Millwood) 2011;30(3):464–71.
9. Shojania KG, Jennings A, Mayhew A, Ramsay CR, Eccles MP and Grimshaw J. The effects of on-screen, point of care computer reminders on processes and outcomes of care. Cochrane Database of Systematic Reviews 2009; 3(3):CD001096.
10. Linder JA, Ma J, Bates DW, Middleton B and Stafford RS. Electronic health record use and the quality of ambulatory care in the United States. Archives of Internal Medicine 2007;167(13):1400–5.
11. Sequist TD, Gandhi TK, Karson AS et al. A randomized trial of electronic clinical reminders to improve quality of care for diabetes and coronary artery disease. Journal of the American Medical Informatics Association 2005; 12(4):431–7.
12. Poon EG, Wright A, Simon SR et al. Relationship between use of electronic health record features and health care quality: results of a statewide survey. Medical Care 2010;48(3):203–9.
13. O'Malley AS, Grossman JM, Cohen GR, Kemper NM and Pham HH. Are electronic medical records helpful for care coordination? Experiences of physician practices. Journal of General Internal Medicine 2010;25(3): 177–85.
14. Sidorov J. It ain't necessarily so: the electronic health record and the unlikely prospect of reducing health care costs. Health Affairs (Millwood) 2006;25(4):1079–85.
15. Tang PC, Fafchamps D and Shortliffe EH. Traditional medical records as a source of clinical data in the outpatient setting. Proceedings of the Annual Symposium on Computer Application in Medical Care 1994:575–9.
16. Ash JS, Berg M and Coiera E. Some unintended consequences of information technology in health care: the nature of patient care information system-related errors. Journal of the American Medical Informatics Association 2004;11(2):104–12.
17. Tufte ER. The Visual Display of Quantitative Information (2e). Cheshire, CT: Graphics Press, 2001.
18. Bauer DT, Guerlain S and Brown PJ. The design and evaluation of a graphical display for laboratory data. Journal of the American Medical Informatics Association 2010;17(4):416–24.
19. Plaisant C, Mushlin R, Snyder A, Li J, Heller D and Shneiderman B. LifeLines: using visualization to enhance navigation and analysis of patient records. Proceedings of the AMIA Symposium 1998:76–80.
20. Zeng Q, Cimino JJ and Zou KH. Providing conceptoriented views for clinical data using a knowledge-based system: an evaluation. Journal of the American Medical Informatics Association 2002;9(3):294–305.
21. Elson RB and Connelly DP. The impact of anticipatory patient data displays on physician decision making: a pilot study. Proceedings of the AMIA Annual Fall Symposium 1997:233–7.

22. Feblowitz JC, Wright A, Singh H, Samal L and Sittig DF. Summarization of clinical information: a conceptual model. Journal of Biomedical Informatics 2011;44(4): 688–99.
23. Blumenthal D and Tavenner M. The 'meaningful use' regulation for electronic health records. New England Journal of Medicine 2010;363(6):501–4.
24. Fries JF. Alternatives in medical record formats. Medical Care 1974;12(10):871–81.
25. Hammond WE and Stead WW. Adopting TMR for physician/nurse use. Proceedings of the Annual Symposium on Computer Application in Medical Care 1991: 833–7.
26. Elson RB, Faughnan JG and Connelly DP. An industrial process view of information delivery to support clinical decision making: implications for systems design and process measures. Journal of the American Medical Informatics Association 1997;4(4):266–78.
27. Wang TD, Wongsuphasawat K, Plaisant C and Shneiderman B. Extracting insights from electronic health records: case studies, a visual analytics process model, and design recommendations. Journal of Medical Systems 2011. (Epub ahead of print.)
28. Shahar Y, Goren-Bar D, Boaz D and Tahan G. Distributed, intelligent, interactive visualization and exploration of time-oriented clinical data and their abstractions. Artificial Intelligence in Medicine 2006; 38(2):115–35.
29. Post AR and Harrison JH Jr. PROTEMPA: a method for specifying and identifying American Medical Informatics Association 2007;14(5): 674–83.
30. Mabotuwana T and Warren J. ChronoMedIt – a computational quality audit framework for better management of patients with chronic conditions. Journal of Biomedical Informatics 2010;43(1):144–58.
31. Goldstein MK, Coleman RW, Tu SW et al. Translating research into practice: organizational issues in implementing automated decision support for hypertension in three medical centers. Journal of the American Medical Informatics Association 2004;11(5):368–76.
32. Chang KC, Overhage JM, Hui SL and Were MC. Enhancing laboratory report contents to improve outpatient management of test results. Journal of the American Medical Informatics Association 2010;17(1): 99–103.
33. Bates DW and Bitton A. The future of health information technology in the patient-centered medical home. Health Affairs 2010;29(4):614–21.
34. Rittenhouse DR, Shortell SM and Fisher ES. Primary care and accountable care — two essential elements of delivery-system reform. New England Journal of Medicine 2009;361(24):2301–3.

CHAPTER 15

INDICATION-BASED PRESCRIBING PREVENTS WRONG-PATIENT MEDICATION ERRORS IN COMPUTERIZED PROVIDER ORDER ENTRY (CPOE)

WILLIAM GALANTER, SUZANNE FALCK, MATTHEW BURNS, MARCI LARAGH, AND BRUCE L. LAMBERT

15.1 BACKGROUND AND SIGNIFICANCE

Use of computerized physician order entry (CPOE) systems for the placement of medication orders is part of the hospital-based and the eligible provider components of the US government's meaningful use incentives. [1] While CPOE has been shown to decrease medication errors [2–4] and in some studies mortality, [5] use of CPOE can also have unintended negative consequences, creating opportunities for or increasing the likelihood of certain types of medication errors. [6–9]

One potential problem with an electronic medical record (EMR) is the risk that a physician will accidentally enter orders in the wrong patient's chart. [8–10] In spite of all their disadvantages, paper charts afforded prescribers multiple visual cues that served to orient them to whether or not they were ordering for the correct patient, including the thickness of the chart, the handwriting, and the patient's problem list. [10] Most of these cues are either missing entirely or are less salient in the electronic environment, increasing the opportunity for wrong-chart errors. Use of patient lists may cause 'pick-list' or other user–interface driven errors, [7,11] and wrong patient selection may be facilitated by system features that allow clinicians to find charts rapidly, such as the ability to select from a list of recently opened charts, or to have multiple patient charts open simultaneously.

A study by Wilcox and Chen estimated that 0.3–0.5% of clinical notes were placed in the wrong patient's electronic chart. [12] A recent study by Adelman et al [13] estimated that for about 1 in 1000 medication orders, clinicians realized that they had placed the order on the wrong patient chart and canceled it prior to any medication administration.

As part of a separate project, we previously developed and implemented a set of clinical decision support (CDS) alerts to prompt prescribers to add problems to the problem list when they were prescribing certain medications in the absence of certain documented problems. When analyzing the effectiveness of these alerts, which did in fact improve the completeness and accuracy of problem lists, [14, 15] we noticed that a small percentage of the time, prescribers canceled medication orders immediately after receiving an indication alert. We suspected that the indication alerts may have improved the prescribers' situation awareness and made them realize that they were about to order a medication for the wrong patient.

15.1.1 OBJECTIVE

Our aim was to determine whether or not indication-based prompts during CPOE of medications might help clinicians to identify and cancel wrong-patient medication orders, thereby intercepting the errors before orders were completed and medications administered.

TABLE 1: Alert groups with corresponding medications

Alert group name	Medications
S/P CVA	Aspirin-dipyridamole
COPD/asthma	Fluticasone, fluticasone/salmeterol, tiotropium
Diabetes mellitus oral	Rosiglitazone, repaglinide, pioglitazone, nateglinide, metformin, glimepiride, sulfonylureas, and combinations of these medications
Factor VIIa	Coagulation factor VIIa
HTN	Aliskiren, amiloride, β blockers except metoprolol-succinate and carvedilol), calcium channel blockers, clonidine, furosemide, guanfacine, methyldopa, metolazone, minoxidil, nitroprusside thiazides, triamterene, and combinations of these medications
HTN/CHF	Carvedilol, hydralazine, isosorbide dinitrate, metoprolol succinate, spironolactone
HTN/BPH	α Blockers
HTN/CHF/nephropathy	ACE, ARB
HIV	NRTIs, NtARTIs or NtRTIs, NNRTIs, protease inhibitors
Hyperlipidemia	HMG-CoA reductase inhibitors, red yeast rice, niacin, fibric acids, ezetimibe, cholestyramine
Intravenous immune globulin	Intravenous immune globulin (IVIG)
Osteoporosis	Bisphosphonates
Ambulatory insulin	Insulins
Pediatric asthma	Albuterol
Proton pump inhibitors (PPI)	PPI
Selective serotonin reuptake inhibitors	Selective serotonin reuptake inhibitors (SSRI)
Hypothyroidism	Levothyroxine; liotrix, thyroid desiccated

15.2 MATERIALS AND METHODS

The University of Illinois Hospital and Health Sciences System (UI-Health) has a 450-bed teaching hospital and a large multi-specialty ambulatory clinic utilizing a commercial EMR (Millennium; Cerner Corporation, Kansas City, Missouri, USA) for problem lists, clinical notes, test results, medication lists, and orders. The EMR is used by all specialties, allowing any clinician to update patient records and problem lists either as free text or using common discrete coded nomenclatures (ICD-9 CM [16] or SNOMED [17]). All medication orders are placed by CPOE which is associated with a commercially available CDS system (Discern Expert; Cerner Corporation) which has been described previously for this and other types of alerts. [14, 15, 18, 19]

Orders for specified medications (table 1) triggered an alert for the clinician to update the medical record for patients whose electronic problem list did not contain an active problem indicated by that medicine. Depending on the medication, alerts displayed one or more possible problems (figure 1). The clinician could select one or more of the offered problems, choose not to enter a problem at all, or cancel the order. Once selected, problems were added automatically to the patient's problem list in the EMR. Clinicians at UI-Health are familiar with similar types of CDS, so we performed no additional physician training.

All specified medication indications triggered alerts in all locations of the medical center, with the exception of insulin, which triggered alerts only in the ambulatory setting, as insulin is very specific to diabetes for outpatients, but in the hospital is frequently prescribed for non-diabetic patients in order to maintain tight glycemic control.

Alerts triggered from April 2006 through February 2012 were analyzed to identify sequences that met the following criteria: (a) an order was started but not completed for a given patient; and (b) within 10 min, [13] the same prescriber submitted an order for the same medication for a different patient. An experienced clinician then completed a chart review of each of these identified instances to decide whether the first order attempt was an intercepted wrong-chart error.

Two criteria were applied during chart review: first, that the patient was not currently being prescribed the medication (this criterion was required due to limitations of automated review and medication lists) and second, that the medication was inconsistent with the clinical condition(s) of the patient and a review of clinical notes. A second reviewer then confirmed all possible intercepted errors by the first chart reviewer.

Intercepted errors were expressed as the number of intercepted errors per 1000 alerts. For each of these proportions measured, the SE of the proportion was determined. Some proportions were compared using χ^2 tests with significance defined with a $p \leq 0.05$.

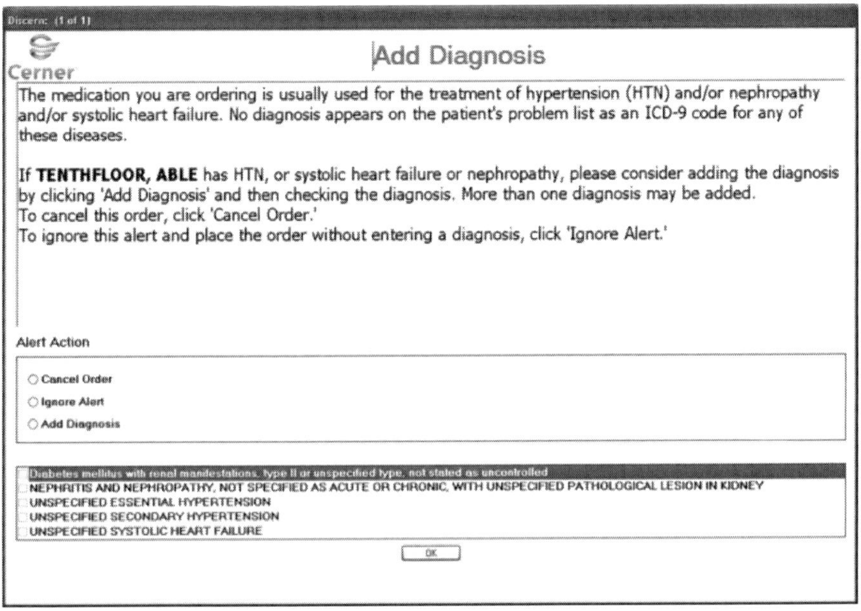

FIGURE 1: Indication alert for angiotensin converting enzymes (ACE) inhibitors and angiotensin receptor blockers (ARB).

This study was approved by the University of Illinois Institutional Review Board. A waiver of consent for both the patient and clinician subjects was obtained.

15.3 RESULTS

Over the nearly 6-year period, from April 2006 to February 2012, the system fired 127 320 alerts on 79 304 encounters with 54 608 unique patients. The distribution by location was 42% inpatient, 38% outpatient, 14% in the emergency department (ED), and 6% undefined. Housestaff received 77% of the alerts, attending physicians 18%, and 5% others (registered nurses, pharmacists, advanced practice nurses, nurse practitioners, medical students, etc). Of these alerts, 3462 (2.72%) were not associated with an order for the medication during the encounter. Chart review was performed on 822 charts involving an order within 2 min prior to and 20 min after the alert due to some slight differences in the alert and order times in our reports.

Chart review identified 32 intercepted wrong chart errors from the 127 320 alerts (table 2). None of these chart errors were for patients who shared the correct patient's last name. In 59%±9% of the interceptions, the clinician had both patient charts open when initiating the first order. Both patients were under the care of the clinician in all but one instance (97%±3%).

TABLE 2: Description of all intercepted wrong-patient medication errors

Medication	Recipient	Location	2 Charts open at same time?*	Caring for both patients	Delay (min)†
Albuterol	Housestaff	Inpatient	Yes	Yes	1
Alendronate	Housestaff	Inpatient	Yes	Yes	0
Amlodipine-valsartan	Attending	Ambulatory	Yes	Yes	1
Diltiazem	Housestaff	ED	Yes	Yes	0
Fluticasone	Housestaff	Ambulatory	No	Yes	9
Glipizide	Nurse	Ambulatory	No	Yes	335‡
Glipizide	Housestaff	Inpatient	Yes	Yes	3
Glyburide	Housestaff	Ambulatory	No	Yes	2
Glyburide	Attending	Ambulatory	Yes	Yes	1
HCTZ	Attending	Ambulatory	Yes	Yes	1
HCTZ	Attending	Ambulatory	Yes	Yes	1
HCTZ	Housestaff	ED	Yes	Yes	5
Insulin regular	Housestaff	ED	Yes	Yes	0
Labetalol	Housestaff	ED	No	Yes	0
Labetalol	Housestaff	Inpatient	Yes	Yes	2
Lisinopril	Housestaff	Inpatient	Yes	Yes	0
Metformin	Housestaff	Ambulatory	Yes	Yes	10
Metformin	Nurse	ED	No	No	5
Metformin	Housestaff	Inpatient	No	Yes	10

TABLE 2: *Cont.*

Medication	Recipient	Location	2 Charts open at same time?*	Caring for both patients	Delay (min)†
Metformin	Housestaff	Inpatient	Yes	Yes	0
Metformin	Housestaff	Inpatient	Yes	Yes	0
Metformin	Housestaff	Inpatient	Yes	Yes	1
Metoprolol	Attending	Ambulatory	No	Yes	1
Metoprolol	Housestaff	ED	Yes	Yes	3
Metoprolol	Housestaff	Inpatient	No	Yes	1
Metoprolol	Housestaff	Inpatient	No	Yes	0
Metoprolol	Housestaff	Inpatient	No	Yes	0
Metoprolol	Attending	Inpatient	No	Yes	0
Metoprolol	Housestaff	Inpatient	Yes	Yes	3
Nifedipine	Housestaff	Inpatient	No	Yes	0
Simvastatin	Housestaff	Ambulatory	Yes	Yes	5
Verapamil	Housestaff	Ambulatory	No	Yes	1

*In the Cerner Powerchart, more than 1 chart can be open at the same time as a site specific preference.
†The events were only captured to the minute and reported to the minute.
‡The error was intercepted based on a verbal order, the attending clinician was notified, and the second order was placed 355 min later. However, review of the chart identified that the decision to replace the order in the correct patient chart was rapid.
ED, emergency department.

The interception rate did not vary as a function of venue or the type of clinician who triggered the alert, but did show significant variation by the type of medication ordered: metformin and metoprolol 0.81/1000 alerts versus others 0.17/1000 alerts ($p<0.001$) (table 3). Interestingly, only 15 medications were involved in the 32 errors, the most common being metoprolol and metformin.

15.4 DISCUSSION

As with any complicated process, medical errors are more likely the result of poor systems and procedures than just mistakes by individuals.[20]

EMR and CPOE systems have created new problems that often are not anticipated or recognized. Many of these are related to poor user–interface design and poor workflow. [6–9 ,11 ,21] One way to improve system quality is through redundant error checking. We have demonstrated one mechanism of error checking by leveraging medication indications with the problem list. The idea of reconciling medication indications with the problem list is not new, and is based on the concept of medication–problem list mismatches. [22 ,23]

TABLE 3: Wrong-patient alerts by venue, clinician type, and medication

Venue	Intercepted errors	Alerts	Rate (interceptions/1000 alerts)
Emergency department	6	17668	0.34±0.14NS†
Inpatient	15	53787	0.28±0.07
Ambulatory	11	48196	0.23±0.07
Ordering clinician			
Housestaff	24	98298	0.24±0.05NS
Attending	6	22453	0.27±0.11
Other	2	6569	0.30±0.22
Medication			
Metformin and metoprolol	13	16084	0.81±0.22*
Others	19	111236	0.17±0.04
Total	32	127320	0.25±0.04

The results of comparisons among the values in this section were not statistically significant.
*$p<0.001$ using the χ^2 statistic.
†The error reported is the SE of a proportion.

CDS systems associated with CPOE typically have attempted to use drug–drug interactions, or more recently drug–laboratory interactions, to reduce medication errors. The drug–problem list alerts described here attempt to exploit the relationship between medications and problems (ie, diagnoses, indications). These alerts have been shown to improve problem list documentation. [14 ,15] Although problem list documentation always has been thought of as a means to improve patient care, [24] and is required by both the Joint Commission [25] and meaningful use, [1] our study demonstrated that drug–problem list alerts have an additional, beneficial effect: they help to intercept wrong-patient medication errors. Safeguards against wrong-patient errors can be implemented at multiple points in the medication ordering sequence, detecting and correcting problems before, during, and after data entry. The indication alerts we studied function during data entry, and can be implemented independently or in combination with other safeguards.

One potential pre-order safeguard against wrong-patient medication errors is to limit the number of charts that a clinician can have open at one time. In our analysis, 60% of the intercepted errors were associated with at least two open charts. However, the chart selection process itself may facilitate wrong patient selection through pick list or other menu selection errors. [11] Without direct study, and ignoring the efficiency benefits of each feature, it is not clear which system promotes more errors, allowing multiple open charts or allowing only one chart but requiring more frequent chart selections. This topic requires more study.

Recently, Adelman et al examined two approaches to help clinicians decrease intercepted wrong-patient medication errors. One was for prescribers to make a single-click confirmation that they had verified patient identity before entering an electronic order. This reduced self-intercepted wrong-patient errors by 16%. The other was to have clinicians re-key a patient's initials, gender, and age before entering an electronic order, which reduced self-intercepted wrong-patient errors by 41%. Self-intercepted wrong-patient errors were measured using a 'retract-and-reorder' logic which looked for all instances where a single provider canceled an order and placed an order for the same medication in another chart within 10 min of signing the initial order. This method was shown to have a positive predictive value of 76%. [13]

Another technique recently published by Hyman et al [26] showed a 40% reduction in wrong-patient errors when a picture of the patient was displayed at the time of final order. The analysis in the study was done on actual non-intercepted errors and showed a numerical reduction, although the errors were self-reported and the total number was small. Nonetheless, the method is promising, and is likely to be more efficient than more interruptive safeguards.

For analysis of post-order safeguards, Carpenter and Gorman evaluated an algorithm which, after patient discharge, compared patient medication prescriptions to the patient's medical record, identifying a 10% mismatch rate. [22] In terms of medical impact, 52% of the mismatches were identified as being clinically relevant. Approximately two-thirds of the mismatches concerned patients whose drug treatment did not have a corresponding medical problem documented in their medical record, and one-third were patients whose prescribed drug treatment of their medical problems was not appropriate.

The relationship between medications, indications, and problem lists or billing diagnoses could be used retrospectively on its own, or as a part of a surveillance system. This relationship could help improve the specificity of a medication–laboratory alert. For instance, knowledge of the presence of atrial fibrillation in patients with congestive heart failure would allow for a more specific alert based on elevated digoxin levels, since the appropriate level of digoxin is dependent on the indication. [27] In studies that examine the risk for drug name confusion (eg, Basco et al [28]), the connections between the medications and the problem list could help improve the specificity of the alerting system.

The present study evaluated indication-based alerts during medication ordering. We found an interception rate of 0.25 errors per 1000 alerts. This is difficult to compare directly with other studies since our alerts are a non-random subset of all medication orders. As one comparison, Adelman et al [13] identified a retract and re-order rate of 0.76/1000, of which 0.58/1000 were estimated to be wrong-patient errors. It would not be reasonable to compare our rate to that of Adelman et al, given that his relied on self-intercepted errors after submission of the order and ours was from interceptions prior to signature. Our interception rate may differ for those errors which may otherwise have been intercepted after submission. It would be very difficult to measure all wrong-patient medication errors as many do not produce harm, so careful measurement of adverse drug events would not suffice.

Because we do not know the magnitude of wrong-patient errors, is it difficult to say how robust our method is at intercepting errors, or whether these errors would have produced adverse events.

None of the individual methods that have been shown to prevent wrong-patient medication errors will be completely effective. Our method is limited to medications for which medication–problem alerts are appropriate, which is not all medications. [15] The methods used by Adelman et al [13] reduced self-intercepted errors by an estimated 40%, but increased clinician order time by over 6 s per order. The absolute error reduction using photographs, as suggested by Hyman et al, [26] is uncertain and effectiveness may vary, as some patients may appear similar when ill, may appear quite different while in the intensive care unit, and neonates often appear very similar. It is likely that a combination of these methods, used more or less simultaneously or at least in an integrated fashion, will be required to achieve optimal reduction of wrong-patient medication errors.

15.5 LIMITATIONS

This study was performed at a single medical center with significant housestaff ordering. Although no differences were found in the housestaff and attending clinician rates, the power to determine this difference was low, thus it is possible the magnitude of the benefit of the intervention might change based on the type of clinician. In addition, the intervention study only used a subset of medications for which the alerts have been built. The data suggested the possibility of variation based on medication, thus a fully developed system with more medications may have a different error interception rate.

15.6 CONCLUSION

Wrong-patient errors, intercepted or not, are known to occur in CPOE. Reduction in these errors can be pursued using a variety of recently published methods. We found that implementing CPOE alerts to help providers improve patient problem list completeness also helped clinicians notice a discordance between a medication's indications and the patient whose medical record they were using, allowing the clinician to recognize and cancel pending wrong-patient errors at a rate of 0.25 per 1000 alerts. Thus indication-based alerts yield the dual benefit of intercepting wrong-patient medication errors and improving the accuracy and completeness of problem list documentation.

REFERENCES

1. Blumenthal D, Tavenner M. The 'meaningful use' regulation for electronic health records. N Engl J Med 2010;363:501–4.
2. Bates DW, Leape L, Cullen DJ, et al. Effect of computerized physician order entry and a team intervention on prevention of serious medication errors. JAMA 1998;280:1311e16.
3. Bates DW, Teich JM, Lee J, et al. The impact of computerized physician order entry on medication error prevention. J Am Med Inform Assoc 1999;6:313e21.
4. Reckmann MH, Westbrook JI, Koh Y, et al. Does computerized provider order entry reduce prescribing errors for hospital inpatients? A systematic review. J Am Med Inform Assoc 2009;16:613e23.
5. Longhurst CA, Parast L, Sandborg CI, et al. Decrease in hospital-wide mortality rate after implementation of a commercially sold computerized physician order entry system. Pediatrics 2010;126:14–21.
6. Bates DW, Cohen M, Leape LL, et al. Reducing the frequency of errors in medicine using information technology. J Am Med Inform Assoc 2001;8:299–308.
7. Campbell EM, Sittig DF, Ash JS, et al. Types of unintended consequences related to computerized provider order entry. J Am Med Inform Assoc 2006;13:547e55.
8. Koppel R, Metlay J, Cohen A, et al. Role of computerized physician order entry systems in facilitating medication errors. JAMA 2005;293:1197–203.
9. Ash J, Sittig D, Poon E, et al. The extent and importance of unintended consequences related to computerized provider order entry. J Am Med Inform Assoc 2007;14:415–23.
10. Ash JS, Gorman PN, Hersh WR, et al. Perceptions of house officers who use physician order entry. Proc AMIA Symp 1999;471–5.
11. Koppel R, Metlay JP, Cohen A, et al. Role of computerized physician order entry systems in facilitating medication errors. JAMA 2005;293:1197–203.
12. Wilcox A, Chen Y-H. Hripcsak minimizing electronic health record patient-note mismatches. J Am Med Inform Assoc 2011;18:511–14.
13. Adelman JS, Kalkut GE, Schechter CB, et al. Understanding and preventing wrong-patient electronic orders: a randomized controlled trial. J Am Med Inform Assoc Published Online First: 29 June 2012 doi:10.1136/amiajnl-2012-001055
14. Galanter WL, Hier DB, Jao C, et al. Computerized physician order entry of medications and clinical decision support can improve problem list documentation compliance. Int J Med Inform 2010;79:332–8.

15. Walton SM, Galanter WL, Rosencranz H, et al. A trial of inpatient indication based prescribing during computerized order entry with medications used off-label. Appl Clin Inf 2011;2:94–103.
16. ICD-9-CM, International Classification of Diseases, ninth revision, Clinical Modification, http://www.cdc.gov/nchs/about/otheract/icd9/abticd9.htm (accessed 3 Dec 2012).
17. SNOMED, Systematized Nomenclature of Medicine, http://www.cap.org/apps/cap.portal?nfpb=true& pageLabel=snomedpage (accessed 3 Dec 2012)
18. Raschke R, Gollihare B, Wunderlich T, et al. A computer alert system to prevent injury from adverse drug events. JAMA 280. 1998;15:317–1320.
19. Galanter WL, Didomenico R, Polikaitis A. A trial of automated decision support alerts for contraindicated medications using computerized physician order entry. J Am Med Inform Assoc 2005;12:269–74.
20. Committee on Quality of Health Care in America. To Err is human: building a safer health ystem. Washington DC, USA: Institute of Medicine, 2000.
21. Committee on Patient Safety and Health Information Technology. Health IT and patient safety: building safer systems for better care. Washington DC, USA: Institute of Medicine, 2012.
22. Carpenter J, Gorman P. Using Medication List-Problem List Mismatches as Markers of Potential Error AMIA. Annual Symposium Proceedings, 2002.
23. Jao C, Hier D, Galanter W. Using clinical decision support to maintain medication and problem lists: a pilot study to yield higher patient safety. Syst Man Cybern 2008:739–43.
24. Weed LL. Medical records that guide and teach. N Eng J Med 1968;278:593–600.
25. Comprehensive Accreditation Manual for Hospitals. The joint commission on accreditation of healthcare organizations. IL: Oakbrook Terrace, 1996.
26. Hyman D, Laire M, Redmond D, et al. The use of patient pictures and verification screens to reduce computerized provider order entry errors. Pediatrics 2012;130:e211–19.
27. Bauman JL, Didomenico RJ, Galanter WL. Mechanisms, manifestations, and management of digoxin toxicity in the modern era. Am J Cardiovasc Drugs 2006;6:77–86.
28. Basco WT Jr., Ebeling M, Hulsey TC, et al. Using pharmacy data to screen for look-alike, sound-alike substitution errors in pediatric prescriptions. Acad Pediatr 2010;10:233–7.

AUTHOR NOTES

CHAPTER 1

Acknowledgments
We thank Alexander McGowan for his technical and audio recording contributions during the interview.

Footnotes
Contributors DFS, JM, and JSA: study concept and design; AW, DFS, JM, JSA, and LLW: analysis and interpretation of data; AW: drafting of the manuscript; AW, DFS, JM, JSA, and LLW: critical revision of the manuscript for important intellectual content; AW, DFS, JM, and JSA: study supervision.

Competing Interests
None.

Provenance and Peer Review
Not commissioned; externally peer reviewed.

CHAPTER 3

Acknowledgments
Funding by Astra Zeneca Pharmaceuticals. Nicola Payne, MPhil, consultant for Providence Medical Group, assisted with statistical evaluation.

CHAPTER 4

Competing Interests
The authors declare that they have no competing interests.

Author Contributions
AW conceived the study, participated in its design, observations, and analysis, and drafted the manuscript. FM coordinated the participants of the study, participated in observations and analysis, and helped with the draft of the manuscript. JF participated in editing and revision of the manuscript, as well as additional analysis of the qualitative data and linking of themes. All authors read and approved the final manuscript.

Acknowledgements and Funding
This work was supported by a grant from the Partners Information Systems Research Council. We are grateful to the participants who allowed us to observe and interview them during our research. We are also grateful to Joan Ash and David W Bates who read early drafts of this manuscript and provided feedback.

The funding of this project was provided by a Partners Healthcare Information System Research Council Institutional Grant.

CHAPTER 5

Competing Interests
The authors declare that they have no competing interests.

Author Contributions
CH created the questionnaire, conducted interviews, collected online responses, transcribed and analyzed the data, and drafted the manuscript. MB participated in designing the study and drafting of the manuscript. DS participated in the review and redrafting process. AW participated in the design and coordination of the study, recruitment of respondents, data analysis, and drafting of the manuscript. All authors read and approved the final manuscript.

CHAPTER 6

Acknowlesgements

This work was supported by a grant from the Partners Community Health-Care Incorporated (PCHI) System Improvement Grant Program and approved by the Partners HealthCare Institutional Review Board. PCHI was not involved in the design, execution or analysis of the study or in the preparation of this manuscript.

Conflict of Interest

The authors declare that they do not have a conflict of interest.

CHAPTER 7

Conflict of Interest

Neither Dr. Wright nor Dr. Bates have any conflicts to report. Dr. Wright had full access to all of the data in the study and takes responsibility for the integrity of the data and the accuracy of the data analysis.

Human Subjects Review

The study was reviewed and approved by the Partners HealthCare Human Subjects Committee.

CHAPTER 8

Acknowledgements

The authors are grateful to the Partners HealthCare Quality Data Warehouse and Research Patient Data Registry teams who provided the data used in the analyses. They are likewise grateful to the Partners High Performance Computing (HPC) team who provided access to the Partners HPC Cluster.

The authors also appreciate the input and advice provided by Howard Goldberg, Cheryl van Putten and Marilyn Paterno who were involved in earlier phases of this project, as well as that of David W. Bates and Gordy Schiff who provided feedback on the methods and approach. Other members of the Partners HealthCare Clinical Informatics Research and Development and Clinical Quality Analysis Groups as well as the Brigham and Women's Hospital Division of General Internal Medicine provided useful comments on the work.

This work was supported by a grant from Siemens Medical Solutions and the Partners Information Systems Research Council. Neither Partners nor Siemens had any role in the design of the study, analysis of the data, interpretation of the results, or the decision to publish.

Dr. Wright had full access to all of the data in the study and takes responsibility for the integrity of the data and the accuracy of the data analysis.

CHAPTER 9

Acknowledgments

We would like to acknowledge the Partners HealthCare Research Patient Data Registry and Quality Data Management teams for supplying data used in this study and Karen Sax McLoughlin, of the Brigham and Women's Physician Organization, for her work in managing the grant. We are also grateful to Elizabeth S Chen, PhD of the University of Vermont for her participation in preparation of the grant application for this project and design of the methods.

Footnotes

Funding This work was supported by a grant from the Partners Community HealthCare Incorporated (PCHI) System Improvement Grant Program. PCHI was not involved in the design, execution or analysis of the study or in the preparation of this manuscript.

Ethics Approval

This study was approved by the Partners HealthCare Institutional Review Board.

Provenance and Peer Review

Not commissioned; externally peer reviewed.

CHAPTER 10

Acknowledgments

We thank the following: Don Bugbee, Betti Rozenman, Regina Breyt, Janak Joshi and Bill Hanley for designing, developing and implementing the MAPLE software; Teal Aroy, Sue Smith, Janet Cygielnik, Dave Dubois, Kira Tsivkin and Roberto Rocha for assistance in knowledge base creation; Howard Goldberg, Mike Vashevko and Molly Schaeffer for providing the problem terminology service; Julie Fiskio, Deb Williams, Yelena Kruglova, Brian Hingston and Alex Turchin for extracting data; E John Orav for statistical consulting; Blackford Middleton for assisting with development and implementation management; and Stanislav Henkin for help with editing of the manuscript.

Footnotes

Funding Partners Community HealthCare Incorporated (PCHI) System Improvement Grant Program.

Ethics Approval

Ethics approval was provided by Partners HealthCare Human Research Committee.

Provenance and Peer Review

Not commissioned; externally peer reviewed.

Data Sharing Statement

AW had full access to all of the data in the study and takes responsibility for the integrity of the data and the accuracy of the data analysis.

CHAPTER 11

Acknowledgements

With special thanks to Lisa Canonge, Marla Lax, R.N. Amy Looi, R.N. and Jennifer Welch C.T. (ASCP) for assistance in the CDS alert development. This study was approved by the University of Illinois at Chicago Institutional Review Board.

The study was in part funded by the National Patient Safety Foundation, James S. Todd Memorial Research Grant (PI: C. Jao). The funding source had no role in the production of this manuscript.

Dr. Galanter was supported by grant number U18HS016973 from the Agency for Healthcare Research and Quality. The content is solely the responsibility of the authors and does not necessarily represent the official views of the Agency for Healthcare Research and Quality.

Contributors: W.L. Galanter helped in CDS concept, CDS design, data analysis, and initital mansucript draft. D.B. Hier helped in CDS concept, data analysis, and mansucript writing. C. Jao helped in CDS concept and mansucript writing. D. Sarne helped in CDS design, data analysis, and manuscript writing.

CHAPTER 12

Acknowledgments

This work is supported by a Deseret Foundation Grant (Salt Lake City, Utah). We would like to thank Min Bowman for her help with the modified Problems module. We would also like to thank Greg Gurr for his advices and his help. Scott Narus and Stan Huff also gave us helpful advice and guidance for which we are grateful. Finally, we are especially grateful to Terry Clemmer whose enthusiasm for the problem list made this study possible.

CHAPTER 15

Footnotes

Funding This project was supported in part by grant number U19HS021093 from the Agency for Healthcare Research and Quality. The content is solely the responsibility of the authors and does not necessarily represent the official views of the Agency for Healthcare Research and Quality.

Ethics Approval
The University of Illinois at Chicago Institutional Review Board approved this study.

Provenance and Peer Review
Not commissioned; externally peer reviewed.

Data Sharing Statement
This was a retrospective observational study and as such no primary data were produced and only routine clinical data, which will not be shared, were analyzed.

INDEX

A

accuracy, xx, 36, 67–68, 73, 75, 77–78, 81, 114, 118–119, 131, 133, 149, 159, 162, 166–167, 170, 172–173, 176–179, 184, 190, 196, 200, 206–207, 224, 226–227, 230, 235–236, 239, 242, 246, 250, 256, 261–262, 264, 269, 275, 300, 310, 315–317

age, 9, 16, 48–51, 88, 92, 95, 97–98, 111–114, 219, 287–288, 307

alcohol, 31, 90

alert, xx, 72, 109, 203, 212, 214–216, 220, 224–225, 232, 234–239, 242, 290, 300–305, 308, 311, 317
  alert reminder, 225

allergies, 54, 127, 184

ambulatory, 45–46, 54–56, 118, 143, 179–180, 206, 240–242, 267–268, 297, 301–302, 304–306

American Health Information Management Association (AHIMA), 80, 84, 87, 118, 134

angiotensin II receptor blockers (ARB), 47–48, 52, 60, 301, 303

antibodies, 168, 172

Apriori algorithm, 154, 160, 178

arthritis, 164–165, 188, 198–200, 212, 220, 222, 283

asthma, 90, 92, 100, 103–104, 106, 115, 139, 188, 190, 198–200, 207, 212, 220, 222, 233, 236, 239, 301

audit, 24, 32, 39–41, 43, 76, 224, 226–227, 230, 242, 248, 298

automated diagnosis, 147

Automated Patient Problem List Enhancement (APPLE), 186–187, 189–190

Automatic Problem List (APL), 246, 249–250

B

Bayesian network, 149, 179

beta-blockers, 47–54

bias, 79, 132, 203–205, 265–266

billing, 59, 66, 71, 74, 123, 132, 184–185, 189–190, 192, 194–197, 199–205, 210–211, 214, 224, 247, 276, 308
  billing diagnosis codes, 211

biomedical informatics, xiv–xv, 16, 147, 298

blood pressure, 56, 224, 280, 284–285, 293–295

Bonferroni correction, 217, 223, 225

C

cancer, 31–32, 73, 85, 90–92, 100, 105, 112, 122, 139, 174, 188, 198–200, 210, 212, 220, 222, 233, 282
  breast cancer, 85, 90–92, 100, 105, 112, 122, 139, 174, 188, 198–200, 210, 212, 220, 222

care coordination, 280, 297
care episode, 45, 252
Center for Knowledge Building Tools, 13
Certification Commission for Health Information Technology (CCHIT), 60–61, 148, 179
coronary artery disease, 100–102, 139, 149, 188, 198–200, 212, 220, 222, 279, 284, 297
chronic disease, xvii, xx, 84, 90–91, 106, 185, 279–281, 283–284, 294, 296
   chronic disease management, xx, 279–281, 283–284, 296
chronic obstructive pulmonary disease (COPD), 163, 188, 190, 198–200, 212, 220, 222, 233, 236, 239, 279, 301
chronology, 73
clinic, 6, 20, 25, 32, 36, 46, 54, 64, 70–71, 76–77, 81, 85, 118, 124–126, 131–133, 177, 179, 206, 214–215, 217, 219, 227, 230, 242, 269, 280, 294, 301
clinical
   clinical charts, 37
   clinical data exchange, 136
   clinical decision support (CDS), xviii–xix, 60, 71, 80, 83, 86, 112, 118, 121, 123, 140, 148, 173, 179, 183–185, 187, 203, 206, 209–210, 225, 229–231, 233–234, 237–241, 243, 280, 282, 287–288, 290, 296–297, 300, 302, 306, 310–311, 317–318
   clinical information system, 14, 150, 173, 180, 245, 247, 267
   clinical research, 80–81, 229, 247, 295

clinical teaching, 27
co-occurrence, 150–151, 180, 186–187, 207, 228
code set, 125
coding, 28, 64, 86–87, 137, 207, 242, 247, 268
computer, 8–11, 16, 19–21, 28, 30–31, 39, 41, 43–44, 59, 75, 118, 134, 136, 142, 150, 161, 206, 228, 241–242, 246, 248, 268, 295, 297–298, 311
   computer science, 150
   Computer-based Patient Record (CPR), 246, 268
computerized, 8, 14, 20–21, 80–81, 118, 133, 143, 179–180, 184, 206, 227, 229, 231, 233, 235, 237, 239, 241–243, 247, 266, 268–269, 274, 297, 299, 310–311
   computerized physician order entry (CPOE), 131, 143, 180, 229, 231–233, 235, 237, 239–243, 266, 299–300, 302, 306, 309–311
congestive heart failure (CHF), 47, 56, 165, 177, 188, 198–200, 202, 209, 212, 220, 222, 279, 284–285, 292–293, 301, 308
continuity, 32, 36, 184, 246
conviction, 156–158, 162–163, 168, 187
cost, 35, 43, 80, 147, 151, 173–174, 185, 225, 240, 266–267, 275, 279, 293–294, 296–297
couplers, 10, 12–13, 15–16
culture, 64, 67–68, 76–77, 130
current practice, 174–175

D

data mining, xix, 143, 147, 150–151, 174, 178–180, 185–186, 210, 229

Index 323

association rule mining, xix, 150–151, 155–156, 158–159, 175, 177, 179, 186
  frequent item set mining, 150–153, 155
data representation, 295
data set, 89, 98, 151, 158, 173–174, 180, 265
decision support, xviii–xx, 16, 60, 71–72, 76, 80, 83, 86, 112, 118, 121, 123, 133, 140, 142, 147–148, 173, 175, 178–179, 183–185, 187, 203, 206, 209–210, 227, 229, 241–243, 265, 280, 282, 287–288, 290, 296–298, 300, 310–311
demographic, 28, 30–31, 47, 50, 72, 98, 111, 113, 116–117, 217, 219
developers, xx, 3, 78, 140, 203
diabetes, 29, 48–50, 60–61, 71, 73, 84, 90–91, 101–102, 107, 127, 137, 139, 149, 153, 155–156, 159–160, 167, 174–175, 177, 185, 188–189, 192, 194–196, 198–200, 202, 210, 212, 215, 220, 222, 224, 233–234, 236, 263, 279–280, 296–297, 301–302
diagnosis, xvii, 22, 28, 34, 47–50, 52–53, 60, 72, 89–91, 103, 108, 114, 123, 130, 147, 149, 211, 224–225, 230, 232–239, 242, 248, 268, 280–281, 283, 290, 293, 295
  diagnostic action, 22
  diagnostic test, 16, 207, 284
digoxin, 48, 52–53, 55, 60, 242, 308, 311
discipline, 5, 37, 39, 41, 43–44, 92, 95, 97, 99
disease management, xx, 54, 279–281, 283–285, 287, 289, 291, 293, 295–297
documentation, viii, xx–xxi, 16, 45, 47, 59–61, 63, 69, 72, 77–78, 85, 118, 121, 129, 131, 133–134, 140, 158, 179, 206–207, 224, 226, 228–231, 237, 240–241, 245–248, 254, 264–266, 306, 310
drug interaction, 140, 306
drug therapy, 33, 84

E

ease of use, 136
education, 4, 7, 14–16, 21, 38–39, 41, 44, 67–68, 75, 87, 206, 241, 276
efficiency, 21, 28, 35, 43, 80, 130, 142, 282, 284, 291, 294–296, 307
electronic chart, 251, 282, 300
electronic medical record (EMR), 16, 46–47, 54, 60–61, 121, 134, 140, 183, 190, 202, 207, 228–231, 234, 237, 240–242, 268, 274–276, 300–302, 306
episodic illness, 30
error, xx, 39, 83, 85–87, 118, 157–158, 174–175, 179, 207, 217, 231, 235, 238–239, 242–243, 245–247, 256, 263, 273, 275–276, 297, 299–311
  error rate, 157–158, 217
ethnographic, 64, 79, 81, 85, 89, 134, 228

F

false negatives, 74, 84, 173, 197, 251
false positives, 74, 84, 149, 173, 177–178, 193, 197, 212, 235–236, 251, 262–263
family history, 72, 85, 90, 92–93, 100, 105, 177
fiscal management, 43
flow sheet, 27, 29, 33

Food and Drug Authority (FDA), 161, 174, 181, 234, 238
formalism, 151
fragmentation, 32, 34, 75
functionality, 15, 112, 118, 131

G

Gamma distribution, 140–141
gaps in care, 275
gender, 48–51, 234, 307
genome-wide association studies (GWAS), 185, 207
geriatrics, 65, 70, 122, 127–128
glaucoma, 164, 188, 198–200, 212, 220, 222
gold standard evaluation, 161, 165
graphics, 281, 297

H

Hawthorne effect, 79, 266
Health Insurance Portability and Accountability Act (HIPAA), 108, 114, 119, 125
heart failure (HF), xviii, 28, 32, 45–56, 60, 80, 84, 118, 133, 165, 177, 179, 188, 198–200, 202, 207, 209, 220, 222, 227, 279, 308
HELP2, 246–248, 250
hemophilia, 104, 168, 188, 190, 197–200, 212
historical data, 20
HIV, 91, 108, 159, 162–165, 170, 172, 233, 236, 301
hospice, 283, 290
hospital, xix–xx, 5, 7–8, 10, 14, 21, 25–26, 42–43, 61, 63, 74, 77, 80, 89, 93, 100, 104, 122–124, 129, 132, 134, 136, 141–143, 152–153, 158, 162, 180, 186–187, 206, 214–215, 230–231, 240–243, 247, 249, 252, 264, 299, 301–302, 310–311, 316
  hospital resources, 43
  hospitalization, 53, 90, 99–100, 105, 111
hypertension, 6, 29, 32–33, 44, 48–51, 54, 61, 139, 153, 159–160, 167, 175, 188, 197–200, 210, 212, 220, 222, 224, 227, 230, 279–280, 298
hypovolemia, 32, 44

I

ICD-9, 86, 184, 189, 202, 206–207, 214, 230–231, 233–234, 238–239, 241–242, 247, 302, 311
infectious disease, 65, 69, 71, 127–128, 279
informatics, 3, 13, 15–16, 59, 83, 119, 135, 141–142, 147, 150, 180, 183, 207, 209, 228–229, 245, 279, 295, 297–299, 316
information retrieval, 162, 207
insulin, 153, 155–156, 159–160, 167, 175, 189, 194–196, 212, 301–302, 304
insurance, 47, 108, 149, 219, 293
intensive care, xx, 228, 249, 281, 285, 309
interestingness, 156–157, 180
internal medicine, 45, 70, 80, 121–122, 127–129, 149, 189–190, 209, 254, 296–297, 316
International Classification of Disease, 47
interviewer, 20, 93–94

J

Joint Commission for the Accreditation of Hospitals (JCAHO), 240, 246–247, 268

Index

K

kidney disease, 201, 207, 224, 228, 282, 287
knowledge base, xix, 14–15, 134, 142, 147–151, 161, 174–176, 183, 185–187, 189, 191, 193, 195, 197, 199, 201, 203, 205, 207, 211, 214, 226, 228, 268, 317
    knowledge-based technique, 174–175
KnowledgeLink, 71

L

lab results, 135–137, 139–141, 143, 150, 177, 285, 287
language, xix–xx, 86, 106, 108, 128, 135, 142, 149, 161, 179–180, 185, 207, 210, 219, 228, 231, 238, 246–247, 267–268, 276
Likert scale, 92, 95
literature review, 175, 189
Logician, 47, 54
longitudinal medical record (LMR), 61–62, 71–73, 75, 117, 122–126, 128–129, 187, 214, 226

M

Mann–Whitney test, 251, 261
meaningful use (MU), 60, 78, 80, 86–87, 118, 121–122, 129–131, 133, 203, 207, 226–228, 294, 298–299, 307, 310
medical
    medical error, xx, 83, 231
    medical informatics, 3, 13, 15–16, 59, 83, 150, 180, 183, 209, 229, 245, 295, 297–299
    medical record, xvii–xxi, 3, 5–8, 13–17, 19, 21–23, 25, 27–29, 31–41, 43–46, 48, 53, 55, 59–61, 67, 75, 80, 83–86, 100, 103–106, 109, 112, 117–118, 121–122, 134, 140, 148, 179, 183–184, 187, 190, 202, 206–207, 209, 214, 228, 230, 235, 241–242, 245–246, 252, 267–268, 274, 297–298, 300, 302, 308–309, 311
medication, xvii, xix–xx, 27, 46–48, 52–55, 70–71, 74, 86, 90, 100, 104, 106, 118, 132, 135–137, 139–143, 147–153, 155, 157–159, 161–163, 165–167, 169, 171–179, 181, 184–187, 189–190, 192, 194, 197, 202, 204–205, 207, 210–211, 214, 224, 228–229, 231–235, 237–243, 247, 280–288, 294–295, 299–311
    medication errors, 118, 231, 239, 299, 301, 303–311
    medication record, 229
Medicine in Denial, 13, 15–16
mental health, 103, 108, 114
meta-analysis, 53
metformin, 153, 156, 174, 177, 194, 210, 233–234, 301, 304–306
Minnesota Multiphasic Personality Inventory (MMPI), 30
mortality, 32, 53, 56, 299, 310
multivariate model, 49, 51, 54

N

narrative, 20–21, 27–28, 185, 247, 283
natural language processing (NLP), xx, 149–150, 179–180, 185, 207, 210, 228, 238, 246–249, 261, 265, 267–268, 276–277
neurology, xiv, 127, 129, 230, 284, 290
New York Heart Association (NYHA), 55, 285, 293

nonsteroidal anti-inflammatory drugs (NSAID), 48, 52
note shares, 129
note volume, 124, 129, 132
nurse practitioner (NP), 63, 65, 92, 94–97, 99, 104, 109, 303

O

obesity, 73, 91, 103, 108
Odds ratio (OR), 51–52
order sets, 142–143, 150, 180, 248
outpatient, 25, 56, 74, 81, 117–118, 122, 124, 133, 136, 158, 177, 179, 190, 206, 214, 227, 240, 242–243, 248, 252, 264, 269, 275, 279, 297–298, 303
ownership, 66, 68–70, 72, 77–78, 80, 113–114, 130

P

pain, 8, 10, 22, 72, 90–91, 101–102, 107, 125, 234, 238, 283–284, 290, 293
paper charts, 47, 54, 281, 300
paramedical, 19, 21, 31, 35, 44
Pareto principle, 135
patient
    patient care, xviii, 15–16, 38–39, 41, 44, 46, 59, 71, 83–86, 112, 117, 178, 184, 206, 225–226, 228–229, 241, 297, 306
    patient outcomes, 46, 80, 227, 241, 266–267, 297
pediatrics, 17, 65, 122, 127–128, 214–215, 243, 301, 310–311
pick list, 239, 247, 307
plurality, 95, 97, 110–113
pneumonia, 29, 32

policy, 13, 77–78, 87, 111, 113–115, 117, 122–124, 130–131, 133, 243
polycystic ovarian syndrome, 153, 174, 177, 233–234
population management, 86, 112
practice variation, 46
predictive value, 132, 162, 173, 193, 195, 198–199, 201, 211–212, 251, 256, 263, 307
primary care provider (PCP), xix, 46, 50, 54, 61, 65, 69–70, 72–73, 76, 78, 92, 94–95, 97–100, 103–104, 109, 112–113, 116, 121–134, 214–215, 227–228, 273, 275, 279–285, 287, 292, 294–296, 298
    primary care management, 279–280
privacy, 108, 114, 119
problem
    problem data, 124, 140, 150, 184
    problem inference, 185–186, 188–189, 197–198, 200, 205, 210, 213, 220, 225–227
    problem list documentation, xx, 121, 129, 179, 229–231, 237, 240–241, 306, 310
    problem list gaps, 89, 149, 178, 277
    problem list maintenance, 109, 226, 230–231, 240
    problem vocabulary, 184
    problem-oriented approach, 22
    Problem-Oriented Medical Information System (PROMIS), 3, 8, 14–16
    problem-oriented medical record (POMR), xvii–xviii, xx, 3, 5–6, 13–16, 32, 45–46, 59, 67, 84, 148, 184, 206, 209, 246
progress notes, 6, 13–15, 22–24, 27, 34–35, 39, 42, 48, 74, 124, 132, 149, 177, 190, 193, 210, 252, 255

Index

proxy methods, 126, 132, 149, 185
psychologists, 31
public health, xiii–xiv, 17, 93, 150, 180

R

radiology, 127, 177, 179, 230, 238, 252, 255, 280, 283–284, 290
Randomized Controlled Trial (RCT), 179, 207, 215, 228, 242, 245, 247, 249, 251, 253–257, 259, 261, 263, 265–267, 269, 310
receiver operating characteristic (ROC), 162
record keeping, 59, 136
REDCap, 94, 119
Research Electronic Data Capture, 94, 119
regression model, 49, 51, 95, 222
relevance, 49, 66–70, 80
reliability, 73–74, 80, 252, 274
responsibility, xvii, 66, 68–70, 72, 75, 77–78, 80, 113, 130–131, 276, 295, 315–318
risk factor, xvii, 184

S

safeguards, 307–308
screen space, 140
search engines, 247
sensitivity, 114, 162, 179, 193–194, 196–202, 204, 207, 211–212, 228, 230, 242, 245, 251, 256–257, 261–264, 267
sepsis, 273–274
smoking, 31
SNOMED, 72, 76, 86, 123, 158, 180, 184, 206, 214, 230–231, 234, 238, 241–242, 247, 268, 302, 311

SOAP (subjective/objective/assessment/plan,), xviii, 3, 13–14
socioeconomic, 63
software, xx, 49, 160–161, 240, 317
somatization, 71
Sparklines, 281
splenectomy, xx, 273–277
standardization, 112
stroke, 188, 198–200, 212, 220, 222, 233, 236
Student's t-test, 126
study cohorts, 60
subclinical, 20, 218
synonyms, 69, 212
systolic dysfunction, 47–48, 53, 55, 84

T

terminologies, 73, 91, 101, 106, 123, 149, 158, 174, 184, 206, 230–231, 242, 267, 317
test results, 47, 161–162, 172, 180, 284, 295, 298, 301
timeliness, 246, 252, 254, 261–262, 266–267
training, 5, 10, 13, 22, 24, 36–38, 44, 61, 67, 75, 77, 87, 95, 113, 123, 190, 194, 196, 198, 201, 211, 215, 254, 275, 302
transitive inference, 159–160
transplant surgery, 127–129
trauma, 128, 273
treatment plan, 83, 86

U

urban, 25–26, 36, 63, 214

V

vaccination, xx, 179, 273–277

validity, 235–236, 239, 268
vasodilator, 48, 50–51, 55
visualisation, 184, 206, 280–290, 292–293, 295, 297–298
vital signs, 27, 197, 211, 214, 284
von Willebrand disease, 190

W

Weed, Larry, xviii, 3, 5, 7, 9, 11, 13, 15, 17, 148

workflow, 66–69, 79, 119, 131, 231, 265, 274, 276, 306
workload, 294

Z

Zipf's law, 135–136, 139–140